서울대 물리학과 출신 30년 경력 번역가의 영문법 정석

# 멘토링 영문법

멘토 **최치남**

꿈과비전
Dream & Vision Books

멘토링
영문법

## 머리말

서울대 자연대 물리학과 출신의 총기와
고대 헬라어를 비롯해 세계 10개 언어를 섭렵한 언어적 이해와
전문 번역사 30년의 경험을 다 쏟아부었다!

서울대 물리학과 4학년 때 과외 금지 조치로 인해 영어 번역 알바를 시작하면서 영어와 질긴 인연을 맺게 되었다. 대학원을 마친 후 감리교 신학대학원에 입학하였고 거기서 희랍어, 히브리어, 라틴어 같은 고대 언어들을 처음 접하였다. 지금 생각해도 신학교 3년 동안은 고대 언어들 공부하던 기억밖에 없다.

미국에 유학해 논문을 쓰고 GRE 준비를 하면서 영어와의 치열한 싸움이 시작되었다. 그 어려운 영단어들을 정복하기 위해 밤낮으로 애쓰던 노력의 결과는 <Word Lord>로 나타났다. 이 책에는 단어들의 희랍어·라틴어 어원 분석을 시작으로 특별한 암기법과 관련 단어들을 함께 넣어 학생들이 단어를 빨리 정확히 외우고 오랫동안 기억할 수 있도록 나의 모든 비법을 쏟아부었다.

이제 남은 건 영문법 책인데, 솔직히 이 책은 쓰고 싶지 않았다. 시중에 너무나 많은 영문법 책이 범람하고 있었기 때문이다. 그런데 막상 애들을 가르치려고 영문법 책을 고르다 보니 문제가 있었다. '어라, 알파벳을 가르치는 영문법 책이 하나도 없네?' 내가 지금까지 여러 언어를 공부했지만, 알파벳을 가르치지 않는 문법책은 본 적이 없다. 그런데 등잔 밑이 어둡다고, 막상 영문법 책엔 알파벳이 없는 것이다. 그러니 애들이 영어 단어 읽는 법도 모르고 헤맬 수밖에. 이게 말이 되는가?

무엇보다도 문법 설명도 문제였다. 영어에 미래 시제가 있다고? 고대 언어 희랍어나 라틴어엔 분명 미래 시제가 있는데, 미안하지만 영어엔 없다! 보라, sing-sang-sung. 여기 어디 미래 시제가 있는가? 그리고 가정법에 현재형, 미래형이 있다고? 오호, 턱도 없는 말씀! 동사의 법(mood)이 뭔지도 모르고…. 그래서 이런 오해를 떨어버리기 위해 부득이 붓을 들었는데, 독자들이여, 30년 경력 번역가의 이 필생의 역작을 통해 부디 영문법에 통달하시라!

2022년
최고로 치는 남자 **최치남**

## 이 책의 활용법

영문법 책은 교과서라기보다는 영어 사전처럼 참고서입니다. 사전은 굳이 a부터 차근차근 배워나갈 필요가 없고, 다만 모르는 어휘가 나오면 찾아보면 됩니다. 그처럼 문법책도 어법상 문제가 생기면 그때마다 이를 해결하기 위해 참고하면 됩니다.

영어를 문법책으로 배우고자 하면 안 됩니다. 우리가 어릴 때 한글을 어떻게 배웠는지 생각하면 됩니다. 제일 먼저 엄마, 아빠, 밥 등의 단어들로부터 시작했죠. 그리고는 필요에 따라 그 단어들을 내뱉게 되었죠. 마찬가지로, 영어도 간단한 일상 회화부터 공부하는 게 좋습니다. Hungry. Gimmi hamburger. I like it. Let's go. Come on. Don't do that. 이렇게 남들로부터 주워들은 말들을 함부로 내뱉다가, 이런 말들을 상대가 잘 알아듣게 하려면 순서대로 잘 배열해야 한다는 사실을 알고 짜증스러워하죠.

문법은 이 짜증적 단계에서 필요한 것입니다. 즉, 여러 개의 단어를 조리 있게 배열해야 할 때 필요합니다. 처음부터 완벽하게 단어들을 배열할 수는 없겠죠. 시행착오를 겪는 동안, 도움을 줄 수 있는 것이 바로 문법책입니다.

이 문법책을 잘 이용하려면 다음 순서를 따르십시오:

(1) 우선 목차를 읽고 무슨 내용이 담겨 있는지 확인하십시오.

(2) 목차를 보다가 그 내용이 무슨 뜻인지 이해하기 어려우면, 페이지를 찾아 그 내용을 한 번 훑어보십시오. 나중에 영어 문장을 읽다가 혹은 글을 쓰다가 이와 유사한 문제가 생길 때, 이 부분들을 다시 찾아 좀 더 자세하게 공부를 하십시오.

(3) 그다음에 책에 있는 표들을 살펴보십시오. 그것은 핵심적 내용을 포함할 수 있으므로 그 내용을 반복해서 훑어볼 필요가 있습니다. (가능하면 표를 복사해 벽에 붙여놓거나 사진 찍어 핸드폰에 저장해 놓아도 좋습니다.)

복잡한 문장 구조를 설명하는 부분은 처음부터 완전히 이해하려 하지 말고, 학교에서 교과서 본문 등과 연결해 천천히 공부하십시오. 예컨대, 분사 구문이나 가정법 같은 부분은 학교 선생님의 설명을 듣고 나서 이 책을 참고하는 게 좋습니다. 즉, 학교에서 문법을 공부하는 진도에 맞춰 해당 부분을 참조하라는 것입니다.

한국에서 중시하는 문법 문제가 미국 혹은 본토에서 중시하는 바와 다를 수 있습니다. 그러므로 유학을 생각한다면 마지막 장과 부록 부분에 있는 미국식 문법 문제도 점검할 필요가 있습니다.

참고서는 어떻게 이용하느냐에 따라 큰 도움이 될 수도 있고 책장에서 먼지만 뒤집어쓰는 애물단지가 될 수도 있습니다. 본 책의 중간중간에 있는 멘토링 구절들도 보면서 좋은 활용법을 찾기 바랍니다. 만약 학교나 학원에서 이 책을 영문법 교재로 활용하고 싶다면, 그 대상으로 중3 또는 고1 학생들을 추천합니다.

멘토 **최치남**

# CONTENT

머리말                      005
이 책의 활용법        006

## 제1장 파닉스 (Phonics)

1. 알파벳(Alphabet)        014
2. 발음(Pronunciation)     016
    A. 자음
    B. 중자음
    C. 자음의 묵음
    D. 모음
    E. 이중모음
    F. 모음의 묵음
    G. 삼중모음
3. 강세(Accent and Stress)    028
    A. 액센트
    B. 문장의 강세
    C. 억양
    D. 끊어 읽기와 이어 읽기

## 제2장 품사 : 문장 구성단위

4. 명사(Noun)               036
    A. 종류
    B. 명사의 수
    C. 성을 표시하는 명사
    D. 명사의 격
5. 관사(Article)             049
    A. 관사의 종류
    B. 정관사의 용법
    C. 관사의 위치
    D. 관사의 생략
    E. 관사의 공통적 사용
6. 대명사(Pronoun)        056
    A. 인칭대명사
    B. 지시대명사
    C. 부정대명사
    D. 의문대명사
7. 전치사(Preposition)      068
    A. 전치사의 종류
    B. 전치사의 용법
    C. 이중 전치사
    D. 전치사의 생략
    E. 전치사를 포함하는 관용 동사구

8. 동사(Verb) ......................................... 085
   A. 완전 자동사: 1형식 동사
   B. 불완전 자동사: 2형식 동사
   C. 완전 타동사: 3형식 동사
   D. 수여 동사: 4형식 동사
   E. 불완전 타동사: 5형식 동사

9. 조동사(Auxiliary Verb) ......................... 096
   A. 기본 조동사
   B. 그 외의 조동사

10. 형용사(Adjective) ............................... 102
    A. 형용사의 형태
    B. 어미를 통한 품사 전환
    C. 형용사의 용법
    D. 수량, 정도를 나타내는 부정 형용사 및 대명사
    E. 형용사의 위치와 순서

11. 부사(Adverb) ..................................... 113
    A. 부사의 형태
    B. 의문부사
    C. 부사의 위치
    D. 주의할 부사의 용법

12. 접속사(Conjunction) ........................... 123
    A. 등위접속사
    B. 종속 접속사

13. 관계대명사(Relative Pronoun) ............. 132
    A. 관계대명사의 한정적 용법
    B. 관계대명사의 특별 용법

14. 관계부사(Relative Adverb) .................. 140
    A. 관계부사의 한정적 용법
    B. 관계부사의 계속적 용법

15. 감탄사(Interjection) ........................... 142

# 제3장 활용(Conjugation)

**16. 동사의 법(Mood)**     147
    A. 직설법(부가의문문, 감탄문)
    B. 명령법

**17. 동사의 시제(Tense)**     159
    A. 단순 현재형
    B. 단순 과거형
    C. 진행형
    D. 미래의 표현
    E. 완료형

**18. 수동태(Passive Voice)**     168
    A. 수동태 만드는 법
    B. 주의해야 할 수동태 용법
    C. 중간태 동사

**19. 부정사(Infinitive)**     175
    A. to부정사의 용법
    B. to부정사의 활용
    C. to부정사의 특별 용법
    D. 원형부정사

**20. 동명사(Gerund)**     186
    A. 동명사의 역할
    B. 동명사의 의미상 주어와 부정
    C. 동명사의 시제와 수동태
    D. 주의할 동명사의 용법
    E. 동명사 관련 관용 표현

**21. 분사(Participle)**     193
    A. 분사의 용법
    B. 분사구문

**22. 비교(Comparison)**     200
    A. 원급
    B. 비교급
    C. 최상급

**23. 가정법(Subjunctive Mood)**     209
    A. 가정법의 종류
    B. 다양한 가정법 표현들

**24. 일치와 화법 (Agreement & Narration)**     215
    A. 서술형태의 일치
    B. 주어와 동사의 일치
    C. 시제의 일체
    D. 화법의 전환

**25. 기교적 표현 (Technical Expression)**     222
    A. 도치
    B. 강조
    C. 생략과 대체
    D. 삽입과 동격

실전 문제(SAT) 230
해답 233

## 표 목록(Table List)

| | |
|---|---|
| 표 1. 영어의 알파벳표 | 015 |
| 표 2-1. 영어 자음의 발음(한가지 소리) | 016 |
| 표 2-1. 영어 자음의 발음(여러 가지 소리) | 017 |
| 표 3. 영어 중자음의 발음 | 019 |
| 표 4. 자음의 묵음 | 020 |
| 표 5. 모음의 발음 | 022 |
| 표 6. 이중모음의 발음 | 024 |
| 표 7. 국제 음성 기호의 발음 | 031 |
| 표 8. 불규칙 복수 명사 | 039 |
| 표 9. 복합명사의 복수형 I | 034 |
| 표 10. 복합명사의 복수형 II | 040 |
| 표 11. 수사 | 042 |
| 표 12. 인칭대명사, 소유대명사, 재귀대명사 | 056 |
| 표 13. be동사의 인칭/수/시제에 따른 활용례(직설법) | 085 |
| 표 14. 수여동사의 종류 | 089 |
| 표 15. 중요 접미사 | 104 |
| 표 16. 중요 접두사 | 106 |
| 표 17. 수량 형용사·대명사 | 108 |
| 표 18. 불규칙 동사표 | 157 |
| 표 19. 불규칙 비교급, 최상급 | 206 |

# 파닉스(Phonics)

# 01

Mentoring English Grammar

# 제1장
# 알파벳과 발음

본격적인 문법 공부에 들어가기 앞서 본 장에선 영어의 기본인 알파벳과 그 읽는 법(phonics)에 관해 살펴본다.

영어 알파벳은 고대 그리스에서 출발해 로마에서 현재의 모습을 거의 갖추었다. 고대 언어들은 매우 복잡한 문법체계를 갖고 있는 반면, 영어는 (문화수준이 낮은) 앵글로 색슨족이 사용하던 언어라 많이 단순화되었다.

예컨대, 그리스어 동사의 활용형은 매우 많고 복잡했다. 현재, 과거형 뿐 아니라 미래형도 있었고 (영어엔 미래형이 없음), 각 시제마다 단수/복수 1인칭(나/우리), 2인칭(너/너희), 3인칭(그, 그녀, 그것/그들) 변화가 다 따로 있었다. (영어엔, 현재형 3인칭 단수 동사에 -s 붙는 정도로 살짝 남아 있다.)

수동태, 중간태(능동과 수동의 중간형태), 완료형, 진행형(미완료)까지 시제와 인칭에 따른 변화가 다 다르고, 명령법과 가정법에서도 그 활용형이 죄다 달랐으니 얼마나 복잡했겠는가! 한 동사의 활용형을 다 모아 놓으면 2페이지 가득이니 말해 무엇하랴? 게다가, 명사와 형용사에서도 남성/여성/중성, 단수/복수, 주격/소유격/목적격/여격 등으로 어미변화를 해대니 먹고 살기도 바쁜 고대인들에게 말 배우기는 퍽 번거로웠을 것이다.

그래서 영국인들은 언어를 확 간소화시켰는데, 우리로서는 다행이 아닐 수 없다. 반면에 여러 나라 말이 섞이다 보니 발음 원칙이 일관적이지 않고, 편의상 소리 내지 않는 묵음도 많이 생겼는데 이건 외국인인 우리로선 오히려 배우기 불편한 점이 되었다.ㅠㅠ

영어는 독일, 프랑스 등의 주변 강대국 영향을 받아 어휘적으로 다양해지던 중에 아메리카 대륙으로 건너오면서 또 한 번 중요한 변화를 겪는다. 발음 면에서 좀 더 부드러워지고 문법적으로 더 융통성을 갖게 되었다. 미국이 세계 최강이 된 후 우리는 미국식 영어를 선호하게 되었으므로, 본 책은 미국식 영어에 기반을 둔다. 영국식 발음을 알기 원하면 인터넷 포털에서 제공하는 사전을 참조하라. (그리고, 이 책을 공부하려는 독자는 최소한 초등학생용 800단어 정도는 마스터해야 함!)

# Unit 01 알파벳 (Alphabet)

알파벳은 그리스 문자의 첫 글자인 알파(α)와 다음 글자인 베타(β)가 합쳐진 말로, 영어에서 사용되는 철자 기호를 가리킨다.

표 1. 영어의 알파벳

| 인쇄체 | 필기체 | 이름 | 인쇄체 | 필기체 | 이름 | 인쇄체 | 필기체 | 이름 |
|---|---|---|---|---|---|---|---|---|
| A a | $\mathcal{A}a$ | 에이 | J j | $\mathcal{J}j$ | 제이 | S s | $\mathcal{S}s$ | 에스 |
| B b | $\mathcal{B}b$ | 비 | K k | $\mathcal{K}k$ | 케이 | T t | $\mathcal{T}t$ | 티 |
| C c | $\mathcal{C}c$ | 씨 | L l | $\mathcal{L}l$ | 엘 | U u | $\mathcal{U}u$ | 유 |
| D d | $\mathcal{D}d$ | 디 | M m | $\mathcal{M}m$ | 엠 | V v | $\mathcal{V}v$ | 비 |
| E e | $\mathcal{E}e$ | 이 | N n | $\mathcal{N}n$ | 엔 | W w | $\mathcal{W}w$ | 더블유 |
| F f | $\mathcal{F}f$ | 에프 | O o | $\mathcal{O}o$ | 오 | X x | $\mathcal{X}x$ | 엑스 |
| G g | $\mathcal{G}g$ | 지 | P p | $\mathcal{P}p$ | 피 | Y y | $\mathcal{Y}y$ | 와이 |
| H h | $\mathcal{H}h$ | 에이치 | Q q | $\mathcal{Q}q$ | 큐 | Z z | $\mathcal{Z}z$ | 지 |
| I i | $\mathcal{I}i$ | 아이 | R r | $\mathcal{R}r$ | 알 | | | |

1. a, e, i, o, u, (y)는 모음(홀소리)이고 나머지는 자음(닿소리)이다. y는 자음과 모음으로 다 쓰일 수 있는데, 단어 맨 앞에 올 때는 항상 자음이고, 단어 맨 뒤에 올 때는 항상 모음이다.

2. 대문자(capital letters)는 문장 맨 앞, 고유명사 맨 앞, 약어 등에 사용된다. "나는"을 뜻하는 I는 문장 중간에서도 항상 대문자로 사용된다.
    · Do you know who I am? My name is D. Trump.

3. 필기체는 이어쓰기에 편리하도록 변형된 글자체이다.
    · This book was written by George.    [인쇄체]
    = *This book was written by George.* [필기체]

## ▌연습문제 1

**01.** 다음 중 대문자와 소문자의 사용이 잘못된 부분을 모두 찾으라.
① Do You like my sister jane?    ② how can i speak this word?
③ there is the han river in seoul.

**02.** 다음 문장을 필기체로 써 보라.
Dear my friend, please help me. I am in a trouble

# Unit 02 발음 (Pronunciation)

## A 자음(Consonants)

### 1. 한 가지 소리만 갖는 자음

**표 2-1. 영어 자음의 발음(한 가지 소리)**

| 표시 | 음 | 보기 | 표시 | 음 | 보기 |
|---|---|---|---|---|---|
| B b | ㅂ | book(북) bubble(버블) | P p | ㅍ | pen(펜) pocket(파킷) |
| F f | ㅍ[1] | father(파덜) fence(펜스) | Q q | 쿠 | quarter(쿼러) quick(퀵) |
| H h | ㅎ | hand(핸드) help(헬프) | R r | ㄹ[3] | read(리드) rock(락) |
| J j | ㅈ | jelly(젤리) jump(점프) | V v | ㅂ[1] | vase(베이스) voice(보이스) |
| K k | ㅋ | skate(스케이트) kick(킥) | W w | (우) | wise(와이즈) write(롸잇) |
| L l | ㄹ[2] | glow(글로우) large(라지) | X x | ㄱㅅ | exit(엑씯) xylophone(자일로폰) |
| M m | ㅁ | magic(매직) milk(밀크) | Y y | (이) | year(이어) yoyo(요요) |
| N n | ㄴ | neck(넥) snow(스노우) | Z z | ㅈ | zoo(주) crazy(크레이지) |

주: 1. f와 v는 윗니로 아랫입술을 살짝 깨물었다 놓으며 발음한다.
　　f는 무성음, v는 유성음. of(어브)는 뒤에 유성음이 자주 오다 보니 f가 유성음화 되었다.
　2. L, l은 앞에 약하게 (을)이란 말을 넣어 발음한다 : love는 (을)럽
　3. R, r은 앞에 약하게 (우)란 말을 넣어 발음한다 : rub는 (우)럽
　　모음 다음에 r이 올 때, 미국에서 "ㄹ" 발음을 하지만 영국에선 잘 안 한다.
　　**cf** father (미) 파덜  (영) 파더

※ **유성음과 무성음:** 유성음은 발음 시 목청이 떨리고, 무성음은 목청이 떨리지 않는다. 목 앞 울대뼈 밑에 손을 대면 목청의 울림을 확인할 수 있다. 자음 중 f, h, k, p, q, w, x는 무성음이고, 나머지는 유성음이다. 모음은 모두 유성음이다. 두 유성음 사이의 무성음은 종종 유성음화된다.

■ **연습문제 2**
다음 중 밑줄 친 부분이 무성음인 것을 고르라

① book　② toy　③ house　④ rose　⑤ swim　⑥ graph　⑦ father
⑧ of　⑨ clean　⑩ tell　⑪ open　⑫ off　⑬ zero　⑭ read

## 2. 여러 소리를 갖는 자음

영어는 여러 언어의 영향을 받아 한 알파벳이 여러 소리를 갖는 경우가 많다. 다음 알파벳들에 대해서는 각 단어마다 발음을 외워두어야 한다.

표 2-2. 영어 자음의 발음(여러 가지 소리)

| 표시 | 음 | 원칙 | 보기 | 참조/예외 |
|---|---|---|---|---|
| C c | ㅋ | 모음 a, o, u, 및 자음 (r, l) 앞에서 *항상* | cat(캣) cry(크라이) clean(클린) | Caesar (씨절) |
|  | ㅅ | 모음 e, i(y) 앞에서 *대개* | cell(쎌) city(씨티) cycle(싸이클) | cello (첼로) |
| D d | ㄷ | *대개* | desk(데슥) dry(드라이) |  |
|  | ㅈ | -dure, -dua 등 [유] 소리 앞에서 *종종* | individual(인디비주얼) endure(인쥬어) | did you (디쥬) |
| G g | ㄱ | 모음 a, o, u, 및 자음 앞에서 *항상* | gate(게잇) golf(골프) glass(글래스) | algae (앨지) |
|  | ㅈ | 모음 e, i(y) 앞에서 *대개* | general(제너럴) engine(엔진) gym(짐) | get(겟) give(깁) |
| S s | ㅅ | *대개* | star(스탈) sell(쎌) sense(쎈스) |  |
|  | ㅈ | 유성음[1]들 사이에서 *종종* | rose(로즈) music(뮤직) |  |
| T t | ㅌ | *대개* (맨 앞, 액센트 앞) | tall(톨) continue(컨티뉴) |  |
|  | ㄹ | 액센트 모음 뒤에서 *대개* | little(리를) water(워럴) | 미국식[2] |
|  | ㅊ | [유] 앞에서 *대개* | nature(네이철) venture(벤처) | Don't you |
|  |  | r 앞에서 *종종* | tree(츠리) truck(츠럭) train(츠레인) | 미국방언 |
|  | 쉬 | -tion, -tous, -tien, -tia 에서 *항상* | nation(네이션) cautious(커셔스) patient(페이션트) | question (퀘스쳔) |

주: 1. 단어 끝의 묵음 e는 유성음으로 작용할 수도 있고 무성음으로 작용할 수도 있다. 단, 복수형이 되어 s가 하나 더 붙으면 모두 유성음화 된다 : house(하우스) → houses(하우지즈)
　2. t가 단어 **중간**에 액센트 없는 모음 앞에 오면 "트"→"드"→"르"로 점차 부드러워지는데 이를 'medial(**중간**) t' 현상이라 한다.
　　t가 "드"로 발음되는 경우도 종종 있다: méteor(미디얼)

### 연습문제 3

다음 중 밑줄 친 부분의 소리가 다른 것을 골라라.

1. ① center ② city ③ candy ④ cylinder
2. ① drain ② India ③ danger ④ procedure
3. ① ice ② snow ③ houses ④ sense
4. ① gift ② ginger ③ giraffe ④ magic
5. ① gentle ② geology ③ gem ④ together
6. ① truck ② nation ③ trip ④ venture
7. ① town ② center ③ continue ④ tall
8. ① statue ② waiter ③ water ④ better
9. ① rose ② music ③ position ④ singer
10. ① father ② of ③ graph ④ chef

## B 중자음(Double Consonants)

1. 자음들이 겹쳐 나오면, 대개 글자 순서대로 발음하면 된다 (겹치는 소리는 하나만 발음): br(브르), bl(블르), cr(크르), cl (클르), ck(크), fr(프르), fl(플르), gr(그르), gl(글르) sm (스므), sl(슬르), st (스트)
   ※ 특별한 중자음의 발음은 표 3을 참조할 것!

   · street(스트릿), clock(클락), decrease(디크리즈), blouse(블라우즈), frog(프락), slipper(슬리펄), smart(스마트)

2. sc는 대개 '스크'로 발음하되, e, i 앞에선 ㅅ 발음이 겹치게 되므로 그냥 '스'로 발음한다:

   · screen(스크린), description(디스크립션)
   · scene(씬), scent(쎈트), scissors(씨절스), science(싸이언스), cf sceptic(스켑틱)

3. -ct는 '크트'로 발음하는데, 앞 음절을 급히 끊고 '트'를 약하게 발음한다 :

   · contact(컨택트)  · sect(쎅트)

### 표 3. 영어 중자음의 발음

| 표시 | 음 | 해당 경우 | 보기 | 참조/예외 |
|---|---|---|---|---|
| ch | ㅊ | 대개 | chair(체어) chicken(치킨) | 대표발음 |
| ch | ㅋ[1] | 라틴어원 단어는 *대개* | anchor(앵커) architect(아키텍트) character(캐릭터) choir(콰이어) Christmas(크리스마스) echo(에코) schedule(스케줄) school(스쿨) stomach(스토막) technique(테크닉) | |
| ch | 쉬 | 외래어(불어) 중 *종종* | chef(셰프) Chicago(시카고) machine(머쉰) mustache(머스태쉬) | |
| gh | ㅍ | 묵음을 예외하고 *대개* | cough(커프) enough(이너프) rough(러프) tough(터프) | f와 동일 |
| ng | ㅇ(응) | g, k 앞에서 n은 항상 '응' | sing(씽) hang(행) pink(핑크) uncle(엉클) | 발음편의상 |
| ph | ㅍ | 항상 | phone(폰) graph(그래프2) | f와 동일 |
| sh | 쉬 | 항상 | sharp(샾) shoes(슈즈) dish(디쉬) | |
| th[2] | ㄷ | 유성음, *대개* | the(더) that(댓) mother(마더) | 혀끝 물고 발음 |
| th[2] | ㅆ | 무성음 *종종(혼용)* | think(씽크) thick(씩) teeth(티스) | 혀끝 물고 발음 |

주: 1. 본래, c가 e, i 앞에서도 'ㅋ'로 발음하게 하려 h를 첨가함
 2. th(ㄷ, ㅆ)는 이빨 사이에 혀를 깨물었다가 놓으며 발음한다. ㄷ는 유성음, ㅆ는 무성음. th가 유성음들 사이에 오면 대개 ㄷ(유성음화)로 된다.

### ▌연습문제 4

다음 중 밑줄 친 부분의 소리가 다른 것을 골라라.

1. ① chrome    ② chicken   ③ chemistry  ④ stomach
2. ① sceptic   ② scenery   ③ scissors   ④ science
3. ① machine   ② Chicago   ③ technique  ④ mustache
4. ① ghost     ② laugh     ③ cough      ④ tough
5. ① other     ② father    ③ they       ④ tooth
6. ① phone     ② fence     ③ of         ④ off
7. ① ink       ② sing      ③ uncle      ④ know
8. ① chair     ② chef      ③ shower     ④ dash

## C 자음의 묵음(Mute Consonants)

### 표 4. 자음의 묵음

| 음 | 예시 |
|---|---|
| b | [m 뒤, t 앞에서] lam_b_(램) bom_b_(밤) tom_b_(툼) deb_t_(뎉) doub_t_(다웉) clim_b_(클라임) com_b_(콤) dum_b_(덤) sub_t_le(써틀) thum_b_(썸) |
| d | [n 앞 뒤에서] We_d_nesday(웬스디) han_d_some(핸썸) han_d_kerchief(행커칩) |
| g | [n 앞에서 종종] campai_g_n(캠페인) forei_g_n(퍼린) rei_g_n(레인) desi_g_n(디자인) assi_g_n(어싸인) cf si_g_nal(시그널) |
| gh | [맨 뒤 혹은 t 앞에서] dau_gh_ter(더러) ri_gh_t(롸잇) hi_gh_(하이) strai_gh_t(스트레잇) thou_gh_(더우) thou_gh_t(써트) ei_gh_t(에잇) kni_gh_t(나잇) |
| h¹ | [맨 앞 뒤 혹은 g, r, x 다음에서] _h_eir(에어) _h_our(아월) _h_onest(어니스트) _h_onor(아널) g_h_ost(고스트) r_h_ythm(리듬) w_h_y(와이) ve_h_icle (비어클) ex_h_ibit(익지빗) cf ex_h_ale(엑스헤일) |
| k | [n 앞에서] _k_nife(나잎) _k_night(나잇) _k_nock(낙) _k_now(노우) _k_nowledge(날리지) _k_nee(니) |
| l | [d, f, k, m 앞에서] wou_l_d(욷) fo_l_k(폭) ca_l_m(캄) ca_l_f(캐프) wa_l_k(웍) ha_l_f(해프) sa_l_mon(새먼) a_l_mond(아먼드) cha_l_k(척) ta_l_k(턱) pa_l_m(팜) cf e_l_m(엘름)² |
| n | [n 앞에서] autum_n_(어럼) colum_n_(컬럼) dam_n_(댐) solem_n_(쌀럼) condem_n_(컨뎀) |
| p | [자음 앞에서] cu_p_board(커버드) cor_p_s(컬) _p_salm(쌈) _p_sycho(싸이코) recei_p_t(리씯) _p_neumonia(뉴머냐) cf cou_p_(쿠) |
| r | i_r_on(아이언) |
| s | [l 앞에서] ai_s_le(아일) i_s_land(아일런드) |
| t | [s, f 뒤에서] fas_t_en(패쓴) lis_t_en(리쓴) sof_t_en(써픈) inter_n_ational(이너내셔널)³ has_t_en(헤이슨) cf has_t_e(헤이스트) |

주: 1. h는 단어 맨 앞과 끝, 모음과 모음 사이, ex 다음, gh나 rh로 시작되는 단어에서 종종 묵음이 된다. wh로 시작되는 단어에서도 h는 발음이 잘 안 된다.

2. elm도 거의 "에엄"처럼 발음해서 l 발음이 잘 들리지 않는다.

3. 미국 일부에선 거친 발음을 피하기 위해 n 다음에 t를 발음하지 않는 경향이 있다 (액센트가 없는 음절일 때) :
cen_t_er(쎄너), wan_t_ to ⇒ wanna(워나), going to ⇒ gonna(고나)
cf cen_t_énnial(쎈테니얼)

1. 자음 세 개가 겹치는 경우, 발음 편의상 하나는 종종 묵음 처리한다 :
   Chri<u>s</u>tmas(크리스마스), che<u>s</u>tnut(체스넛), mor<u>t</u>gage(머기지)
   ca<u>s</u>tle(캐쓸), whi<u>s</u>tle(위쓸), mu<u>s</u>cle(머쓸) **cf** mu<u>s</u>cular(머스큘러)

2. 단어 끝의 t, th는 잘 발음하지 않되 숨을 잠시 끊었다가 읽는다.
   beas<u>ts</u>(비슷/츠), ten<u>ts</u>(텐/쓰), mon<u>ths</u>(먼/쓰)
   · I <u>can</u> go. (아이캔고)
   · I <u>can't</u> go. (아이캔/고)

3. 단어 마지막의 묵음은 접미사가 첨부될 때 발음이 살아날 수도 있다 :
   solem<u>n</u>(살럼) → solem<u>n</u>ize(쌀럼나이즈)
   autum<u>n</u>(어럼) → autum<u>n</u>al(어텀널)
   colum<u>n</u>(컬럼) → colum<u>n</u>ar(컬럼널)
   condem<u>n</u>(컨뎀) → condem<u>n</u>ation(컨뎀네이션),
   **cf** condem<u>n</u>ed(컨뎀드), condem<u>n</u>ing(컨데밍)

### ▌연습문제 5
다음 중 밑줄 친 부분의 소리가 다른 것을 골라라.

1. ① lum<u>b</u>er ② plum<u>b</u>er ③ su<u>b</u>tle ④ dou<u>b</u>t
2. ① campai<u>g</u>n ② assi<u>g</u>n ③ <u>g</u>naw ④ si<u>g</u>nal
3. ① ais<u>l</u>e ② a<u>l</u>mond ③ sa<u>l</u>mon ④ fo<u>l</u>k
4. ① <u>p</u>sycho ② cor<u>ps</u> ③ cou<u>p</u> ④ cou<u>p</u>le
5. ① <u>h</u>air ② <u>h</u>eir ③ <u>h</u>our ④ <u>h</u>onest
6. ① da<u>m</u>nation ② conde<u>m</u>ned ③ autu<u>m</u>nal ④ colu<u>m</u>nar
7. ① ba<u>l</u>m ② pa<u>l</u>m ③ ca<u>l</u>m ④ e<u>l</u>m
8. ① cou<u>gh</u> ② ei<u>gh</u>t ③ thou<u>gh</u> ④ ni<u>gh</u>t
9. ① has<u>t</u>en ② fas<u>t</u>en ③ island ④ has<u>t</u>e
10. ① han<u>d</u>kerchief ② We<u>d</u>nesday ③ woul<u>d</u> ④ han<u>d</u>some

## D 모음(Vowels)

영어의 모음은 다음 표와 같이 여러 소리를 갖는데, 처음 보는 단어는 대표발음으로 발음해 본다. 단, 액센트를 갖지 않는 모음은 대개 '어[a]'로 약하게 발음한다.

예 advénture(어드벤쳐), équal(이퀄), pálace(팰리스)

**표 5. 모음의 발음**

| 표시 | 음 | 해당 경우 | 보기 | 참조/예외 |
|---|---|---|---|---|
| A a | 애 | 단음절은 대개 | mat(맽) gas(개스) bag(백) | 대표발음 |
|  | 에이 | 끝의 e 앞에서[1] | cake(케익) page(페이지) |  |
|  | 어 | -al 등의 경우 | ball(벌) call(컬) fall(펄) false(펄스) hall(헐) salt(썰트) chalk(처크) | '오'와 '어' 중간음 |
|  | 아 | -ar[2] 의 경우 대개 | art(알트) hard(할드) |  |
| E e | 에 | 단음절은 대개 | egg(엑) error(에러) bed(벧) | 대표발음 |
|  | 이 | 끝의 e 앞에서 | gene(진) scene(씬) evening(이브닝) | recipe (레서피) |
|  | 어 | er 형태[2] | service(썰비스) certain(썰튼) |  |
| I i | 이 | 단음절은 대개 | ill(일) ink(잉크) dish(디쉬) | 대표발음 |
|  | 아이 | 끝의 e 앞에서[1] | ice(아이스) find(파인드) |  |
|  | 어 | ir 형태[2] | bird(벌드) circus(썰커스) |  |
| O o | 아 | 단음절은 대개 | hot(핫) color(칼러) top(탑) | 대표발음 |
|  | 오우 | 끝의 e 앞에서[1] | over(오벌) rope(로웊) gold(골드) | do(두) |
|  | 어 | of-, on-, or- 형태 | office(어피스) on(언) order(어덜) |  |
| U u | 어 | 단음절은 대개 | sun(썬) but(벝) study(스터디) | 대표발음 |
|  | 유 | 끝의 e 앞에서[1] | use(유즈) sugar(슈갈) duty(듀티) | bury(베리) |
|  | 우 | ue 혹은 ul 경우 | bull(불) glue(글루) push(푸쉬) |  |
| Y y | 아이 | 단음절은 대개 | bye(바이) dye(다이) sky(스카이) | 자음 뒤의 y는 모음 |
|  | 이 | 단어 중간이나 끝 | busy(비지) day(데이) only(언리) |  |

주: 1. 단어 맨 뒤에 묵음 e가 올 때, 그 바로 앞 모음은 대개 자기 이름처럼 발음한다. 예컨대, a는 '에이,' i는 '아이', u는 '유'로 발음.

2. ar은 '알'(or '얼')로 발음하며, er, ir, or, ur 등은 대개 '얼'로 발음된다.
    단, 끝에 e가 오면 대개 다음과 같이 발음된다:
    -are(에얼) : bare(베얼)    -ere(이얼) : mere(미얼)
    -ire(아이얼) : fire(파이얼)  -ore(오얼) : sore(쏘얼)
    -ure(유얼) : cure(큐얼)    -yre(아이얼) : tyre(타이얼)

### ▌연습문제 6
다음 중 밑줄 친 부분의 소리가 다른 것을 골라라.

1. ① c<u>a</u>t      ② m<u>a</u>t       ③ p<u>a</u>ge     ④ h<u>a</u>t
2. ① <u>a</u>side    ② <u>a</u>bide     ③ <u>a</u>gain    ④ <u>a</u>tom
3. ① b<u>a</u>ll     ② h<u>a</u>ll      ③ c<u>a</u>lm     ④ s<u>a</u>lt
4. ① <u>e</u>quation ② g<u>e</u>ne      ③ m<u>e</u>t      ④ <u>e</u>vening
5. ① d<u>i</u>sh     ② f<u>i</u>nd      ③ d<u>i</u>ffer   ④ d<u>i</u>splay
6. ① s<u>o</u>n      ② h<u>o</u>t       ③ p<u>o</u>t      ④ b<u>o</u>ttle
7. ① b<u>u</u>t      ② h<u>u</u>nter    ③ s<u>u</u>n      ④ d<u>u</u>ty
8. ① <u>o</u>ff      ② <u>o</u>f        ③ d<u>o</u>       ④ <u>o</u>n
9. ① sk<u>y</u>      ② pupp<u>y</u>     ③ d<u>y</u>e      ④ m<u>y</u>
10. ① f<u>ar</u>ther ② b<u>ar</u>       ③ c<u>ar</u>t     ④ v<u>ar</u>y
11. ① b<u>ir</u>d    ② d<u>ir</u>e      ③ g<u>ir</u>l     ④ c<u>ir</u>cle
12. ① s<u>u</u>gar   ② st<u>u</u>dy     ③ p<u>u</u>re     ④ <u>u</u>se

## E 이중모음(Double Vowels)

이중모음은 일반적으로 각 모음의 대표 발음을 이어서 발음하되, 다음 표의 경우들은 외워두자.

표 6. 이중모음의 발음

| 알파벳 | 발음 | 해당 경우 | 참조/예외 |
|---|---|---|---|
| au | 어:¹ | autumn(어럼) fault(펄트) caught(커트) daughter(더럴) August(어거스트) | 대표발음 |
| | 애 | aunt(앤트) laugh(래프) | gauge(게이지) |
| ea | 이:¹ | mean(민) meat(미트) heat(히트) read(리드) seat(씨트) leave(리브) neat(니트) | 대표발음 |
| | 에 | dead(델) deaf(데프) jealous(젤러스) health(헬쓰) meadow(메도우) sweater(스웨털) ready(레디) feather(페덜) weather(웨덜) wealth(웰쓰) heavy(헤비) threaten(쓰레튼) instead(인스텐) | create(크리에잍) great(그레잇) pearl(펄) |
| ee | 이:¹ | beef(비:프) teen(틴:) seen(씬:) | been(빈) |
| ei | 에이 | eight(에잇) neighbor(네이벌) weight(웨잇) | 대표발음 |
| | 이:¹ | ceiling(씰링) receive(리시브) seize(씨즈) | deity(디어티) |
| | 아이 | geist(가이스트) height(하잇) | 독일 외래어 |
| eo | 이어, 이아 | geology(지얼러지) video(비디어) | 대표발음 |
| | 에 | leopard(레펄드) Leonard(레널드) jeopardy(제펄디) | people(피플) |
| ey | 이 | honey(하니) key(키) money(마니) | eye(아이) |
| ie | 이:¹ | field(피필드) niece(니스) piece(피스) | lie(라이) |
| oa | 오우 | boat(보웉) coat(코웉) soap(소웊) | |
| oe | 우:¹ | canoe(커누) shoe(슈) | does(더즈) |
| | 오우 | doe(도우) foe(ㅍ호우) toe(토우) | |
| | 오위 | poet(포윗) poetry(포윗츄리) | poem(포엄) |

| | | | |
|---|---|---|---|
| oo | 우:[1] | b<u>oo</u>k(북:) s<u>oo</u>n(순:) f<u>oo</u>t(풋:) r<u>oo</u>t(룻:) | -oor의 발음은 주 2 참조 |
| | 우 | l<u>oo</u>k(룩) w<u>oo</u>d(욷) c<u>oo</u>k(쿡) | |
| | 어 | bl<u>oo</u>d(블런), fl<u>oo</u>d(플럿) | |
| ou | 아우 | <u>ou</u>t(아웉) r<u>ou</u>nd(라운드) s<u>ou</u>nd(사운드) | 대표발음 |
| | 어:[1] | b<u>ou</u>ght(버:트) c<u>ou</u>gh(커:프) c<u>ou</u>rt(컬:트) f<u>ou</u>r(펄) j<u>ou</u>rnal(저널) | t<u>ou</u>ch(터치) t<u>ou</u>gh(터프) |
| | 우:[1] | gr<u>ou</u>p(그룹:) s<u>ou</u>p(수:프) y<u>ou</u>(유:) | c<u>ou</u>ld(쿨) |
| | 오우 | d<u>ou</u>ghnut(도우넡) m<u>ou</u>ld(모울드) s<u>ou</u>l(소울) | |
| ui | 우이 | r<u>ui</u>n(루인) s<u>ui</u>te(쉍) t<u>ui</u>tion(튜이션) | c<u>ui</u>sine(퀴진) |

주: 1. (:) 표시는 장음을 나타낸다.
  2. 이중모음 다음에 r이 오면 다음과 같이 발음하고, 그 외에 표 5 아래 주 2도 참조하라:
  pa<u>ir</u>(페얼), ae<u>r</u>obic(에어러빅), meteo<u>r</u>(미디얼), liquo<u>r</u>(리컬),
  floo<u>r</u>(플로어), doo<u>r</u>(도얼), ea<u>r</u>(이얼), pea<u>r</u>(페얼), bee<u>r</u>(비얼),
  hei<u>r</u>(에얼), choi<u>r</u>(콰이얼), doe<u>r</u>(두얼) cf po<u>or</u>(푸얼), mo<u>or</u>(무얼)

※ 특이한 발음을 가진 이중모음
  m<u>ae</u>stro(마이스트로), d<u>ai</u>ry(데어리), alg<u>ae</u>(앨지), C<u>ae</u>sar(시저), f<u>ia</u>ncee(피앙세),
  s<u>ai</u>d(쌔드), vac<u>uu</u>m(배큐엄), fr<u>ui</u>t(푸룻), bl<u>ue</u>(블루), s<u>ow</u>, (쏘우), h<u>ow</u>(하우)

■ 연습문제 7

다음 중 밑줄 친 부분의 소리가 다른 것을 골라라.

1. ① l<u>augh</u>     ② <u>au</u>tumn     ③ f<u>au</u>lt      ④ c<u>augh</u>t
2. ① <u>ai</u>m      ② p<u>ai</u>nt     ③ s<u>ai</u>d      ④ d<u>ay</u>
3. ① m<u>ea</u>t     ② s<u>ea</u>t      ③ sw<u>ea</u>t     ④ p<u>ea</u>k
4. ① w<u>ei</u>ght   ② f<u>ei</u>nt     ③ c<u>ei</u>ling   ④ n<u>ei</u>ghbor
5. ① g<u>eo</u>logy  ② l<u>eo</u>pard   ③ n<u>eo</u>n      ④ n<u>eo</u>lith
6. ① mus<u>eu</u>m   ② <u>Eu</u>rope    ③ f<u>eu</u>dal    ④ n<u>eu</u>ron
7. ① d<u>i</u>ary    ② As<u>i</u>a      ③ d<u>i</u>amond   ④ g<u>i</u>ant
8. ① f<u>ie</u>ld    ② n<u>ie</u>ce     ③ p<u>ie</u>ce     ④ l<u>ie</u>
9. ① b<u>ee</u>f     ② f<u>ee</u>d      ③ m<u>ee</u>t      ④ b<u>ee</u>n
10. ① c<u>oa</u>t    ② b<u>oa</u>t      ③ <u>oa</u>k       ④ r<u>oa</u>r
11. ① h<u>o</u>ney   ② k<u>ey</u>       ③ <u>ey</u>e       ④ m<u>o</u>ney
12. ① sh<u>oe</u>    ② h<u>oe</u>       ③ d<u>oe</u>       ④ f<u>oe</u>
13. ① s<u>ou</u>nd   ② b<u>ou</u>nd     ③ c<u>ou</u>nt     ④ c<u>ou</u>gh
14. ① gr<u>ou</u>p   ② s<u>ou</u>p      ③ s<u>ou</u>l      ④ y<u>ou</u>
15. ① f<u>u</u>el    ② cl<u>u</u>e      ③ bl<u>u</u>e      ④ gl<u>u</u>e
16. ① f<u>oo</u>d    ② m<u>oo</u>d      ③ d<u>oo</u>r      ④ b<u>oo</u>k
17. ① t<u>u</u>ition ② fr<u>u</u>it     ③ r<u>u</u>in      ④ s<u>u</u>ite
18. ① h<u>ow</u>     ② <u>ow</u>n       ③ s<u>ow</u>       ④ rainb<u>ow</u>
19. ① h<u>ea</u>lth  ② r<u>ea</u>dy     ③ gr<u>ea</u>t     ④ h<u>ea</u>vy
20. ① f<u>ar</u>     ② <u>ear</u>       ③ p<u>air</u>      ④ b<u>eer</u>

## F 모음의 묵음(Mute Vowels)

1. 단어 맨 끝의 e는 거의 발음이 되지 않는다. 이 경우, 바로 앞의 모음(액센트가 있을 때)은 대개 자기 이름대로 발음된다.
   ic<u>e</u>(아이스), dy<u>e</u>(다이), pi<u>e</u>(파이), pag<u>e</u>(페이지), cut<u>e</u>(큐트)
   **cf** giv<u>e</u>(깁), wer<u>e</u>(월), recip<u>e</u>(레써피)

2. i의 묵음
   bru<u>i</u>se(브루즈), fr<u>i</u>end(프렌드), su<u>i</u>t(수트), fru<u>i</u>t(프룯)

3. u의 묵음
   b<u>u</u>ild(빌드), b<u>u</u>y(바이), b<u>u</u>oyant(버이언트), g<u>u</u>ard(가드), g<u>u</u>ess(게스), g<u>u</u>est(게스트), g<u>u</u>ide(가이드), g<u>u</u>itar(기타), g<u>u</u>y(가이)

## G 삼중모음(Triple Vowels)

다음의 발음들은 외워두자.
l<u>ieu</u>(루), b<u>eau</u>tiful(뷰리펄), bur<u>eau</u>cracy(뷰라크러시), continu<u>ou</u>s(컨티뉴어스)

---

**연습문제 8**

다음 중 밑줄 친 부분의 소리가 다른 것을 골라라.

1. ① br<u>ui</u>se   ② fr<u>ui</u>t   ③ b<u>ui</u>ld   ④ s<u>ui</u>t
2. ① <u>i</u>ce   ② h<u>a</u>ve   ③ d<u>i</u>ve   ④ rec<u>i</u>pe
3. ① b<u>u</u>y   ② g<u>u</u>itar   ③ p<u>u</u>re   ④ g<u>u</u>ide
4. ① g<u>i</u>ve   ② l<u>i</u>ne   ③ n<u>i</u>ght   ④ b<u>y</u>e
5. ① f<u>i</u>t   ② s<u>i</u>t   ③ fr<u>i</u>end   ④ b<u>e</u>hind

# Unit 03 강세 (Accent and Stress)

## A 액센트(Accent)

영어는 각 단어마다 기본적으로 강세를 갖는데, 이를 액센트라 한다. **액센트**는 모음(a, e, i, o, u, y)에만 붙는다(단어 끝 묵음 e는 음절로 취급하지 않음). 단음절 단어는 하나 있는 모음에 액센트가 있는 반면, 모음이 둘 이상인 단어에는 액센트가 있는 모음과 없는 모음이 정해져 있다. 액센트가 있는 모음은 또렷하고 강하게 발음하고(앞의 **표 5, 6 참조**) **액센트가 없는 모음은 약하게 '어, 으, 이' 등으로 발음한다.** 각 단어의 액센트의 위치는 무조건 외우자. 그래도 굳이 법칙을 찾자면 다음과 같다:

1. 두 음절로 된 **명사**는 대개 **앞**에 액센트가 있다.
   · wáter(**워**러), íncome(**인**컴)
   **cf** abýss(어**비**스), recéipt(리**씨**트), guitár(기**탈**)

2. 두 음절로 된 동사는 대개 **뒤**에 액센트가 있다.
   · retúrn(리**턴**), forgét(풔**겥**) **cf** vísit(**비**짙)

3. 접미사 -al, -ar, -ed, -er, -est, -ing, -ive, -ly, -ry 등에는 액센트가 붙지 않는다.

4. -tion로 끝나는 단어에선 바로 **앞** 모음에 액센트가 붙는다.
   · vibrátion(바이브**레**이션), condítion(컨**디**션)

5. 긴 단어에는 두 개의 액센트가 (사이에 모음을 하나 건너) 붙을 수 있는데, 발음기호 상에서 둘 중 더 강한 모음엔 (´), 약한 모음엔 (`)를 찍는다.
   · hélicòpter(**헬**리캅털)

6. 합성어에선 연이은 음절에 모두 강한 액센트가 붙을 수 있다.
   · shé-góat(**쉬고트**)      · mánsérvant(**맨서번트**)

7. 단어에 접두사나 접미사가 붙으면 액센트 위치가 변할 수 있다.
   · átom(**애**럼) → atómic(어**타**믹)

### B 문장의 강세(Sentence Stress)

문장을 말할 때, 주의를 요하는 단어들(**명사, 본동사, 의문사, 지시대명사, 감탄사** 등)은 좀 더 강하게 발음하고, 덜 중요한 단어들(**전치사, 접속사, 관사, 인칭대명사, 조동사, be동사** 등)은 약하게 발음하는데, 말하는 사람의 주관에 따라 강세가 달라질 수 있다.

- *What* is that? This is my **book**. [사물 강조]
- *Whose* book is that? This is **my** book. [소유자 강조]

### C 억양(Intonation)

1. 일반적으로 모든 영어 단어는 읽을 때 **끝을 살짝 내려준다.**
   cow(카우↘), well(웰↘), canál(커낼↘)

2. **yes, no** 대답을 요구하는 의문문은 문장 **끝을 올린다.**
   - Did you have lunch↗?

3. 의문사(who, whose, whom, what, when, where, which, how)로 시작되는 의문문은 문장 **끝을 내린다.**
   - Where did he go↘?

4. **not, never** (didn't, isn't 등)에는 강세를 둔다.
   - I am **not** a fool. [아임 **나러** 풀]
   - Tom **isn't** working now. [이**슨** 워킹 나우]

   ※ can과 can't의 구별: n 다음의 t는 발음이 거의 안 되므로, can과 can't의 구별은 실제 회화에서 쉽지 않은데, can't는 not을 강조하기 위해 끝을 **살짝 올리는 게** 다르다.
   - You **can** be here. [유 캔비 히어]
   - You **can't** be here. [유 캔/비 히어]

## D 끊어 읽기와 이어 읽기 (Pausing & Linking)

1. 영어에선 여러 단어를 붙여 이어 말하는 경향이 강하다. 약하게 발음되는 **대명사, 접속사, 전치사** 등은 붙여 읽고, **조동사와 be동사**도 not이 포함되지 않는 한 약하게 붙여 발음한다(not에는 강세), 한 단어에서도 **액센트가 없는 음절은 앞 말에 붙여 읽는 경향**이 있으므로 주의한다.

   · He is **about** to leave. [히이써 **바**우투리브]

   · If you go with us, we will have a lot of advantages.
   [이퓨 **고**위더스,   위월해버     라어벗   **배**니지스]

   · I have never thought that he would be arrested again in America.
   [아허브   **네**버썻         댓히웃비어   **레**스티더 **개**니너 **메**리카]

2. 구두점(, . ; :) 뒤에서 혹은 접속사(when, where, what, if) 앞에서 대체로 끊어 읽는다. 반대로, 의미상 큰 변화를 주지 않는 단어들은 한꺼번에 이어 읽는다.

   · Say hello / when she comes here.
   · As it were, / he is a famous singer.

### ▮ 연습문제 9

**01.** 다음 단어들에서 강한 액센트가 있는 음절에 ( ´ ) 표시를 하라.

topic, cemetery, backpack, behind, mobile, mediterranean, cashier, consideration, committee, employee, concentrate, figure, deter

**02.** 다음 글을 이어읽기를 적용해 읽어보라.

He was again attacked by Americans who had been amusing themselves.

## 표 7. 국제 음성 기호의 발음

| 발음기호 | 소리 | 비고 | 발음기호 | 소리 | 비고 |
|---|---|---|---|---|---|
| [a] | 아 |  | [b] | ㅂ |  |
| [e] | 에 |  | [d] | ㄷ |  |
| [i] | 이 |  | [j] | (이) | 자음 |
| [o] | 오 |  | [l] | ㄹ | 혀끝을 입천장에 대고 발음 |
| [u] | 우 |  | [m] | ㅁ |  |
| [w] | (우) | 자음 | [n] | ㄴ |  |
| [ʌ] | 아 | 아/오 중간 | [r] | ㄹ | 혀뿌리를 목젖에 대고 발음 |
| [ɔ] | 어 | 아/어 중간 | [f] | ㅍ | 아랫입술을 윗니로 깨물며 (무성) |
| [ɛ] | 에 |  | [v] | ㅂ | 아랫입술을 윗니로 깨물며 (유성) |
| [æ] | 애 |  | [z] | ㅈ | 부드럽게 |
| [ɑː] | 아ː | 장모음 | [ʒ] | ㅈ | [z] 보다 좀 거칠게 |
| [eː] | 에ː | 장모음 | [dʒ] | ㅉ | [ʒ]보다 좀 더 거칠게 |
| [iː] | 이ː | 장모음 | [tz] | ㅉ |  |
| [uː] | 우ː | 장모음 | [ð] | ㄷ | 혀를 깨물고 발음(유성음) |
| [ɔː] | 어ː | 장모음 | [θ] | ㅆ | 혀를 깨물고 발음(무성음) |
| [ai] | 아이 |  | [h] | ㅎ |  |
| [ei] | 에이 |  | [g] | ㄱ |  |
| [ɔi] | 어이 |  | [ŋ] | 응 | 끝소리로만 사용 |
| [au] | 아우 |  | [k] | ㅋ |  |
| [ou] | 오우 |  | [p] | ㅍ |  |
| [iɔ] | 이어 |  | [s] | ㅅ |  |
| [uɔ] | 우어 |  | [t] | ㅌ |  |
| [ɛə] | 에어 |  | [ʃ] | 슈 |  |
| [eə] | 에어 |  | [tʃ] | 츄 |  |

주: 국제 음성 기호에는 [으] 소리가 없다: [st] = 스트

# 품사:
# 문장 구성단위

# 02

Mentoring English Grammar

# 제 2 장
# 문장의 요소 (품사)

우리는 영어, 한국어 등의 언어가 어떻게 생겨났는지 정확히 모른다. 그래도 우리 자신이 익히고 아이들을 가르치는 과정을 통해 언어의 생성 과정을 대충 짐작할 수 있다.

모든 언어는 단어(word)로부터 시작한다. 우선 눈에 보이는 사물들을 지칭하는 단어들이 생겨났는데, 그것이 명사(noun)이다. 명사의 반복을 피하기 위해 이를 대용하는 대명사(pronoun)도 거의 같이 생겨났을 것이다.

다음에는 그 명사의 움직임을 나타내는 동사(verb)가 만들어지고, 명사의 상태를 나타내는 형용사(adjective)가 나왔다. 언어 체계가 더 복잡해지면서, 단어들을 연결하는 접속사(conjunction)가 나오고, 동사와 형용사를 더 자세히 설명하는 부사(adverb)가 생겨났다.

영어에는 우리 한국어에 없는 전치사(preposition)가 있어 명사와 결합해 형용사나 부사의 역할을 만든다. 그 외, 독립적으로 사용되는 감탄사(interjection)가 분화하며 문장을 구성하는 요소들 곧 품사(speech parts)들이 다양해졌다.

의미 전달을 위해선 이 품사들을 제대로 늘어놓아야 하는데, 이렇게 품사들을 늘어놓는 규칙이 바로 문법(grammar)이다. 영어는 그 배열 방식이 한국어와 상당히 다르다. 본 장에서는 영어의 각 품사가 어떻게 배열되는지 알아보고, 각각의 특성도 살펴본다.

### 1. 영어 문장의 기본 구조

영어를 비롯한 대부분의 유럽 언어들은 동사를 중심으로 이뤄진다. 즉, 동사의 종류에 따라 핵심 문장 성분들이 달라지는 것이다. 동사(verb, V)가 목적어(objective, O)를 필요로 하면 목적어를 넣고, 보어(complement, C)를 필요로 하면 보어를 넣는다. 물론 목적어나 보어를 필요로 하지 않는 동사도 있다. 이렇게 동사의 성질에 따라 목적어(O) 혹은 보어(C)를 찾아야 문장을 정확히 이해할 수 있다. 편의상, 영어 문장은 다음과 같이 5 가지 구조로 분류된다:

> ① 1형식 문장: S(주어) + V(동사) [이때 동사는 **완전 자동사**]
> ② 2항식 문장: S + V + C [이때 동사는 **불완전 자동사**]
> ③ 3형식 문장: S + V + O [이때 동사는 **완전 타동사**]
> ④ 4형식 문장: S + V + O + O [이때 동사는 **수여동사**]
> ⑤ 5형식 문장: S + V + O + C [이때 동사는 **불완전 타동사**]
> 단, 이런 형식 구분은 일본식이고 실제 미국에선 시행되지 않는다!!

### 2. 영어의 8 품사

① **명사(noun)**: 사람이나 사물의 이름을 나타내는 말로, 문장 내에서 동사의 주어나 등으로 사용된다. 대개 관사(a, the)와 함께 쓰인다.
② **대명사(pronoun)**: 명사의 반복을 피하기 위해 이를 대신하는 말로, 문장 내에서 명사와 같은 역할을 한다.
③ **동사(verb)**: 행위를 표현하는 말로, 반드시 그 앞에 행위의 주체 곧 주어(subject, S)를 필요로 한다.
④ **형용사(adjective)**: 명사를 꾸미는 말로 명사의 앞/뒤에서 그 명사의 상태나 감정을 표현한다. 독립하여 보어가 될 수도 있다.
⑤ **접속사(conjunction)**: 단어와 단어, 구와 구, 절과 절을 연결해 준다.
⑥ **부사(adverb)**: 동사, 형용사, 다른 부사 등을 수식하며, 문장에서 주어, 목적어, 보어가 될 수 없다.
⑦ **전치사(preposition)**: 명사 앞에 붙어서 형용사구, 부사구를 만든다.
⑧ **감탄사(interjection)**: 느낌이나 부름/응답을 표현하는 독립어로, 다른 품사들과의 연결 없이 사용된다.

# Unit 04 명사 (Noun)

## A 명사의 종류

### 1. 보통명사(Common Noun)
일반 인물이나 사물을 나타내는 명사로, 복수형을 만들 수 있다.
girl, car, cup, tree 등.

### 2. 고유명사(Proper Noun)
인명이나 지명을 나타낸다. 대문자로 시작하며, 원칙적으로 복수로 할 수 없고 대개 관사(a, the)를 붙이지 않는다. Seoul, Mary, Mt. Everest 등

- ❶ 고유명사에 관사가 붙는 경우
    a Mr. Smith(스미스 씨라는 어떤 사람)
    an Einstein(아인스타인 같은 인물)
    the Jacksons(잭슨 네 가족), the late Mr. Kennedy(고 케네디 씨)
    the National Museum(국립 박물관)
    the Atlantic Ocean(대서양), the Mississippi(미시시피강)
    the Rocky Mountains(로키 산맥), the Korean Peninsula(한반도)
    the LA Times(타임지), the Titanic(타이타닉호), the Central Line(중앙선)
    the United Kingdom(영국), the Netherlands(네덜란드)
    the United States(미국), the Sudan(수단)

### 3. 물질명사(Material Noun)
일정한 모양이 없는 물질로, 일반적으로 복수형을 쓰지 않는다.
sugar, salt, meat, gold, water, paper, snow, milk, butter 등.

- ❶ 물질명사의 수량을 나타내는 방법: 단위 사용
    a glass of wine, a cup of tea, a piece of cake, an ounce of oil,
    two sheets of paper, two pounds of sugar, a loaf of bread

❷ 규격화된 제품이나 친숙한 종류의 물질은 복수형을 만들 수 있다.
· Don't throw **stones** at the cat.   · I want two regular **coffees**.
· These **papers** are stained.

## 4. 추상명사(Abstract Noun)
비가시적 개념 등을 나타내는 명사로, 일반적으로 복수형을 쓰지 않는다.
art, life, beauty, truth, love, hatred, information, news 등.

※ 구체적 종류나 행위의 실례를 나타낼 때 보통명사화 할 수 있다.
· Mary was **a beauty**(미인) and showed us **a mercy**(자비 행위).

## 5. 집합명사(Collective Noun)
사람이나 사물의 모임을 나타내는 명사로, 하나의 통일된 단위로 작용하면 단수 취급하고, 구성원들 각각을 고려할 때는 복수로 취급(이때는 '군집명사'라 부르기도 함).

예 people, police, family, class, crew, group, herd, team, audience(청중), management(경영진), faculty(교수진), crowd, band, committee, party, school(고기 떼), cattle(소, 항상 복수 취급) 등.

· Korean **people** has different origin from Chinese.   [집합명사]
· Korean **people** are very diligent.   [군집명사]
· Her **family** is composed of 6 members.   [집합명사]
· Her **family** except Mary were very tired after hiking.   [군집명사]

---

▌ **연습문제 10**

괄호 속 단어 중 알맞은 것에 ○표하라.

1. I found a lot of (sugars, sugar) in the room.
2. The cattle in the field (are, is) mine.
3. We ordered two cups of (coffee, coffees).
4. Mr. Smith is from (a, the) United Kingdom.
5. Jewish people (is, are) very smart.
6. Bring us two large (Coke, Cokes).
7. John has diverse (information, informations) about the moon.
8. The news from all over the world (is, are) very useful for us.

## B 명사의 수(Number)

영어에선 1개의 사물을 나타내는 단수(singular)와 2개 이상을 나타내는 복수(plural) 명사를 구분한다. 복수형 만드는 법은 다음과 같다:

### 1. 복수형 만들기

❶ 명사 끝에 -s를 붙인다. 무성음(k, p, t 등) 다음에선 s가 [스]로, 유성음 다음에선 [즈]로 발음된다.
  book - books(북스), part - parts(팥츠), pen - pens(펜즈)
  car - cars(칼즈), table - tables(테이블즈)

❷ 명사가 -s, -z, -sh, -x, -ch로 끝나면, -es 를 붙이고 발음은 [이즈].
  bus - buses(버씨즈), fox - foxes(팍씨즈)
  church - churches(철치즈)

❸ -o 로 끝나는 명사는 대개 -es 를 붙여 복수형을 만든다.
  potato - potatoes, hero – heroes
  echo – echoes, tomato - tomatoes
  **cf** piano - pianos, photo - photos
      radio – radios, studio - studios

❹ (자음)+y 의 복수형은 -y 대신 -ies로 바꾼다.
  city - cities, baby - babies
  candy - candies, lady - ladies
  ※ (모음)+y 의 복수형은 그냥 –s 만 붙인다: boy - boys

❺ -f, -fe 로 끝나는 명사는 복수형에서 종종 -ves 로 바뀐다(유성음화).
  calf – calves, elf – elves, half - halves
  knife – knives, leaf – leaves, life - lives
  loaf – loaves, self – selves, thief - thieves
  wife – wives, wolf - wolves
  **cf** chief - chiefs, staff – staffs(간부), relief - reliefs
      roof - roofs, safe - safes(금고), gulf - gulfs

## 2. 불규칙 복수형

**표 8. 불규칙 복수 명사**

| 단수 | 복수 | 단수 | 복수 | 단수 | 복수 |
|---|---|---|---|---|---|
| axis | axes | genius | -es, genii | index | indices |
| basis | bases | nucleus | nuclei | mouse | mice |
| crisis | crises | radius | -es, radii | bison | bison |
| diagnosis | diagnoses | stimulus | stimuli | corps | corps |
| emphasis | emphases | genus | genera | crossroads | crossroads |
| thesis | theses | brother | -s, rethren | deer | deer |
| parenthesis | parentheses | child | children | fish | -es, fish |
| agendum | agenda | ox | oxen | headquarters | headquarters |
| bacterium | bacteria | foot | feet | means | means |
| datum | data | goose | geese | moose | moose |
| medium | media | tooth | teeth | series | series |
| millennium | millennia | man | men | sheep | sheep |
| criterion | criteria | woman | women | species | species |
| phenomenon | phenomena | this | these | Chinese | Chinese |
| alumnus | alumni | that | those | Japanese | Japanese |
| focus | -es, foci | alga(앨거) | algae(앨지) | Swiss | Swiss |

## 3. 항상 복수형으로 쓰는 명사

❶ **학문 이름: 단수 취급** _ mathematics, economics, politics
  ※ statistics가 '통계학'을 뜻할 때는 단수, '통계자료'를 뜻할 땐 복수.
    · Statistics *is* not taught in this college.
    · Statistics *show* that the population of Incheon is decreasing.

❷ **질병 이름: 단수 취급**
   hiccups(딸꾹질), measles(홍역), diabetes(당뇨병)

❸ **게임 이름: 단수 취급**
   billiards(당구), marbles(구슬치기)
   · Rock, paper, scissors is a funny game.

❹ **짝 물건: 복수 취급하되, a pair of, a couple of 는 단수 취급.**
   glasses(안경), pants(바지), jeans, shoes, scissors(가위)
   · A pair of scissors *was* found on the desk.
   · My glasses *were* steamed up. (내 안경에 김이 서렸다)

❺ **~년대**: *the* 1980s(1980년대), *the* 2010s(2010년대)

❻ **기타**: goods(상품), clothes(옷), arms(무기), ruins(유적)

## 4. 복합명사의 복수형

❶ **중요 단어**에 –s 붙임

표 9. 복합명사의 복수형 I

| 단수형 | 복수형 | 의미 |
|---|---|---|
| father-in-law[1] | fathers-in-law | 장인, 시아버지 |
| by-stander | by-standers | 옆에 선 사람 |
| passer-by | passers-by | 통행자 |
| commander-in-chief | commanders-in-chief | 총사령관 |

주: 1. in-law는 자연적이 아닌 법률적 관계를 말한다. 즉, father-in-law는 혼인 등을 통해 새로이 아버지가 된 사람으로, 장인 혹은 시아버지를 가리킨다.

❷ **대등한 관계**이면 둘 다 혹은 맨 뒤에 –s 붙임

표 10. 복합명사의 복수형 II

| 단수형 | 복수형 | 의미 |
|---|---|---|
| man-servant | men-servants | 남자하인 |
| man-eater | men-eaters | 식인종 |
| merry-go-round | merry-go-rounds | 회전목마 |
| forget-me-not | forget-me-nots | 물망초 |

## 5. 시간, 가격, 거리, 무게 등이 하나의 단위로 사용될 때는 단수로 취급.

· Two miles *is* not a good distance to walk.
· Five thousand dollars *is* enough to buy the car.

## 6. 복수형 어미 –s 가 생략되는 경우

❶ **단위명사가 수사 다음**에 와서 뒤의 명사를 꾸며줄 때:

a **two-mile** race(2마일 경기), a **two-horse** coach(쌍두마차)
· I weigh about **seventy kilogram**. (몸무게가 70kg 정도다)

❷ dozen, hundred, thousand, percent 등이 **수 단위**로 쓰일 때:
· 325 = three **hundred** and twenty five
· About 20 **percent** of the Korean people are Christians.

## 연습문제 11

괄호 속 단어 중 알맞은 것에 ○표하라.

1. The (foxs, foxes) are cute.
2. There are three (churchs, churches) in this town.
3. Look at the (pianos, pianoes) over there.
4. My (potatos, potatoes) are nice, but his (tomatos, tomatoes) aren't.
5. John took many (photos, photoes) in the park.
6. Do not give (candys, candies) to the (babys, babies).
7. The (boys, boies) are playing with (toys, toies).
8. Give me two (loafs, loaves) of bread.
9. I put down the (leafs, leaves) on the (roofs, rooves).
10. (Wifes, Wives) are cutting the cheese with (knifs, knives).
11. She has two (childs, children).
12. (Thiefs, Thieves) tried to steal the (safes, saves) in the bank.
13. These (axes, axis) are bent.
14. He wrote two (theses, thesis) on the (oxes, oxen).
15. Wash your (tooths, teeth) and (foots, feet) before going to bed.
16. These (goose, geese) are healthy.
17. The cat caught three (mouses, mice).
18. The (deer, deers) are cared with (bison, bisons).
19. These (sheep, sheeps) are owned by the (Japanese, Japaneses).
20. Mathematics (is, are) difficult.
21. Statistics about the disease (is, are) not available now.
22. Hiccups (is, are) easy to cure.
23. Billiards (is, are) hard to learn.
24. Where did you get (that, those) jeans?
25. Her clothes (is, are) very expensive.
26. There were many (passers-by, passer-bys).
28. Two litters of water (is, are) enough for our picnic.
29. We saw many two (horse, horses) coaches in the fair.
30. Two (hundreds, hundred) and two kids were injured in the accident.

표 11. 수사

| 숫자 | 기(본)수 | (순)서수 | 숫자 | 기(본)수 | (순)서수 |
|---|---|---|---|---|---|
| 0 | zero, ou | zeroth | 21 | twenty-one | twenty-first |
| 1 | one | first | 30 | thirty | thirtieth |
| 2 | two | second | 31 | thirty-one | thirty-first |
| 3 | three | third | 40 | forty | fortieth |
| 4 | four | fourth | 41 | forty-one | forty-first |
| 5 | five | fifth | 50 | fifty | fiftieth |
| 6 | six | sixth | 51 | fifty-one | fifty-first |
| 7 | seven | seventh | 60 | sixty | sixtieth |
| 8 | eight | eighth | 61 | sixty-one | sixty-first |
| 9 | nine | ninth | 70 | seventy | seventieth |
| 10 | ten | tenth | 71 | seventy-one | seventy-first |
| 11 | eleven | eleventh | 80 | eighty | eightieth |
| 12 | twelve | twelfth | 81 | eighty-one | eighty-first |
| 13 | thirteen | thirteenth | 90 | ninety | ninetieth |
| 14 | fourteen | fourteenth | 91 | ninety-one | ninety-first |
| 15 | fifteen | fifteenth | 100 | one hundred | one hundredth |
| 16 | sixteen | sixteenth | 1,000 | one thousand | one thousandth |
| 17 | seventeen | seventeenth | 10,000 | ten thousand | ten thousandth |
| 18 | eighteen | eighteenth | 1,000,000 | one million | one millionth |
| 19 | nineteen | nineteenth | $10^9$ | one billion | one billionth |
| 20 | twenty | twentieth | $10^{12}$ | one trillion | one trillionth |

※ 배수: '~번, ~배'를 나타낼 때는 (기수)+time(s)를 붙인다.

  · one time (= once)     · two times (= twice, double)     · three times

# 숫자 읽는 법

**1. 일반 숫자:** 콤마(,)를 기준으로 끊어 읽는다. 0은 보통 '오우'로 읽는다.
· 5,601,912 → five million six hundred one thousand nine hundred (and) twelve
· 201-5061 → two ou(zero) one (dash) five ou(zero) six one
· 007 → double ou seven    · 6669 → triple six nine

**2. 연도:** 원칙적으로 두 자리씩 끊어 읽는다.
· 1956 → nineteen fifty six.    · 2002 → two thousand two 혹은 twenty ou two

**3. 시각:** 그냥 순서대로 읽어도 되고, '~분 전'이나 '~분 후'로 읽기도 한다.
· 04:25 → four, twenty five.    · 12:10 → twelve ten 혹은 ten past twelve
· 08:50 → eight fifty 혹은 ten to nine(9시 10분 전)

**4. 분수와 소수:** 분수의 분자는 기수로, 분모는 서수로 쓴다. 소수점은 point로 읽는다.
· 1/2 → a(one) half    · $2\frac{2}{3}$ → two and two thirds    · 2.51 → two point five one
· One third of soldiers were dead.    · Two thirds of salt was stolen.

**5. 수식:** 수학에서 자주 사용되는 수식 읽기
· 2+3=5 → 2 plus 5 equals 5    · 2-3=-1 → 2 minus 3 equals negative 1
· 2×3 → 2 times 3 혹은 2 multiplied by 3         · 2÷3 → 2 divided by 3
· 2:3 → 2 to 3              · $2^2$ → 2 squared    · $2^3$ → 2 cubed
· $2^4$ → 2 to the power 4 혹은 2 to the fourth (power) 혹은 2 to the four
· 2/$x$ → 2 over $x$
· ($x$-1)(y+1)/z → ($x$-1), (y+1) over z

**6. 기타**
· World War II → World War Two        · George II → George the Second
· m²/sec → square meter per second,    · m³/min → cubic meter per minute
· -10℃ → minus(or negative) 10 degrees Celsius
    ※ 섭씨(C: Celsius)/ 화씨(F: Fahrenheit)는 온도 계량형을 만든 사람의 한자식
      성씨(氏)에서 온 말이다. 즉 섭씨=Mr. 攝, 화씨=Mr. 華

## C 성을 표시하는 명사(Gender)

명사에서 남성과 여성을 표시하는 방법은 다음과 같다:

### 1. 여성 접미사(-ess, -ine)를 붙이는 경우

duke ↔ duch**ess**,  prince ↔ princ**ess**,  host ↔ host**ess**,
waiter ↔ waitr**ess**,  hero ↔ hero**ine**,  cf **male** ↔ **fe**male

### 2. 성을 나타내는 접두사, 접미사를 붙이는 경우

**boy**-friend ↔ **girl**-friend,  **man**-servant ↔ **maid**-servant
**he**-goat ↔ **she**-goat,  land**lord** ↔ land**lady**

### 3. 다른 용어를 쓰는 경우

son ↔ daughter,  king ↔ queen,  man ↔ woman,
lad(청년) ↔ lass,  brother ↔ sister,  husband ↔ wife,
nephew ↔ niece,  deer ↔ doe(암사슴),  rooster ↔ hen
stallion ↔ mare(암말),  ram ↔ ewe(암양),  bull ↔ cow

### ■ 연습문제 12

**01.** 괄호 속 단어 중 옳은 것을 골라라.

① I have (three, third) apples in my bag.
② Tom saws that movie (twice, second).
③ There were two (hundred, hundreds) people in the train.
④ Two thirds of the silver (is, are) mine.
⑤ Hurry up. It's ten (to, before) six.

**02.** 다음 명사의 여성형을 쓰라.

① duke
② waiter
③ steward
④ actor
⑤ prince
⑥ ram
⑦ nephew
⑧ rooster
⑨ man-servant
⑩ he-goat
⑪ lad
⑫ male

## D 명사의 격(Case)

명사는 문장에서 늘 특정 역할(주어, 목적어)을 한다. 영어의 명사는 **주격**, **목적격**, **소유격**은 형태가 다 같은데 (인칭대명사는 다름), 다만 소유를 나타내는 방법이 조금 다를 뿐이다. 상대를 부를 때 쓰는 호격은 독립적으로 쓰이며 형태는 역시 주격과 같다.

1. **소유격 만들기:** 소유격은 일종의 형용사로, 그 다음에 명사를 수반한다.

   ❶ **사람과 동물**의 소유격은 소유하는 명사 끝에 **'s**를 붙인다.
      -s 로 끝나는 명사에는 '(apostrophe)만 붙인다:
      boy's cap, cat's leg, Jesus' words, girls' highschool(여고)

   ❷ **무생물**인 경우, 소유하는 명사 앞에 of 를 써서 소유격을 만드는 게 원칙이다.
      window of house(집의 창문),
      voice of love(사랑의 목소리)

   ❸ **상황**에 따라 사람도 of 로 소유격을 만들 수 있다.
      · I saw the girl's dog in a red dress.(✗) (드레스 입은 개?)
      ⇒ I saw the dog of the girl in a red dress.(○) (드레스 입은 소녀의 개)

   ❹ **시간, 거리, 지명, 조직, 활동** 등의 비인칭 명사도 (표현의 단순화를 위해) 's 로 소유격을 만들 수 있다:
      two hours' delay(두 시간의 지체), today's paper(오늘의 신문)　　　　[시간]
      ten miles' distance(10마일의 거리)　　　　[거리]
      Korea's future, world's best player(세계 최고 선수)　　　　[지명]
      the school's history, the government's policy　　　　[조직]
      the plan's importance, the report's conclusion　　　　[활동]

2. **공동 소유와 개별 소유**
   Tom and Jerry's room (두 사람이 함께 쓰는 방)
   Tom's and Jerry's rooms(각 사람이 쓰는 방들)

## 3. 소유명사

소유격 뒤에 명사가 오지 않으면 그 소유격은 소유 명사가 되며 해석은 "~의 것"이 된다.

· This hat is not my **mother's**. (이 모자는 내 어머니 것이 아니다.)

## 4. 이중소유격(Double Possessive)

소유 대상 앞에 a(an), this, that, some, any 등이 올 때는
(소유격)+(명사) 대신 **(명사)+of+(소유[대]명사)** 형태를 쓴다.

· this my father's book (×) → this book of my father's (○)
· Tom is a my friend. (×) → Tom is a friend of **mine**. (○)
　　　　　　　　　　　= Tom is one of my friends. (○)
· Do you know any son **of the farmer's**? (그 농부의 아들들 중 아무나)

## 5. 소유격 뒤의 명사 생략

반복 단어거나 house나 shop 같이 익숙한 장소는 생략할 수 있다.

· This phone is my **sister's** (phone).
· He went to the **butcher's** (shop) to buy some pork. (정육점)

### ▌연습문제 13
괄호 속 단어 중 옳은 것을 골라라.

1. (He, His) works in the toy factory.
2. He told (me, my) not to cry.
3. We want (she, her) to go with us.
4. This is not (my, mine) book.
5. The building is a (girl's, girls') highschool.
6. Where is (today's, of today) newspaper,
7. John and Jill's house (are, is) very pretty.
8. She met (a friend of mine, a my friend) in the party.
9. I like (that Tom's bike, that bike of Tom's).
10. Bill bought the beef at the (butcher, butcher's).

# 종합문제 1

**01 다음 문장에서 어색한 부분을 찾아 바르게 고치라.**

1. Yesterday I met a my old friend on the street.
2. May I use this Tom's camera?
3. Use your scissor to cut the paper.
4. They are looking for a ten-years-old boy.
5. This singer was popular in 1990s.
6. This is Tom's and Jerry's room.
7. We got two hour's delay because of snow.
8. Your answer for the nineth question is wrong.
9. I know a girl who came from the China.
10. The waters are leaking from the tanks.

**02 괄호 속 단어들 중 알맞은 것에 ○표하라.**

1. My cap is cheaper than (John, John's).
2. Tom Cruise is the (hero, heroine) of the movie.
3. I want (today, today's) newspaper.
4. He is (a friend, one) of my friends.
5. She is the (landlord, landlady) of this farm.
6. I ate one third of milk, so two thirds (is, are) left.
7. One third of the people (is, are) black.
8. Elizabeth became the (king, queen) of England.
9. As the mare is sick, (he, she) cannot run in the race.
10. I like this hat of (her, hers).

**03 괄호 속에 있는 말을 이용해 다음 우리말을 영작하라.**

1. 나는 나의 이 옛 친구를 잊을 수 없다. (this old friend)

2. 10달러는 이 자전거를 사기에 충분치 않다. (enough)

3. 그 기차는 20분의 지체 후에 출발했다. (delay, start)

4. 스미스 씨 네는 어제 비행기로 중국에 갔다. (Mr. Smiths, by plane)

5. Tom의 가족은 키가 크다. (family, tall)

6. Tom의 가족은 Canada 출신이다. (from Canada)

7. 나는 빨간 모자를 쓴 소녀의 핸드백을 보았다. (with a red hat)

8. 내 친구들 중 1/3은 미국인이다. (American)

**영어 노래 부르기:** 언어 학습의 핵심은 반복이다. 그런 면에서 팝송이나 영어 동요는 영어 공부에 안성맞춤인 도구이다. 같은 문구를 수십 번 반복하는 건 지겨울 수 있지만, 노래는 얼마든지 반복할 수 있다. 영어 노래의 또 다른 장점 중 하나는 저절로 액센트를 익힐 수 있다는 것이다. 영어 노래에서 고음은 거의 단어의 강세 위치와 일치하기 때문이다. 음악의 고저와 가사의 강세가 일치하지 않는 노래는 사람들에게 잘 불릴 수 없다.

# Unit 05 관사 (Article)

'관사'의 '관'은 '모자'를 뜻하는데, 명사의 머리 위에 붙어 다니므로 그런 이름이 붙었다.
관사(a, the)가 보이면 다음에 명사가 온다는 신호가 된다. 예컨대, "I am serving boy." 라는 문장의 경우, 관사가 없어 글의 뜻이 모호하다. 여기에 관사 a를 넣어 보는데, 그 위치에 따라 뜻이 전혀 달라진다:
· I am a serving boy(나는 시중드는 소년이다).   · I am serving a boy(나는 한 소년을 시중들고 있다).

관사는 **일종의 형용사**지만, 명사와 불가분 관계이므로 먼저 공부한다.

## A 관사의 종류

### 1. 부정관사 a, an(하나의, 어떤)

'부정(indefinite)'이란 '정해져 있지 않다'는 뜻으로, 특정되지 않은 존재를 가리킨다. 부정관사를 쓰면 그와 동일하거나 유사한 명사가 여럿 있을 수 있음을 나타낸다. 모음으로 시작하는 말 앞에선 발음 편의를 위해 an을 쓴다.

**예** a pen, an apple, an egg, an umbrella

※ an hour, an honest man                                          [h가 묵음]
※ a useful book, a university                                     [u가 자음 [j]로 발음되므로]

· I met a nice girl(어떤) and we are of an age(같은).
· I need an honest friend rather than a useful one.

### 2. 정관사 the(그)

이는 본래 특정 사물을 가리킬 때 사용된다. 정관사 the는 자음 앞에서는 [ðə](더), 모음 앞에선 [ði](디)로 발음된다. 부정관사는 고대 언어에 존재하지 않았던 것으로 그 용법이 비교적 단순하지만, 정관사는 다음과 같은 다양한 용법이 있다.

❶ 앞에 언급된 명사를 다시 받을 때:
　· I bought a dog. The dog is very cute.

❷ 처음 언급되더라도 서로 알고 있거나 따로 설명되는 명사를 가리킬 때:
　· Will you close the window?                                    [서로 알고 있는 '그 창문']
　· The book *on the table* is mine.                              [따로 설명되는 '그 책']
　· The sun is rising.                                            [모두가 알고 있는 '태양']
　· The cow is a useful animal.                                   [일반적으로 알려진 동물]

❸ 서수, 형용사 최상급, only 등 앞에서(유일하므로):
- I won **the third** prize in the contest.
- Tom is **the tallest** boy in our class.
  - **cf** I will *try* **a** *third* time. ([두 번 실패 후] 한 번 더 도전)

## 3. 관사의 특수 용법

❶ **관사 + (고유명사)**
여러 지역에 걸쳐있는 **산, 강, 바다, 호수, 사막, 철도, 도로, 터널, 복수형태 지명, 관청, 일반 명사에서 유래한 고유명사**엔 the 가 붙을 수 있다. 사람 이름 앞에 a(an)이 붙으면 "**~라는 사람, ~ 같은 사람**"을 뜻한다.
- The Sahara(사하라사막)
- The White House(백악관)
- The Philippines(필리핀)
- The Alps(알프스)

❷ **a + (단위)**: ~마다(per)
- He works 10 hours **a** day. (하루당)

❸ **many a + (단수명사)**: 많은 ~
- **Many a** *man* was killed in the war.      [동사도 단수형]
- Jack tried **many a** *time* but failed. (여러 번)
- a Ms. Kim(김씨라는 여자)

❹ **a number of + (복수명사)**: 많은 ~(=many)
- **A number of** students *were* at the meeting.      [동사도 복수형]
  - **cf** The number of students at the meeting *was* 30. (숫자)

❺ **관사의 공통적 사용**: 한 사람이 둘 이상의 직업이나 직위를 가질 때, 관사는 한 번만 사용한다.
- He is **a** singer and actor. (가수이자 배우)
  - **cf** A singer and **an** actor were present. (가수 한 명과 배우 한 명)

❻ **신체를 접촉할 때**, (전치사) + the + (신체)를 쓴다:
· Tom hit *me* on the head. (Tom은 내 머리를 때렸다.)
= Tom hit *my* head.

❼ **the + 형용사 = 보통명사**: 대개 복수지만 단수도 될 수 있다.
the rich = rich people, the second = the second one

❽ **악기 앞에는 the를 붙인다**:
· She plays the violin.　　　　　　　　[음악가가 사용하는 악기는 대개 정해져 있음]
　**cf** 운동 앞에는 관사를 붙이지 않는다.
· He plays basketball.　　　　　　　　[운동선수가 사용하는 공은 자주 바뀌므로]

❾ **기타 정관사를 쓰는 경우**
in the morning, in the afternoon, in the evening　　**cf** at night
in the 1980s(1980년대에), by the pound(파운드 단위로)
· Beef was sold by the pound in the 1960s.

### ▎연습문제 14

괄호 속 단어들 중 알맞은 것에 ○표하라.

1. We have (a, an) hour till departure.
2. The workers get payment once (a, the) week.
3. Look at (a, the) sun rising in the east.
4. She touched me on (a, the) head.
5. You should help (a, the) poor.
6. In (a, the) morning, I brush my teeth.
7. Do you sell the sugar by (a, the) pound?
8. There (were, was) many a toy on the table.
9. A number of people (was, were) wounded in the accident.
10. The number of houses (was, were) 20 at that time.

## B 관사의 위치

관사는 명사 혹은 명사구(형용사 포함)의 맨 앞에 놓는 게 원칙인데, 특별한 용어와 함께 쓰이면 위치가 바뀔 수도 있다.

· a *very good* time　　· the *beautiful white* flowers

**1. as, so, too, how 등이 쓰이면 형용사는 부정관사 앞으로 나온다.**

· It is **too** *good* an opportunity *to* lose. (잃어버리기 아까운 좋은 기회)
· Mike is **as** *clever* a boy *as* his brother. (그의 형처럼 영리한 소년)
· She is not **so** *pretty* a girl *as* she used to be. (과거처럼 예쁜 소녀)
· **How** *lovely* a girl she is! (= What a lovely girl she is!)　　[감탄문]

**2. such, quite, many 가 쓰이면 부정관사는 그 바로 뒤에 온다.**

· I have never seen **such an** animal. (그러한 동물)
· 10 years was **quite a** long time for her. (아주 오랜 시간)

**3. all, both, double 등과 쓰이면 정관사는 그 뒤에 온다.**

· **All the** members were present. (모든 회원)
· **Both the** parents were dead. (부모님 두 분 모두)
· He paid **double the** price. (가격의 두 배)
　**cf** the double price (이중 가격)
※ twice는 항상 부사로 쓰이고, double은 주로 형용사, 명사로 쓰인다.


## C 관사의 생략

관사는 써 주는 게 원칙이나, 빈번히 사용되는 명사에선 생략되기도 한다.

**1. 상대를 부를 때(호칭)**

· **Sir,** may I help you?

**2. 자기 가족 구성원을 가리킬 때**

· **Mother** loves cooking pizza.　　　　　　　　　　[Mother = My mother]

### 3. 건물, 기구가 본연의 목적으로 쓰일 때

go to school(공부하러), go to church(예배드리러), go to bed(잠자러)

· I go to school by bus.

cf Father came to the school to pick me up.

### 4. 교통수단

by bus, by subway, by train, by boat, by plane

cf on foot (걸어서)

### 5. 식사, 운동, 질병, 학과목 이름

· I have breakfast at seven.
· He plays badminton everyday.   cf I played *the* piano.
· She died of cancer.
· John is good at math.

### 6. 대귀(Couple Words)

bread and butter(버터 바른 빵)   knife and fork(칼과 포크)
hand in hand(서로 손을 잡고)   arm in arm(서로 팔을 끼고)
from morning till night(아침부터 저녁까지)

### 7. 기타(관사가 없어도 명사임에 분명할 때)

· We elected him chairman.(그를 의장으로 선출했다)
· The mouth of dog is larger than that of cat.
· I like apple better than banana.

---

### ▌연습문제 15

괄호 속 단어들 중 알맞은 것에 ○표하라.

1. Tom is so (a smart, smart a) boy that he will never be lost.
2. It was (a quite, quite a) long time.
3. To get the ticket, I had to pay (the double, double the) price.
4. I usually go to (bed, a bed, the bed) at 10.
5. She died of (cancer, a cancer, the cancer).
6. They marched arm in (arm, an arm) on the street.

# 종합문제 2

**01 다음 문장에서 어색한 부분을 찾아 바르게 고치라.**

1. A sun is larger than a moon.
2. I usually have a breakfast at 8:00.
3. There is an university in that block.
4. Let's play a tennis after school.
5. Jane can play piano very well.
6. I will pay the double price that he has offered to you.
7. A black and white dog are running after me.
8. The rich is not always happy.
9. How a lovely flower it is!
10. I will never make a such mistake.
11. The both brothers were very brave.
12. Peace and happiness always go a hand in a hand.
13. A water of this pool is very clean.
14. I lost the my bag.
15. He knows the all boys in my class.
16. I found this a pen on the floor.
17. I met this your friend in the park.
18. Tom is a fastest runner in his class.
19. Let's meet together at this bench after a hour.
20. Every a Sunday, he goes to church by a bus.

**02 괄호 속에 있는 말을 이용해 다음 우리말을 영작하라.**

1. 그는 아침부터 밤까지 기타를 친다. (from ~ till)

2. 그들은 Trump를 미국 대통령으로 선출했다. (elect)

3. 우리는 열 시에 취침한다. (go, bed)

4. 그는 배우이자 작가이다. (and)

5. 누가 그렇게 큰 피자를 만들었니? (who, such)

6. 그들은 1년에 100 대의 자동차를 만든다. (make, a year)

7. 월요일은 한 주의 두 번째 날이다. (Monday, second)

8. 그 노인은 말라리아로 죽었다. (die, malaria)

9. 그녀는 1980년대에 유명한 배우였다. (in the 1980s)

10. John은 그의 형처럼 멋진 소년이다. (handsome, as)

**Article의 의미:** 영어에서 '관사'를 뜻하는 article이 무슨 의미인지는 확실치 않다. '팔, 주먹'을 뜻하는 art에 '작다'는 뜻의 접미사 -cle이 붙은 형태인데, 직역하면 '작은 팔 혹은 주먹'이란 말이다. 짐작컨대, 헬라어의 관사 ὁ (남성) 또는 ἡ (여성)가 단어가 짧으면서 모양이 주먹 혹은 팔처럼 생겨서 그런 이름이 붙은 것 같다.

# Unit 06 대명사 (Pronoun)

대명사는 명사를 대신하는 말로, 그 종류는 편의상 인칭대명사, 지시대명사, 의문대명사, 부정대명사, 관계대명사 등으로 구분하며 관사는 붙이지 않는다.

## A 인칭대명사(Personal Pronoun)

고대 언어의 성·수·격에 따른 명사 변화 흔적이 유일하게 남아 있는 부분인데, 여기서 **1인칭**은 **말하는 자신**(나·우리), **2인칭**은 **듣는 자**(너·너희), **3인칭**은 **그 외 존재**(그, 그녀, 그것·그들)를 가리킨다.
(각 인칭대명사에 대한 be동사의 변화는 표 13, 14를 보라.)

### 표 12. 인칭대명사, 소유대명사, 재귀대명사

| 인칭 | 수 | 격 | 주격 (~가) | 소유격 (~의) | 목적격 (~를) | 소유대명사 (~의 것) | 재귀대명사 (~자신) |
|---|---|---|---|---|---|---|---|
| 1 | 단수(나) | | I | my | me | mine | myself |
|   | 복수(우리) | | we | our | us | ours | ourselves |
| 2 | 단수(너) | | you | your | you | yours | yourself |
|   | 복수(너희) | | you | your | you | yours | yourselves |
| 3 | 단수 | 남성(그) | he | his | him | his | himself |
|   |    | 여성(그녀) | she | her | her | hers | herself |
|   |    | 중성(그것) | it | its | it | (its) | itself |
|   | 복수(그들) | | they | their | them | theirs | themselves |

1. **인칭대명사의 격변화: 주격**은 동사의 **행위를 하는** 주체, **목적격**은 동사의 **행위를 받는** 객체, **소유격**은 다른 대상에 대한 **소유 관계**를 나타낸다.
   ※ 소유대명사와 재귀대명사는 격변화를 하지 않는다.

- We love him and his family.
  (주격)   (목적격) (소유격)
- If your towel is wet, use mine.   It is next to yours.
  (소유격)              (소유대명사)  (주격)    (소유대명사)
- She thinks of herself only.
              (재귀대명사)
- She herself built her house.
    (재귀대명사)   (소유격)

## 2. 일반 주어로서의 we, you, they

we, you, they 는 막연히 일반 사람을 가리키는 데 사용될 수 있다.

- **We(You)** should obey **our(your)** parents. (부모에게 순종해야 한다)
- **They** say that Socrates was wise. (소크라테스는 현명했다고 한다)

## 3. 소유대명사(Possessive Pronoun)의 용법

명사의 반복을 피하기 위해 사용되는데, 이중 소유격(of+소유격)에서 종종 사용된다.
단, 소유대명사 its는 거의 사용되지 않는다.

- This hat is **hers**(=her cap). (그녀의 것)
- Did you see *any* friends **of mine**?                    [이중 소유격]
  = Did you see *any of my* friends?

## 4. 재귀대명사(Reflexive Pronoun)의 용법

❶ **재귀적** 용법: 재귀란 '되돌아 온다'는 뜻으로, 주체가 행하는 동작의 대상이 주체 자신이 된다는 말이다.
  - I told **myself** to be brave.
  - I heard (that) she killed **herself**.
  - Help **yourself** to the cake. (남이 도와주지 않아도 스스로 챙겨 먹어라)

❷ **강조적** 용법: 명사나 대명사를 강조하기 위해 반복할 때 사용된다.
  - You **yourself** did it. (너 자신이 그걸 했다)
  - Tom did it **himself**. (Tom이 스스로 그걸 했다)

❸ **관용적** 용법:
  by oneself(혼자 외로이), for oneself(혼자 힘으로), of oneself(저절로)
  ※ 이 세 가지는 혼동되어 쓰이는 경향이 있다.
  - I stayed there by myself. (나 혼자 외로이)
  - He finished the work for himself. (그의 힘으로)
  - The window opened of(or by) itself. (저절로)

▌**연습문제 16**

괄호 속 단어들 중 알맞은 것에 ○표하라.

1. Do you know what is (our, us) bus?
2. Is this your book? / Yes, it's (my, mine).
3. She loves (herself, himself) very much.
4. John visited (me, my) with (him, his) family.
5. Look at (they, them) on the beach.
6. Do you know any friend of (my, mine)?
7. I am a big fan of (her, hers).
8. (He, They) say Einstein was a genius.
9. Tell (you, yourself) that it is the time to rise again.
10. The door opened (for, of) itself.

## 5. it의 특별 용법

❶ **날씨, 시각, 거리, 계절, 요일** 등을 나타내는 비인칭 주어

- It is cold outside. (날씨)
- It is already 9 o'clock. (시각)
- It is 50 miles from here to New York. (거리)
- It is summer now. (계절)
- What day is it today? / It is Tuesday. (요일)

❷ **가주어 및 가목적어**: 주어나 목적어가 길어질 때, 이를 대신해 it을 쓰고 진짜 주어나 목적어는 뒤쪽으로 보낸다.

- To study Chinese is hard. ⇒ <u>It</u> is hard <u>to study Chinese</u>.
                                (가주어)      (진주어)

- That he was dead is true. ⇒ <u>It</u> is true <u>that he was dead</u>.
                                 (가주어)      (진주어)

- I think <u>it</u> easy <u>to copy the file</u>.
         (가목적어)    (진목적어)

❸ **강조**를 위한 It is ~ that 의 용법: 강조 부분을 **앞으로** 내놓는다.
   · Tom met Jane at the park yesterday.
      → It is(was) *Tom* that(*or* who) met Jane at the park yesterday.
      → It is(was) *Jane* that(*or* whom) Tom met at the park yesterday.
      → It is(was) *at the park* that(*or* where) Tom met Jane yesterday.
      → It is(was) *yesterday* that(*or* when) Tom met Jane at the park.

▌**연습문제 17**

괄호 속 단어들 중 알맞은 것에 ○표하라.

1. (It, This) is hot today.
2. What day is (it, this) today?
3. I think (it, that) difficult to learn English.
4. How far is (it, that) from Seoul to Busan?
5. (It, That) was John that I met yesterday in the park.
6. I know (it true, true it) that he is married.

## B 지시대명사(Demonstrative Pronoun)

대상을 **가리킬 때** 사용하는 대명사. 가까운 것은 this(these) 먼 것은 that(those)으로 표현하며, 격변화는 하지 않는다.
   · **This** is my phone and **that** is yours.
   · **These** were made in Korea and **those** (were made) in China.

### 1. 후자와 전자를 나타내는 this 와 that
   · I have a cat and a dog; <u>this</u> is big and <u>that</u> is small.
      [this = 후자, 즉 dog: 나중에 언급되었으므로 현재 말하는 관점에서 가깝다.]
      [that = 전자, 즉 cat: 먼저 언급되었으므로 현재 말하는 관점에서 멀다.]

### 2. 전화상에서 본인과 상대를 나타내는 this와 that
   · Hello, **this** is Tom speaking. Is **that** you, Mary?

## 3. 현재와 과거를 나타내는 this(these)와 that(those)

this year(올해), that year(과거 그 해),
these days(요즘), those days(과거 당시)

## 4. 문장 전체를 받는 this와 that

· Let me say **this**: he is a lucky guy.　　　　　　　　　　[this는 앞·뒤 문장을 다 받음]
· He came back safely. **That** made me happy.　　　　　　[that은 앞 문장만]

## 5. 명사의 반복을 피하기 위한 that(those)

· The tail of fox is longer than **that** of rabbit.　　　　　　[that = tail]
· Korean bears are smaller than **those** in America.　　　　[those = bears]

## 6. 관계대명사와 함께 "~한 사람들"의 의미로 쓰이는 those

· Heaven helps **those** who help themselves.

---

### ▌연습문제 18

괄호 속 단어들 중 알맞은 것에 ○표하라.

1. (This, That) year, I will study English hard.
2. Hello, (this, that) is Roy speaking.
3. Your score is higher than (this, that) of Tom.
4. Happy are (these, those) who are poor in spirit.
5. I will say (this, that) to you: "Don't cheat me."

---

## C 부정대명사(Indefinitive Pronoun)

불특정 사람이나 사물을 대신할 때 쓰며, 격변화는 하지 않는다.

### 1. one(복수 ones)의 용법

**❶ 일반** 사람을 가리킬 때

· **One** should do **his/her** best. (= **Ones** should do **their** best.)
· Many people spend Christmas Eve with their beloved **ones**.
· I know **the ones**(=those) who never give up.

❷ **특정되지 않은 보통명사를 받을 때 쓰며, 지정된 경우엔 it을 쓴다.**
· Do you have **a** book? / Yes, I have **one**.
   cf Do you have **the** book? / Yes, I have **it**.

❸ **no one과 none**: no one은 대개 **단수**로 받지만, none of는 그다음에 복수 명사가 오면 **복수**로 쓰인다.
· **No one** *knows* our future.
· **None** of the passengers *were* safe in the accident.

## 2. nobody의 용법

❶ nobody는 대개 단수로 받는다.
· **Nobody** *wants* to hear your silly story.

❷ nobody는 not anybody로 바꿔 쓸 수 있지만, 문두에서는 불가하다.
· I saw **nobody** in the room.
= I did**n't** see **anybody** in the room.
· **Nobody** answered my question.
   cf **Anybody** did *not* answer my question. (✗)

## 3. each와 every의 용법

항상 단수로 취급한다. every는 단독으로 사용되지 않고 -one, -body, -thing 등과 결합되는데, 개별성을 나타내면서도 예외가 없음을 강조한다.

· **Each** of them has his or her own cap.
· **Everyone(Everybody)** was present at the meeting.

## 4. some과 any의 용법

보통명사와 물질명사에 다 사용될 수 있는데, 보통명사를 대신할 경우는 복수가 된다. some은 **긍정문**에, any는 **부정문, 의문문, 조건문(if 절)**에 쓰이는 게 원칙이다.

· Do you have pens? / Yes, I have **some**.
· I have no pens. Do you have **any**? / No, I don't have **any**.
· I have no money. If you have **any**, please lend me **some**.
· **Some** of visitors **were** Korean, but I **didn't** know **any** of them.

❶ some이 **의문문**에 쓰이면, **청유**의 뜻이 된다.
  · I have fresh milk. Do you want **some**? (좀 드시겠어요?)

❷ any가 **긍정문**에 쓰이면, '누구라도, 무엇이라도'라는 뜻이 된다.
  · **Any** (of) Korean students will do it.
   = Every Korean student will do it.

❸ not ~ any 구문은 쓰이지만, any ~ not 구문은 잘 쓰지 않는다.
  · He **didn't** answer **any** of the questions.
   = He answered **none** of the questions.
  · **Any** of them were **not** diligent. (×)   [부정은 가능한 한 빨리 표현]
   ⇒ **None** of them were diligent. (○)

❹ some과 any는 -one, -body, -thing과 결합하기도 한다.
  · **Someone** is waiting for you in the room.
  · Please do not touch **anything** in this room.
  · It is **anybody**'s guess how long it will take. (아무도 모른다)

## 5. other, another, the other(s) 용법

another는 an+other로서 '다른 하나'(단수)를 뜻한다. the other(s)는 특정된 다른 것, 곧 **나머지**를 뜻한다. the other는 물질명사에는 사용되지 않는다.

· She doesn't want to meet **others**. (막연히 '다른 사람들')
· I don't like this hat. Show me **another**. ('다른 하나')
· There were **two** apples. I ate **one** and gave him **the other**.
· Some of the cats were white, and **the others** were black.
  **cf** I drank **some** *milk* in the bottle and gave **the rest** to my cat.

## 6. 상호대명사 each other, one another (서로서로)

원칙적으로 each other는 둘, one another는 셋 이상에 적용되나 실제론 별 구별 없이 사용.

· They helped **each other**(or one another).
· The band shook hands with **one another**.

## 7. all과 both의 용법

both는 '둘 다', all은 셋 이상에 대해 '모두'를 나타낸다.

- **Both** (of) the brothers are lawyers. (두 형제 모두)
- **All** (of) the girls were pretty. (셋 이상의 소녀들 모두)

## 8. either(둘 중 하나)와 neither(둘 다 아닌) 항상 단수이다.

- **Either** of them *is* lying. (둘 중 하나는 거짓말을 하고 있다)
- **Neither** of them *is* innocent. (둘 다 결백하지 않다)

## 9. 부분부정과 전체부정

not + every, all, both 은 부분부정,
not + any, either 혹은 neither는 전체부정이 된다.

- I don't know **everything**. (모든 걸 다 아는 건 아니다)    [부분부정]
  - cf I don't know **anything**. (아무것도 모른다)    [전체부정]
- I don't know **all** of them. (그들 모두를 아는 건 아니다)    [부분부정]
  - cf I don't know **any** of them. (아무도 모른다)    [전체부정]
- I don't know **both** of them. (둘 다 아는 건 아니다)    [부분부정]
  - cf I don't know **either** of them. (둘 다 모른다)    [전체부정]

### ■ 연습문제 19

괄호 속 단어들 중 알맞은 것에 ○표하라.

1. Everybody welcomes the friendly (ones, those).
2. Do you have a computer? / Yes, I have (it, one).
3. (No one, None) of them were safe.
4. (Every, Each) of students was wearing a cap.
5. Do you have sugar? / Yes, I have (any, some)
6. Though he already had two eggs, he took (other, another) one.
7. Of the two balls, I took one and Tom got (another, the other).
8. I lost my watch. If you find (it, one), please tell me.
9. (Both, Each) of them were so pretty.
10. As a stranger, I didn't know (anything, everything) about here.

## D 의문대명사(Interrogative Pronoun)

**1. who(누구)의 용법:** 소유격 whose, 목적격 whom, 소유대명사 whose.
사람 이름이나 가족 관계를 물을 때 사용한다.

- **Who** is he? / He is *Harry Porter*.
- **Who** is the girl? / She is *my sister*.
- **Whose** is this car? / It is *mine*.
- **Who(m)** do you want to go with?　　　　　[구어에선 who를 쓰기도 함]
- With **whom** do you want to go?　　　　　[전치사와 함께 쓰면 항상 whom]
- **Who** is older, you or Tom?

  **cf** 강조형 whoever(대체 누가), whomever(대체 누구를)도 쓰인다.
  - **Whoever** can do such a thing? (대체 누가 그런 짓을 할 수 있는가?)

  **cf** 상대방 이름을 물을 때 "Who are you?"는 좀 무례한 표현이라 삼간다.
  - Who are you? (무례) ⇒ May I have your name? (정중)

**2. what(무엇)의 용법:** 소유격은 없고 목적격은 what이다. 사람과 사물에 다 사용될 수 있는데, 사람에 대해선 직업이나 신분을 물을 때 쓴다.

- **What** is it? / It is a tablet PC.
- **What** is he? (=**What** does he do?) / He is a *doctor*.
- **What**'s the matter? = **What**'s up? = **What**'s wrong? (무슨 일이냐?)

※ 우리와는 다른 표현 방식들에 유의하자!
- **What** is the capital of China?　　　　　　　　　　[where가 아님]
- **What** is the price? (= How much is it?)
- **What** is your age? (= How old are you?)
- **What** is your height? (= How tall are you?)
- **What** brought you here? (= Why did you come here?)

**3. which(어느 것)의 용법:** 소유격은 of which, 목적격은 which이다. 사물에 대해 대상을 선택할 때 쓰며 what을 대신 쓰기도 한다.

- **Which** of these do you want, blue one or red one?
- **Which**(*or* **What**) is better, bus or train?

4. **의문형용사** : 의문사가 단독으로 쓰이지 않고 명사 앞에 붙으면 의문형용사가 된다.
   - **Whose** car is that?
   - **What** book is this? (= *What kind of* book is this?)
   - **Which**(*or* **What**) color do you like best?

5. **의문사 주어인 경우 동사의 위치** : 의문사가 주어이면 동사를 도치시키지 않는다.
   - **Who** is watching us? (○)            **cf** Is **who** watching us? (×)

### ▌연습문제 20

**01.** 다음 빈칸에 적당한 의문대명사를 넣어라.

1. _____ does she do?   /   She is a teacher.
2. _____ do you prefer, Jack or Tom?
3. _____ is this cell phone?   /   It's mine.
4. _____ is she?   /   She is my aunt.
5. _____ is better, pizza or hamburger?
6. _____ is taller, Tom or Jerry?
7. _____ is the matter with you?
8. _____ book is this?   /   That is Sally's.
9. With _____ do you study?   /   With John.
10. _____ are you waiting for?   /   My mom.
11. _____ are you researching on?   /   On the democracy.
12. _____ cap is yours?   /   That yellow one.

**02.** 괄호 속 단어들 중 알맞은 것에 ○표하라.

1. (Who is, Is who) running on the playground?
2. (Whose, What) glasses are these?   /   They are mine.
3. (Which, What) is the box made of?
4. (Whom, What) do you like better, Chris or Mike?
5. (What, How) is the price of this bag?

# 종합문제 3

**01 다음 문장에서 어색한 부분을 찾아 바르게 고치라.**

1. Each of students were given a lunch box.
2. My hat is bigger than your.
3. Living alone, he killed him due to severe depression.
4. I solved the problem by oneself.
5. That is difficult climbing up this mountain.
6. I have an apple and a banana; this is round and that is long.
7. They fought one the other to take the money.
8. I am very busy those days. so I can't go there.
9. There are three boys outside, and I know neither of them.
10. The people should do his best when participating in this project.
11. Whose a book is this?
12. With who do you want to play tennis?
13. You two must help each one to win this game.
14. Where is the capital of Canada?   /   It is Ottawa.
15. You don't know something about Jane.
16. This my picture is very old.
17. All of you have to take care of every another.
18. If you have some question, come to me anytime.
19. Ears of rabbit are longer than that of cat.
20. As far as I know, neither of them are sincere.

**02 괄호 속에 있는 말을 이용해 다음 우리말을 영작하라.**

1. Valentine Day에 우리는 사랑하는 이들에게 선물을 준다. (beloved)

2. 물을 조금만 사발에 부어주세요. (some, bowl)

3. 내가 그 케이크를 다 먹은 건 아니다. (all)

4. 케이크 일부는 Tom에게 주고 나머지는 Jane에게 주었다. (some, rest)

5. 방에 있는 이들은 서로 악수를 나누고 있다. (shake hands, another)

6. 나는 Bill의 오랜 친구지만 그에 관해 다 아는 건 아니다. (everything)

7. 그는 이 계획에 관해 아무것도 모른다. (anything)

8. 그들 중 누구도 뚱뚱하지 않다. (none)

9. 이 임무를 위해 우리가 대체 누구를 보낼 건가? (whomever)

10. 당신 이름이 무엇입니까? (may)

**야구 영어:** 유독 외래어를 많이 쓰는 분야가 스포츠이다. 그래서 스포츠를 많이 보면 영어에 익숙해질 수 있다. 야구에서도 pitcher, catcher, first base man, home run 등 많은 영어가 등장한다. 예전에 우리 방송에서 four(4) ball이라 부르던 걸 요즘은 base on balls라 하고, dead ball이라 하던 걸 hit by pitched ball이라 부른다. 이렇게 영어투성이인데, line-up에서 "1번 타자, 2번 타자…" 등은 계속 한국말을 고집한다. 이들은 미국에서 뭐라 부를까? first batter, second batter…라고 부른다. 그런데 first batter는 "제일 잘 때리는 선수"처럼 들릴 수 있는 게 문제다. 그래서 중계 방송에서는 1번 타자를 lead-off(맨 앞에 있는 선수), 4번 타자를 clean-up batter라 부르고, 나머지는 그냥 이름을 부른다.

# Unit 07 전치사 (Preposition)

'전치사'란 '앞에 놓는 말'이란 뜻인데, 명사나 대명사 앞에 붙어서 함께 **형용사**나 **부사** 역할을 한다. (단, to는 동사 앞에도 붙는데, 이에 관해선 <19. 부정사>에서 다룬다.) 명사·대명사가 전치사 뒤에 올 때는 **목적격**이 된다. 전치사는 명사/대명사와 밀접한 관계이므로 일찍 여기서 다룬다.

## A 전치사의 종류

### 1. 장소, 방향 전치사

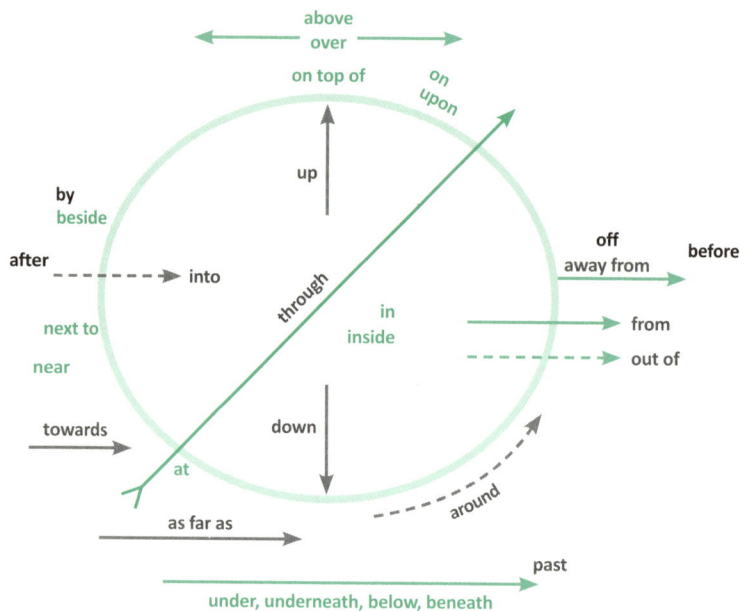

❶ at(~에서): 비교적 좁은 장소
- Please wait **at** the door or **at** the corner.

❷ in(~안에): 비교적 넓은 장소
- The zoo is **in** the National Park **in** Seoul.

❸ on(~위에): 면에 접촉한 곳
- The key is **on** the table.

❹ **over**(~너머): 대상을 넘어간다는 의미
  · The car went **over** the hill.

❺ **above**(~위에): 상당히 떨어진 위, 측량 등에 사용
  · The house is located at 300m **above** the lake.

❻ **under, underneath**(~바로 아래): 가까이 붙은 아래
  · The farm was buried **under** the snow.
  · The river flows **underneath** the bridge.

❼ **below, beneath**(~아래): 상당히 떨어진 아래, 측량 등에 사용
  · The temperature dropped **below** zero.
  · The tunnel lies 500m **beneath** the surface.

❽ **by, beside, near**(~옆에)
  · Stand **by**(*or* **beside**) the tree.
  · The bookstore is **near** the post office.

❾ **up**(~위로, ~로 거슬러)
  · They went **up** the creek.

❿ **down**(~아래로)
  · He came **down** the stairs.

⓫ **into**(~안으로): in+to가 합친 말
  · The dog ran **into** the room.

⓬ **to**(~으로, 까지)
  · Let's go **to** the park.
  · Read the book from page 1 **to** 5.     [p.5 전까지만 읽음, ☞ through]

⓭ **toward(s), for**(~향해)
  · She drove the car **toward** the west.
  · The train left Seoul **for** Busan. (서울을 떠나 부산을 향해)

❹ from(~로부터)
- I am from Korea.

❺ out of(안에서 밖으로)
- They came out of the village.

❻ round, around(~주위에)
- They gathered together round the campfire.
- Mary traveled around the world.

❼ before, in front of(~앞에)
- She sat before me.
- The shop is in front of the bank.

❽ after, behind(~뒤에)
- I will go after you.
- Hide yourself behind the wall.

❾ between(둘 사이에)
- He stood between Jack and Jill.

❿ among(셋 이상 사이에)
- The birds are singing among the trees.

㉑ through(~통하여, 까지)
- We went to mountain through the woods.
- Read the book from page 1 through 5.

[p.5도 읽음]

㉒ along(~따라서): ad(to) + long = 긴 방향으로
- We walked along the street.

㉓ off(~에서 분리되어)
- I got off the train without my bag. (내렸다)
- He is off duty today. (오늘 비번이다)

㉔ across(~가로질러): ad(to) + cross = 교차하는 방향으로
· The can ran **across** the road.

㉕ next to(~바로 다음에)
· His house is **next to** the post office.

㉖ as far as(~까지)
· The ball went up **as far as** 5 meters from the ground.

### ▌연습문제 21
괄호 속 단어들 중 알맞은 것에 ○표하라.

1. Where are you (for, from)? / I'm Canadian.
2. (In, On) his way home, John lost his purse.
3. The robber hid himself (over, under) the bridge.
4. Jane walked (along, on) the river.
5. The bird came (into, out of) its cage and flew away.
6. As I read it from page 3 (to, through) page 5, I read 3 pages.
7. The girl stood (between, among) the two trees.
8. The moon goes (around, across) the earth.

## 2. 시간 전치사

❶ at(~에): 짧은 기간·시각
· We met **at** noon.
· Don't go outside **at** night.        [밤은 잠만 자는 단순한 기간으로 여김]
· **At** first, I thought it was a cat.

❷ on(~에): 날, 다소 긴 기간
· **On** Sunday, I go to church.
· Let's meet **on** Monday morning.

❸ **in**(~에): on보다 더 긴 시간
　　in April, in 1987, in the morning, in the afternoon, in the afternoon
　　　cf **특정한 날**의 morning, afternoon, evening에는 on을 붙일 수 있다.
　　　　· **On(In)** the morning of Feb 12, he will arrive in Seoul.

❹ **before**(~전에)
　　· I studied English **before** lunch.

❺ **after**(~후에)
　　· I played basketball **after** school.

❻ **in, within**(~이내에)
　　· I will finish my homework **in(within)** an hour.

❼ **from**(~부터): 출발점을 나타냄
　　· He walked **from** 5 till 7 o'clock.

❽ **since**(~부터 쭉): 완료형에 사용됨
　　· It has rained **since** last week.

❾ **till, until**(~되기 전까지): 동작이 계속되는 시한
　　· I waited him from Monday **till** Saturday.

❿ **by**(~까지): 동작이 완료되는 시한
　　· Please come home **by** nine.

⓫ **for**(~동안): 일정 길이의 시간
　　· She talked on the phone **for** an hour.

⓬ **during**(~동안): 상태나 행사의 지속 기간
　　· He slept **during** the lecture.

⓭ through(~동안 내내)
- The train ran **through** the night. (밤새)
- The shop opens from Monday **through** Saturday. [토요일 포함 6일간]
  cf from Monday **till** Saturday (토요일이 될 때까지) [토요일 불포함 5일간]

## ■ 연습문제 22
괄호 속 단어들 중 알맞은 것에 ○표하라.

1. The bus will arrive (at, on) 8 PM.
2. He died (at, on, in) Sunday and was buried (on, in) the church.
3. You have to finish your work (by, till) six.
4. She has lived here (for, since) 3 years.
5. Mary stayed in Jeju (during, at) her vacation.
6. The plan will start (before, within) 3 days.
7. It snowed (at, through) the night.


## 3. 방법 전치사

❶ by(~에 의해, ~로, 단위로)
- She goes to school **by** bus. (~로)
- This letter was written **by** Kim. (~에 의해)
- The potatoes are sold **by** the pound.

❷ with(~와 함께, ~을 가지고) ↔ without(~없이)
- I will go **with** you. (~와 함께)
- Please cut the paper **with** scissors. (~을 가지고)
- John was standing there **with** his hat off. (~한 상태에서)
- **Without** the compass, we can hardly find our way.

❸ through(~를 통하여)
- The idea spread **through** the internet.

### 4. 원인, 이유, 대상, 상태 전치사

**❶ at**(~에 대해, ~때문에, ~한 상태로)
- I was surprised **at** the news. (때문에)
- She shouted **at** me. (향해)
- Mary bought the shirt **at** half price. (반값으로)
- The train runs **at** the rate of 30km/h. (~의 비율로, 속력으로)

**❷ for**(~을 위해, ~ 때문에, ~에게 있어)
- Thank you **for** calling. (때문에)
- He waited **for** me for 3 hours. (위해)
- I bought a doll **for** my sister. (위해)
- He paid 3 dollars **for** a chair. (위해)
- He bought a chair **for** 3 dollars. (가격)
- The test was too difficult **for** Tom. (Tom에게 있어서)

**❸ because of**(~때문에)
- I cannot go there **because of** weather.

**❹ in**(~을 입은)
- Mary is **in** a red dress.

**❺ on**(~에 관해, ~중인)
- He presented a report **on** the moon. (~관한)
- On my way home, I met a policeman **on** *guard*. (경비 중인)

**❻ except, but**(~예외하고)
- Everyone **except**(*or* **but**) Kim loved her.

**❼ for**(찬성하는)**, against**(반대하는)
- Are you **for** the plan or **against** it?

**❽ instead of**(~대신에)
- He ordered chicken **instead of** pork.

❾ **about**(~에 관해, ~근처에)
  · We talked **about** our future.  · He is **about**(*or* **around**) my age. (내 나이 정도다)

❿ **per**(~당): per 다음엔 대개 관사가 붙지 않지만 per가 생략되면 a가 쓰임
  · It costs 5 dollars **per** hour. = It costs 5 dollars **an** hour.
  · He comes here twice **per** week. = He comes here twice **a** week.

⓫ **in spite of, despite** (~에도 불구하고)
  · **Despite(In spite of)** her old age, Mary is still in good health.

### ▌연습문제 23
괄호 속 단어들 중 알맞은 것에 ○표하라.

1. She goes to work (by, in) train.
2. (With, Without) air, nobody can survive.
3. Sam looked at me (with, in) his arms folded.
4. The sauce is sold (by, in) the ounce.
5. I bought the camera (by, for) 30 dollars.
6. We were surprised (at, by) the terrible accident.
7. Look at the man (in, on) the yellow suit.
8. I don't know anything (at, on) the matter.
9. Everyone (and, but) Kim was present in the party.
10. Fighting (against, for) my country is honorable.
11. Mr. Park told us (about, for) his youth days.
12. Cindy came to school (instead, in spite) of her illness.

## B 전치사의 용법

**1. 형용사구**(명사 수식)를 만든다.
- The *flower* **on the table** is very beautiful.
- Look at the *girl* **with a dog**.

**2. 부사구**(동사 수식)를 만든다.
- I will *go* there **by subway**.
- They *played* tennis **after school**.

**3. 전치사의 목적어**로 동사를 쓸 때는 반드시 **동명사**(ing 형)를 쓴다.
- He went to bed after *finishing* homework.
- cf He went to bed after *to finish* homework. (✕)

## C 이중 전치사(Double Prepositions)

**1. from behind**(뒤에서부터):
- A bear came **from behind** the tree.

**2. from above**(위로부터):
- A bird fell **from above** the mountain.

**3. from below**(아래로부터):
- The water came **from below** the iceberg.

**4. until before**(~전까지):
- They swam in the river **until before** dark.

**5. till after**(~후까지):
- I worked **till after** sunset.

**6. in down**(안으로 들어가 밑으로):
- He jumped **in down** the sea.

**7. from among**(~중에서부터):
- Take one **from among** these books.

## D 전치사의 생략

자주 사용되는 말 앞의 전치사는 반복하기 싫어 아예 생략해 버린다.
이 경우 해당 명사는 부사가 된다.
~~on~~ today(yesterday, tomorrow), ~~to~~ home(downtown, upstairs, overseas), ~~on~~ next(every, last, this, some) day, ~~per~~ a year, ~~in~~ this year

· On my way **home**, I met my teacher.
· Every Sunday, I go to church.
· He earns 10 dollars a day.
· Let's go **downstairs** to watch TV.


## E 전치사를 포함하는 관용 동사구

자동사가 전치사와 결합해 타동사처럼 행동한다. (☞ 11 부사. **C**. (6))

1. account for (~을 설명하다, ~를 차지하다)
   · The snow **accounts for** the car accident.
   · Asia accounts for 90% of rice consumption.

2. agree to (사물)(~에 대해 동의하다)
   · I **agree to** this plan.

3. agree with (사람)(~와 의견이 같다)
   · I cannot **agree with** my father.

4. arrive in(at)(~에 도착하다)
   · Tom **arrived in** Seoul at 9 PM.

5. be absent from(~에 결석하다)
   · Yesterday I **was absented from** school.

6. be crowded with(~로 붐비다)
   · The street **was crowded with** people.

7. **be different from**(~와 다르다) = differ from
   · My thought **is different from** yours.

8. **be familiar with**(~에 익숙하다)
   · I **am not familiar with** this application.

9. **be filled with, be full of** (~로 가득 차 있다)
   · The room **is filled with** bad smells.
   = The room **is full of** bad smells.

10. **be fond of** (~을 좋아하다)
    · I **am fond of** country music.

11. **be good at** (~을 잘하다) ↔ **be poor at** (~을 잘못하다)
    · He **is good at** swimming but **poor at** running.

12. **be interested in**(~에 흥미를 갖다)
    · I **am interested in** your music.

13. **belong to**(~에 속하다)
    · This bag doesn't **belong to** me.

14. **be pleased with** (~에 기뻐하다), **be satisfied with** (~에 만족하다)
    · Dad **was pleased(satisfied) with** my high grade in math.

15. **be made from**(~로부터 만들어진) : 원재료
    **be made of**(~로 이루어진): 물리적 구성 물질
    · This table is **made of(from)** wood.　　　　　　　　　[원료인 나무의 재질이 현존]
    · The wine is **made from** grapes.　　　　　　　　　　　　[포도가 원료]
    　**cf** The wine is **made of** grapes. (×)　　　　　　[포도 재질은 현존하지 않으므로]

16. **be surprised at**(~에 놀라다)
    · I **was surprised at** the news.

17. **be(get) through with**(~을 다 마치다)
    · I **got through with** my homework.

18. **believe in**(~을 믿다): 신앙의 대상. 종종 in 없이도 사용됨
    · I **believe in** Jesus.
    **cf** I **believe** the *story*.

19. **cling to**(~에 매달리다)
    · The puppy **clung to** me.

20. **come across**(~와 우연히 마주치다)
    · I **came across** a friend of my sister's in the park.

21. **complain of(about)** (~에 관해 불평하다)
    · Jack **complained of(about)** the high price in Seoul.

22. **consist of** (~로 구성되다)
    · Our team **consists of** seven members.

23. **deal with**(~을 다루다, 처리하다)
    · This book **deals with** Korean War.

24. **depend on**, rely on(~에 의존하다)
    · The patient **depends on** her family.

25. **die of** (질병) (~로 죽다)
    · The ducks **died of** bird flu.

26. **do without** (~없이 지내다)
    · Nobody is able to **do without** food.

27. **concentrate on, focus on**(~에 집중하다)
    · It is hard for me to **focus on** the movie because of noises.

28. get rid of (~을 제거하다)
    · You must **get rid of** the trash.

29. go on (~을 계속하다)
    · We must **go on** studying English.

30. graduate from (~를 졸업하다)
    · I **graduated from** this middle school.

31. hear of (~에 관해 소식을 듣다), hear from (~로부터 소식을 듣다)
    · I **heard of** Jane **from** her son. (그 아들로부터 Jane 소식을 들었다)

32. interfere with(~를 방해하다)
    · You may enjoy the music but let it not **interfere with** my study.

33. laugh at (~를 비웃다)
    · She **laughed at** my foolish behavior.

34. listen to (~의 말을 귀담아듣다)
    · **Listen to** your teacher during the class.

35. long for (~을 갈망하다)
    · I **longed for** seeing you. (만나 뵙길 고대했습니다)

36. look after (~을 돌보다) = take care of
    · Yesterday I **looked after** my kid brother. (동생을 돌봤다)

37. look at (~을 보다): look은 "~처럼 보인다"는 자동사
    · **Look at** the picture on the desk.
    cf You **look** sad.

38. look for (~을 찾다)
    · What are you **looking for**?

39. object to (~에 반대하다)
   · He **objects to** genetically modified organisms(GMOs).

40. pay for (~을 위해 지불하다)
   · How much did you **pay for** the jeans?

41. refer to(~을 언급하다, 인용하다, 참조하다)
   · To know about Indian history, we **referred to** the encyclopedia.
   · "Superfood" **refers to** the nutrient-rich food.

42. search for (~을 찾다, 수색하다)
   · They **searched for** the lost child in the woods.

43. speak in (~으로 말하다): in 없이 타동사로도 쓸 수 있다.
   · He could **speak (in)** French but decided to **speak (in)** English.

44. speak of (~에 관해 말하다)
   · He **spoke of** children on the battlefield.

45. subscribe to(~을 구독 신청하다)
   · Tom decided to **subscribe to** the Times Magazine.

46. succeed in (~에 성공하다)
   · He **succeeded in** crossing the Pacific.

47. sympathize with (동정하다, 공감하다)
   · I **sympathized with** the girl in her grief.

48. take after (~를 닮다, 본받다)
   · Mary **takes after** her grandma.

49. think of(about) (~에 대해 생각하다): 전치사 없이 타동사로도 쓰임
   · I **think of** Tom from time to time.                    [Tom 자체가 생각의 대상]
   cf I **think** Tom **(to be)** honest.                    [Tom이 정직하단 사실이 생각의 대상]

50. waite for(~를 기다리다)
- Mom **waited for** me till midnightht. (자정까지 기다렸다)

■ 연습문제 24
**01.** 괄호 속의 뜻에 맞도록 빈칸에 알맞은 전치사를 넣어라.

1. Look _____ the chicken eggs in the yard. (찾으라)
2. Chinese account _____ about 5% of its population. (차지하다)
3. I heard a voice from _____ the wall. (뒤에서 나오는)
4. Please stop talking and listen _____ me. (말을 듣다)
5. They are not familiar _____ Korean culture yet. (익숙하다)
6. The dog was run _____ by a car. (치였다)
7. His sister is very good _____ cooking. (잘한다)
8. Who do you take _____ among your family? (닮았니?)
9. Whenever seeing you, I think _____ your mom. (생각하다)
10. We tried to get rid _____ a tree blocking the road. (제거하다)
11. I will not object _____ you in this project. (반대하다)
12. Many children died _____ hunger in the war. (굶어 죽다)
13. The house was crowded _____ mice. (가득 차다)
14. How are you going to deal _____ this problem? (다루다)
15. After several trials, I succeeded _____ making a kite. (성공하다)

**02.** 괄호 속 말 중 알맞은 것에 ○ 표하라.

1. I cannot agree (of, with) him in the problem.
2. While waiting (to, for) a bus, I fell asleep.
3. I can hardly sympathize (in, with) your point of view.
4. You'd better not depend (in, on) your friends.
5. Jane graduated (in, from) this school.
6. Students must pay (to, for) books and tuition.
7. The history teacher spoke (at, of) the reformation in 1517.
8. "Millennials" refer (of, to) people born between 1980 and 2000.
9. Everyone longs (at, for) happiness.
10. The meal consists (with, of) diverse side dishes.

# 종합문제 4

**01 다음 문장에서 어색한 부분을 찾아 바르게 고치라.**

1. On today, I will visit my uncle.
2. She goes to home after school to take care of her sister.
3. They walked 10km on everyday.
4. On the morning, I brush my teeth after breakfast.
5. Tom arrived L.A. last night.
6. Think in your parents who are waiting for you.
7. He is listening music in his room.
8. I am not good in tennis.
9. How much did you pay to the watch?
10. None of us were surprised by the news.
11. I am not agree of him.
12. Jane is very interested by your music.
13. He graduated this high school.
14. They drove the car at night to reach at the port in time.
15. Everybody laughed to the funny scene.
16. My grandpa died with cancer.
17. Are you satisfied by my explanation?
18. I was looking after my lost glasses in the park.
19. Jim finally succeeded for entering the college.
20. This book belongs with me.

**02 괄호 속에 있는 말을 이용해 다음 우리말을 영작하라.**

1. 그의 방은 낡은 책으로 가득 차 있다. (filled)

2. 우리는 강을 따라 한 시간 정도 걸었다. (along, about)

3. 그 소녀는 너의 나이 정도였다. (around)

4. 새싹들이 땅 밑에서부터 올라온다. (from beneath, ground)

5. 이 플라스틱은 석유로부터 만들어진다. (made, petroleum)

6. 어제 그는 아파서 학교에 결석했다. (absent, because of, illness)

7. 아빠는 뜰에서 잡초를 제거하고 계신다. (yard, weeds, rid)

8. 그는 문 뒤에서부터 오는 이상한 소리를 들었다. (strange, from behind)

9. 모든 생물은 공기 없이 지낼 수 없다. (every, without)

10. 어제 나는 걸어서 집에 왔다. (foot)

---

from~to와 from~through: "~부터 ~까지"를 뜻하는 from~to와 from~through는 약간의 차이가 있다. "from A to D"라면 거기 적용되는 범위는 A, B, C인 반면, "from A through D"라면 A, B, C, D까지 포함된다. 즉, "to D"는 D 앞에 도달하면 멈추라는 뜻이고, "through D"는 D를 통과하여 멈추라는 뜻이다.

# Unit 08 동사 (Verb)

동사는 문장의 골격을 결정하는 핵심적 품사로, 다음 5가지로 구분된다:
① **완전 자동사**(Perfect Intransitive Verb): 목적어나 보어를 갖지 않음
② **불완전 자동사**(Imperfect Intransitive Verb): 보어(C)만 가짐
③ **완전 타동사**(Perfect Transitive Verb): 목적어(O)를 하나만 가짐
④ **수여동사**(Dative Verb): 목적어를 두 개(O+O) 가짐(완전 타동사의 일종)
⑤ **불완전 타동사**(Imperfect Transitive Verb): 목적어(O)와 보어(C)를 가짐

## A 완전 자동사: 1형식 동사

목적어나 보어가 필요 없는 동사로서, 그 기본 문장 구조는 S+V (1형식)가 된다.
예) come, go, (there) is(are), cough, disappear, arrive, run, get up, stand up, sit down

- He **goes** to school everyday.
- **There are** two books on the table.  　　　　　　　[도치형, there는 부사]
- Father **coughs** badly.
- I **arrived** at the station at 7:30. ⇒ I *reached* the station at 7:30.

## B 불완전 자동사: 2형식 동사

목적어 없이 보어만 필요로 하는 동사로, 문장 구조는 S+V+C가 된다. 대표적 동사는 be 인데, 이 동사는 영어 동사들 가운데 유일하게 인칭 변화를 한다.

표 13. be동사의 인칭·수·시제에 따른 활용례(직설법)

| 인칭 \ 시제 \ 수 | 현재 단수 | 현재 복수 | 과거 단수 | 과거 복수 |
|---|---|---|---|---|
| 1인칭 | I *am* a boy | We *are* boys | I *was* a boy | We *were* boys |
| 2인칭 | You *are* a girl | You *are* girls | You *were* a girl | You *were* girls |
| 3인칭 | He *is* a boy<br>She *is* a girl<br>It *is* a book | They *are* boys | He *was* a boy<br>She *was* a girl<br>It *was* a book | They *were* boys |

1. 원형 be는 **조동사**와 함께 사용되거나 to-**부정사**로 쓰일 때만 나타난다.
   - You *are* foolish. ⇒ You must *be* foolish. (바보임에 틀림없다)
   - I *am* a doctor. ⇒ I want to *be* a doctor. (의사가 되고 싶다)

2. be 이외에 불완전 자동사들이 있는데, 문법 문제에 자주 나오니 꼭 외우자:
   feel(느껴지다), smell(냄새나다), look(보이다), taste(맛이 나다), sound(들린다), turn(~로 변하다), become(되다), get(되다), grow(자라서 ~되다), seem(~처럼 보이다), appear(~처럼 보이다), turn out(되다), prove(~로 입증되다), go(되다), remain(남아 있다), keep(유지하다), stay(머무르다), continue(지속하다), lie(누워있다), stand(서 있다)

   - The leaves **turn** *red* in the autumn. (붉게 변한다)
   - The bear **grew** *big* soon. (크게 자랐다)
   - Jack **proved** (to be) *guilty*. (유죄로 판명되었다)
   - We can **stay** *warm* in this house. (따뜻하게 머물 수 있다)
   - This area will **continue** *windy*. (계속 바람이 불 것이다)

3. 보어(C)는 주어(S)와 동격이며, 해당 동사 대신에 be 동사를 썼을 때 뜻이 통해야 한다.
   즉, 보어로 **형용사**나 **명사**가 와야지 부사가 오면 안 된다.

   - This soup **smells** *delicious*. (○) ⇒ This soup is *delicious*. (○)
   - ※ This soup **smells** *deliciously*. (×) ⇒ This soup is *deliciously*. (×)
   - Mary **kept** *silent*. (○) ⇒ Mary was *silent*. (○)
   - ※ Mary **kept** *silently*. (×) ⇒ Mary was *silently*. (×)

4. 위에 언급된 2형식 동사들 중에는 1형식 동사(완전 자동사)나 목적어를 갖는 타동사(3-5형식)로 쓰이는 것도 있으니 주의하라.

   - I **went** to school.                              [1형식]
   - This fish **went** bad. (상했다)                    [2형식]
   - It **tastes** good.                                [2형식]
   - He **tastes** the wine. (맛보다)                    [3형식]
   - It **feels** soft. (느껴진다)                       [2형식]
   - He **feels** pain. (느낀다)                         [3형식]

   ※ 형식 구분은 모호할 수 있으므로, 문맥에서 타동사·자동사 구분만 잘하자!

▌ **연습문제 25**

괄호 속 단어들 중 알맞은 것에 ○표하라.

1. Everyday he goes (school, to school) by bike.
2. We came (home, to home) early.
3. There (is, are) your glasses on the desk.
4. I (am, was) in the library last night.
5. She could not sleep (deep, deeply) because of the noise.
6. This fabric feels (soft, softly).
7. I (arrived, reached) at the airport in time.
8. I (am, is) a student and he (is, are) a teacher.
9. We (are, were) late for school yesterday.
10. Tom studies (English, of English) very hard.
11. This chicken tastes (good, well). I'll take it for lunch.
12. This dog smells so (good, well) that I'll take him to my hunt.
13. He seems (happy, happily) with his new cell phone.
14. The report turned out (true, truly).
15. Let's go swimming.  /  It sounds (nice, well).
16. He (looks, looks at) sad after losing his brother.
17. This beef in the refrigerator went (bad, badly).
18. Jane remained (sad, sadly) till midnight.
19. She lies (sick, sickly) in bed with the flu.
20. He cannot stand (straight, straightly) because of accident.

## C 완전 타동사: 3형식 동사

보어 없이 목적어만 갖는 동사이다. 문장 구조는 S+V+O 로, 대부분의 타동사가 여기 속한다.

예 want, eat, drink, read, write, like, think, reach, have, take, bring, marry

· She **drinks** *mocha coffee* everyday.

· I **want** *him* more than ever. (어느 때보다 더 그를 원한다)

· I **want** *to go* there with him. (그와 거기 가기를 원한다)

### 1. 자동사로 혼동하기 쉬운 타동사

**❶ enter, attend**(참석하다)**, join, inhabit** (거주하다): in(into) 없이 사용.
- We **entered** the convention center to **attend** the meeting.
- He **joined** the Peace Corps to help those **inhabiting** the lake.

**❷ discuss, address**(연설, 제기하다)**, explain, mention**: about 없이 사용.
- I **discussed** my plans with teacher.
- He **addressed** a complaint to the police.
- He **explained** *(about)* the schedule to me.　　　　[about을 쓸 수도 있음]

**❸ accompany**(동반하다)**, contact**(연락하다)**, marry**: with 없이 사용.
accompany는 수동태로 많이 쓴다.
- Children under 6 must be **accompanied** by their parents.
- Whenever you have problems, feel free to **contact** me.

**❹ approach, reach, follow, resemble, ask, answer**: to 없이 사용.
- The cat **approached** the mouse secretly till he **reached** it.
- Please **answer** me why you **followed** my bike.

**❺ await (= wait for)**
- We have been eagerly **awaiting** his arrival.
  = We have been eagerly **waiting for** his arrival.

### 2. 신체 접촉 동사: S+V+(접촉당하는 대상)+(전치사)+(접촉되는 신체 부분)
catch, grasp, hold, beat, hit, touch, kiss, pat, look, stare 등.
여기서 전치사 이후의 부분은 추가적 설명인 셈이다.

- He **hit** me. / (Where?) / He **hit** me on the head.
- Tom **held** me by the hand.　　　　　　　　[나를 잡았다는 사실이 중요]
  = Tom held my hand.　　　　　　　　　　　　[내 손이 중요]
- I **touched** the dog on the back. (개의 등을 만졌다)
- He **looked** her in the eyes. (그녀 눈을 쳐다보았다)

▌**연습문제 26**

괄호 속 단어들 중 알맞은 것에 ○표하라.

1. They (entered, went) the forest to hunt the bear.
2. John was (awaiting, waiting) for his teacher.
3. Please contact (me, to me) after 6 o'clock.
4. She married (a man, with a man) named Bill.
5. Jane hit me on (my, the) shoulder.

## D 수여동사(Dative Verb): 4형식 동사

목적어를 둘 가질 수 있는 완전타동사로, 문장 구조는 S+V+IO(사람)+DO(사물)이 된다. '~에게' 를 뜻하는 앞의 목적어는 **간접 목적어**(Indirect Object, IO), '~를' 을 뜻하는 뒤의 목적어는 **직접 목적어** (Direct Object, DO)라 부른다.

**간접 목적어**를 **전치사**와 함께 뒤로 보내 4형식 문장을 **3형식** 문장으로 바꿀 수 있는데, 동사에 따라 전치사의 종류가 달라진다: give 류는 *to*, buy 류는 *for*, ask 류는 *of*. 단, leave는 *to/for* 를 둘 다 쓸 수 있다.

· <u>She</u> <u>gave</u> <u>me</u> <u>a book</u>. ⇒ <u>She</u> <u>gave</u> <u>a book</u> to me.
　S　V　IO　DO　　　　S　V　　O

· <u>Jack</u> <u>bought</u> <u>her</u> <u>a doll</u>. ⇒ <u>Jack</u> <u>bought</u> <u>a doll</u> for her.
　S　V　IO　DO　　　　S　V　　O

· <u>He</u> <u>asked</u> <u>me</u> <u>a favor</u>. ⇒ <u>He</u> <u>asked</u> <u>a favor</u> of me.
　S　V　IO　DO　　　　S　V　　O

cf Tom **played** <u>us</u> <u>a trick</u>. ⇒ Tom **played** <u>a trick</u> on us. (속이다)
　　　　　IO　DO　　　　　　　　　O

표 14. 수여동사의 종류

| | | |
|---|---|---|
| give류 | give, send, grant(부여하다), offer(제시하다), award(수여하다), issue(발급하다), tell, teach, show, assign, lend, hand(건네주다), sell, assure, bring, leave(남겨주다) | to |
| buy류 | buy(사주다), cook, make(만들어주다), order(주문해주다), find(찾아주다), get(갖다 주다), take(~가 걸리다), spare, save | for |
| ask류 | ask(청하다), inquire(심문하다), require(요구하다) | of |

**■ 연습문제 27**

**01.** 다음을 3형식 문장으로 고치라.(밑줄 부분만)

1. I sent <u>Mary a letter yesterday.</u>  ⇒ _____
2. They sold <u>him a broken car.</u>  ⇒ _____
3. Will you cook <u>me a steak?</u>  ⇒ _____
4. She asked <u>me two questions.</u>  ⇒ _____
5. You played <u>her a trick.</u>  ⇒ _____

**02.** 다음을 4형식 문장으로 고치라.(밑줄 부분만)

1. I will show <u>the way to the station to you.</u>  ⇒ _____
2. Father left <u>nothing for me.</u>  ⇒ _____
3. The test will take <u>about 3 hours for you.</u>  ⇒ _____

### 1. 3형식으로 바꿀 수 없는 수여동사

cost, envy, forgive, last, bet, fine**(벌금 매기다)** 등은 목적어를 2개 가질 수 있지만, 간접목적어를 뒤로 빼내 3형식으로 만들지는 않는다.

- The accident **costed** *him* his life. (사고 때문에 목숨을 잃었다)
  - **cf** The accident **costed** his life to *him*. (×)
- I envy *you* (for) your wealth.
  - = I envy your wealth.
- Forgive *me* (for) my ignorance.
  - = Forgive my ignorance.
- 100 bucks will last *us* (for) about **3** days. (100불이면 3일쯤 견딘다)
- I bet *Tom* **$10** (that) our team would win. (이길 거라는 데에 10불 걸고 Tom과 내기했다)
- The police **fined** *her* **$20** for illegal parking. (20불 벌금 매겼다)

### 2. 수여적 의미를 가진 3형식 동사들: 항상 목적어 한 개만 사용

**❶ S+V+O(사물)+on(수령자)**

bestow(수여하다), impress(인상을 주다), impose(부과하다), confer(수여하다) 등

- The king **conferred** the highest honor **on** the knight.

- We have **bestowed** much energy **on** the project.
- The government **imposed** heavy taxes **on** cigarettes.
- The preacher **impressed** his charisma **on** audiences.
  = The preacher **impressed** audiences **with** this charisma.

## ❷ S+V+O(수령자)+with(사물)
provide(제공하다), entrust(맡기다), fill(채우다), furnish(갖추다) 등

- Mary **entrusted** *me* **with** her dog.
  = Mary **entrusted** her dog **to** me.
- He **provided** *his son* **with** good education.
  = He **provided** good education **to(for)** his son.
- Mom **filled** *the cup* **with** milk.
  = Mom **filled** *milk* **in** *the cup*.

## ❸ S+V+O(사람)+of(사물)
inform(통보하다), remind(상기시키다), warn(경고하다), assure(확신시키다), convince(납득시키다), accuse(비난하다), rob(강탈하다), clean, clear(제거하다), empty(비우다), deliver(분만시키다), ease, relieve(경감시키다), rid(제거하다), deprive(박탈하다), strip(벗기다), cure(치유하다) 등

- The college **informed** *the applicant* **of** his admission.
- He **accused** *me* **of** cheating at the game.
- I **warned** *him* **of** the dangers of smoking.
- A highwayman **robbed** *passengers* **of** their money.
- They **cleaned** *the tree* **of** leaves and **stripped** *it* **of** the bark.
- No one could **cure** *the queen* **of** her blindness.
- This medicine will **relieve(ease)** *you* **of** headache. (경감시킬 것이다)
- You must **rid** *your heart* **of** hatred and jealousy.
  = You must **get rid of** hatred and jealousy **from** your heart.
- The doctor **delivered** *Mary* **of** her baby boy. (분만아를 받았다)

### 3. 목적어가 2개 이상인 **일반 타동사**

수여동사만이 목적어를 2개 갖는 것은 아니다. 준동사(to부정사, 동명사)를 목적어로 갖는 동사의 경우, 그 준동사의 주어도 목적어가 될 수 있으므로 목적어를 2개 갖는 셈이 된다.

- I want h**im**. (그를 원한다)    · I want **to go** there. (가길 원한다)
⇒ I want **him to go** there. (그가 가길 원한다)

### 📗 연습문제 28

**01.** 다음에서 어색한 부분을 찾아 고쳐 쓰라.

1. The book costed five dollars to me.
2. I don't envy of his success.
3. The food will last two weeks to the refugee.
4. Tom bet 10 dollars to me on his success.
5. The state fined 100 dollars to the smuggler.

**02.** 괄호 속 단어들 중 알맞은 것에 ◯표하라.

1. The dictator imposed heavy burdens (on, to) his people.
2. I want to impress my image (for, on) Mary.
3. Kim impressed me (on, with) his honesty.
4. She furnished my room (by, with) new furniture.
5. Mother provided fresh milk (to, with) me.
6. The girl reminds me (of, for) my dead sister.
7. He tried to convince me (with, of) my error.
8. She cleared the table (with, of) dishes.
9. This medicine will ease you (from, of) headache.
10. The wicked king deprived people (for, of) their liberty

## E 불완전 타동사: 5형식 동사

목적어와 목적보어를 다 가질 수 있는 동사로, S+V+O+C 구조를 갖는다. 이때 보어는 목적어와 동등 관계로서 O와 C 사이에 (to be)가 생략된 상태이다.

1. **사역동사**: make, have, let 등 타인에게 어떤 일을 시킬 때 쓰는 동사
   - He made *me* (to be) happy. (나를 행복하게 만들었다)
     **cf** He made *me* happily. (기꺼이 나를 창조했다)
   - I will make *him* (to be) a man. (그를 사나이로 만들겠다)
   - I had *my hair* cut. (이발했다)

2. **그 외 5형식 동사**: call, get, name, keep, leave, find, think, elect 등
   - I found *the book* (to be) easy. (그 책이 쉬움을 알았다)
     **cf** I found *the book* easily. (쉽게 그 책을 찾았다.)
   - He kept *me* not (to be) comfortable.
   - She named *the girl* (to be) Jane.

▎**연습문제 29**

괄호 속 단어들 중 알맞은 것에 ○표하라.

1. I think the monkey very (smart, smartly).
2. Mary made me (sad, sadly) in the decision.
3. They elected (he, him) president last week.
4. Nobody could get the machine (work, working).
5. Don't leave the door (open, to open).
6. I heard a dog (barking, to bark).
7. They (called, told) me Jack.

**사역동사 문장은 몇 형식?**: 사역동사는 제 5형식 문장을 만드는 대표적 동사이다. 그러나 문장 성분과 상태에 따라 형식은 달라질 수 있다. She made John happy. 혹은 She made John a singer. 등은 제 5형식(S+V+O+C) 문장이다. 반면에 부정사를 포함하는 She made John sing. 같은 문장은 John과 (to) sing 이 모두 목적어가 될 수 있으므로 제 4형식이라 할 수 있다. 이처럼 문장의 형식은 상황에 따라 달라질 수 있으므로, 참고로만 알아두자.

## 종합문제 5

**01** 다음 문장에서 어색한 부분을 찾아 바르게 고치라.

1. He went school with his friends.
2. I sat down the chair and read the newspaper.
3. She coughed bad during the lunch.
4. I want to marry with Jane.
5. Jane wants to go to there with me.
6. The trees grow slow in the winter.
7. He left the room silent and fast.
8. The leaves turned redly after two weeks.
9. He looked the car, dreaming his bright future.
10. In the restaurant, dad ordered a hamburger to me.

**02** 다음 문장을 3형식 문장으로 고쳐 쓰라. (밑줄 부분)

1. He offered me a great job. ⇒
2. It will take us a whole day to fix the car. ⇒
3. Jack left me a lot of work. ⇒
4. She found me a math book. ⇒
5. I will ask you a question. ⇒

**03** 괄호 속에 있는 말을 이용해 다음 우리말을 영작하라.

1. 나는 그 문제가 매우 어렵다는 걸 발견했다. (difficult)

2. 그는 나에게 속임수를 썼다. (play, trick)

3. 우리는 그녀를 대통령으로 선출했다. (elect, president)

4. 그는 나에게 엉터리 물건을 팔았다. (sell, lemon)

5. 나에게 그런 질문을 하지 마라. (ask, question, such)

6. 우리는 John을 살아 있는 전설이라 불렀다. (call, legend)

7. Mary는 나의 볼에 키스했다. (me, on)

8. 그에게 너무 많은 것을 요구하지 마라. (require, too much)

9. 방과 후에 나는 배고픔을 느꼈다. (feel)

10. 지하철역 가는 길을 좀 알려주세요. (show, way)

11. 이 쿠폰은 우리에게 5달러를 절약해 준다. (save)

12. 부디 나의 무례를 용서해 주십시오. (forgive, me)

> **영작의 중요성:** 영어 Test(TOEIC, TOEFL)를 준비하는 사람은 듣기(Listening)이 어렵다고 하소연한다. 그런데, 듣기는 2~3개월만 훈련해도 훨씬 좋아질 수 있는 반면, 정말 어려운 건 말하기이다. 한 때 동양 아이들이 TOEFL 시험에서 만점을 많이 받으니까 이를 떨어뜨리려고 ETS가 쓰기/말하기를 추가시켰다. 꾸준한 영작 연습이 진정한 영어의 강자를 만들 수 있다.

# Unit 09 조동사 (Auxiliary Verb)

일반 동사 앞에서 그 동사의 의미를 보조해 준다. 조동사 두 개는 겹쳐 쓸 수 없다. 때문에 종종 일반 동사 형태의 대용어를 갖는다. 조동사 다음에 오는 본동사는 항상 원형이다. do와 have를 제외한 모든 조동사는 현재 3인칭 단수에서 -s를 붙이지 않는다.

## A 기본 조동사

### 1. do(과거 did)

"~을 하다"라는 의미를 갖는 동사로, 다음 경우 조동사로 쓰인다:

❶ 일반 동사의 의문문, 부정문을 만들 때
  · You love Mary. → (부정문) You **do not** love Mary.
                    (의문문) **Do** you love Mary?

❷ 동사를 강조할 때
  · I **do** love Mary. (나는 정말로 메리를 사랑합니다.)

❸ 대동사: 다른 동사를 대신해서 사용
  · Tom loves Mary.  /  So **do** I. (do = love)

### 2. can(과거 could)

❶ **능력, 가능**(~할 수 있다): 대용어는 be able to
  · I **can** ride a bike. = I **am able to** ride a bike.
  · I *will* **can** ride a bike.(✗) ⇒ I *will* **be able to** ride a bike. (○)

❷ **강한 부정적 추측**(~할 리가 없다): not과 함께 쓰일 때
  · She **cannot** be a spy.                    [can과 not은 붙여 쓴다]

### 3. must(과거형 없음)

❶ **의무**(~해야 한다): 대용어는 have to, [단, don't have to = need not]
  · You **must not** go through a red light. (빨간 불에 지나가면 안 된다)
  · I **must** go there.(현재형) ⇒ I **had to** go there. (과거형)
  · You **don't have to** go there. ⇒ You **need not** go there. (필요 없다)

❷ **강한 추측**(~임에 분명하다): 과거형은 must have p.p(**과거분사**)
- You **must** be hungry. (너 배고프구나)
- You **must have been** hungry. (너 배고팠구나)

## 4. may(과거 might)

❶ **허가**(~해도 좋다) : 대용어는 be allowed to
- **May** I come in? / Yes, you **may**.
  / No, you **may**(or **must**) not.

❷ **약한 추측**(~일지도 모른다): must보다 약함
- It **may** rain tomorrow.

❸ **기원**(~되기를)
- **May** God bless you!

❹ **may**를 포함한 관용어
- He worked hard **so that** he **may** become rich. (부자가 되기 위해)
  = He worked hard **in order to** become rich.
- He **may well** do so. (그가 그렇게 하는 것도 일리가 있다.)
- We **may as well** start now. (오늘 출발해도 괜찮겠다.)

## 5. will(과거 would)

'의지'에서 온 말로, 주로 미래를 나타내기 위해 사용된다.

❶ **결심, 의도**(~하려고 한다): 미래의 의미 없음 (특히 과거형으로 쓰일 경우)
- I **will** not betray my country.  [현재의 다짐]
- Tom **would** not enter the school. (들어가려 하지 않았다)  [고집]
- She **would** persuade me but failed. (설득하려 했지만 실패했다)  [의도]
- **Will** you please pass me the soy sauce?  [의향]

❷ **미래**(~할 것이다) : (~할 것이다): 대용어는 **be going to**
- It **will** rain tomorrow. = It is going to rain tomorrow.
- I **will** be lonely without you.

## 6. shall (과거 should)

'격식상의 의무'를 표현하는 말로, 주로 법률적, 종교적 의무를 가리킨다. 따라서 이 말은 법관이나 성직자 입에서 나오는 경우가 많다.

**❶ 의무**(~해야 한다): **계약서**나 **법조문**에 쓴다.
- Both parties of contract **shall** sign on the document. (서명할지어다)

**❷** 1인칭 의문문에서 will의 대용: 자신의 의지를 남에게 묻는 게 어색하므로 will 대신 shall을 쓰는데, 미래의 뜻보단 상대의 의향을 묻는 말이다.
- **Will** I go there? ⇒ **Shall** I go there? (제가 거기 가야 할까요?)
- **Will** we dance? ⇒ **Shall** we dance? (춤추시겠습니까?)

## B 그 외의 조동사

### 1. ought to (~해야 한다)

강한 의무를 나타낸다. 부정형은 **ought not to**

- We **ought to** help each other.
- You **ought not to** waste your time.

### 2. should (~해야 한다)

shall의 가정법 형태로 다소 부드러운 의무 표현 (☞ 23. 가정법)

- You **should** listen to your teachers. (혹시 할 수 있거든)

### 3. would (~하려 하다)

will의 가정법 형태로 정중한 의지 표현 (☞ 23. 가정법)

- **Would** you close the window? (혹시 할 수 있거든)
- I **would** like (to eat) pizza. (될 수 있으면)

### 4. be going to (~할 예정이다)

'~로 가고 있다'는 의미에서 '미래'를 '예정'을 나타내는 대용 조동사이다. 주어의 **의지와 관계없이** 일정이 잡혀 있는 미래에는 이를 쓰는 게 원칙이다.

- I **am going to** inherit this land. (이 땅을 물려받기로 예정됨)
- We **are going to** visit grandpa this weekend. (방문 스케줄이 잡힘)

## 5. need (필요하다)와 dare (감히 ~하다)

**긍정문**에선 **본동사**로, **의문문과 부정문**에선 **조동사**로 쓰이나, 대개는 본동사로 사용된다.

- She **needs to** work.                                                    [본동사]
- She **need not** work. [조동사] = She **doesn't** *need to* work.          [본동사]
- **Need** she work? [조동사] = **Does** she *need to* work?                 [본동사]
- He **dares to** say such a thing. (감히 한다)                              [본동사]
- He **dare not** say such a thing. (감히 하지 않는다)                       [조동사]
- How **dare** he say such a thing? (어찌 감히 하는가?)                      [조동사]

## 6. be about to (막 ~하려 하다)

'~하는 주변에 있다'는 의미로, 임박한 미래를 표현한다.

- The train **is** about **to** leave. (막 떠나려 한다)

※ have는 간혹 조동사처럼 행동하기도 하지만 조동사는 아니다.

- He **has** *not* a book. [영국] ⇒ He *doesn't* **have** a book. [미국]

### ▎연습문제 30

괄호 속 단어들 중 알맞은 것에 ○표하라.

1. He (can, cans) speak English well.
2. She (isn't. doesn't) study hard.
3. Jack (will, can) be able to walk soon.
4. She (has, have, must) to go home now.
5. You need not (go, to go) to school tomorrow.
6. You ought not (cross, to cross) the road on red light.
7. He (will, is going) to work in the farm.
8. (Would, Should) you mind my opening the window?
9. (Will, Shall) we go on a picnic?
10. (Don't, Aren't) you need a book?
11. She (dare, dares) not accept his suggestion.
12. I (will, would) like to go shopping.
13. (Need, Needs) he study now?
14. This door (should, would) not open. Please help me open it.
15. (May, Might) God help you during the travel!

## 종합문제 6

**01 다음 문장에서 어색한 부분을 찾아 바르게 고치라.**

1. Does he goes to school by bike?
2. Do you can believe this?
3. She had to finished the work within a week.
4. I can be able to play tennis better than him.
5. You need not to go there if you don't want to.
6. Dare you to fight against me?
7. Does she need come here after school?
8. I will be going to wait for Mary till she comes.
9. You ought not make noises in the library.
10. He do loves Jane however poor she is.
11. I studied hard so that I may pass the exam, but failed.
12. Who wrote this letter?  /  Tom was.
13. You must to take care of your kid brother.
14. You should clean your room before you went out.
15. Would you helping me with my homework?
16. Must I come to work on Sundays?  /  No, you must not.
17. As you have walked long, you must have been thirsty now.
18. I insist that the criminals may be punished.
19. According to the weather forecast, it would snow tomorrow.
20. We are going to got tired after climbing the mountain.

**02 괄호 속에 있는 말을 이용해 다음 우리말을 영작하라.**

1. 그녀는 내 말을 들으려 하지 않았다. (would, listen)

2. 비가 막 오려고 한다. (about)

3. 너는 내일 도서관에 올 필요가 없다. (have to)

4. 커피 좀 드시겠습니까? (would)

_____

5. 나는 저 아름다운 산을 영원히 사랑할 것이다. (forever)

_____

6. 한 시간만 저와 이야기할 수 있습니까? (could, for)

_____

7. 저녁 식사 후 우리 영화나 보러 갈까요? (shall)

_____

8. 네가 나에게 화내는 것도 일리가 있다. (may well)

_____

9. 그가 친구 돈을 훔칠 리가 없다. (cannot, steal)

_____

10. 그녀는 과거에 부자였음에 틀림없다. (must, past)

_____

---

**영어 문장에서 기본 요소(S, O, C) 파악이 중요한 이유:** 한글에서는 주어, 목적어, 부사 등이 조사를 통해 거의 다 구별된다: "엄마가(주어) 시장에(부사) 가서 꽃을(목적어) 사신다." 그런데 영어엔 조사가 없으므로 특정 단어가 문장에서 무슨 역할을 하는지 구별하기가 쉽지 않다: "Mother(S) goes to market(ad) and buys flowers(O)." 많은 경우, 전치사가 한글의 조사처럼 명사의 의미를 보완하곤 하는데, 이런 전명구(형용사, 부사 역할)는 그 뜻이 대체로 명확하므로 오히려 문장 이해에서 큰 중요성을 갖지 못한다.

반면에 전치사가 없는 명사는 그 뜻을 금방 파악하기 어려운데, 영어 문장 기본 요소 중 S, O, C가 전치사 없이 단독으로 쓰이는 명사들이다.

그래서 이런 명사들이 문장에서 무슨 역할을 하는 지 아는 것이 문장 이해에 핵심적 열쇠가 되는 것이다.

# Unit 10 형용사 (Adjective)

형용사는 명사를 수식(한정)하는 말로 그 성질, 상태, 종류 등을 보여준다.

## A 형용사의 형태

1. **고유 형용사**:
   - 예) wise, pretty, new, big, wide, nice, bright 등
     · I went up a **high** mountain, which was very **nice**.

2. **명사 전용 형용사**: 명사나 대명사가 형용사로 전용(轉用)되는 경우

   ❶ **명사의 전용**(수사 포함): 앞의 명사가 뒤의 명사를 꾸며 준다.
   - 예) a **silver** coin, the **gold** watch, the **bus** stop
     the **car** tire, **two** books, **second** chance
     · Tom bought a **car** *seat* for his baby.
     · I have two **table** *covers*.

   ❷ **대명사의 전용**: 지시대명사, 의문대명사, 부정대명사의 전용
   - 예) **this** pen [지시형용사]　　　**what** time [의문형용사]
     **some** flowers [부정대명사]　**any** card
     **many** people　　　　　　　**few** students

     · **This** *book* is bigger than **that** *one*.
     · **Which** *color* do you like, red or blue?

3. **분사 형용사**: 동사를 **분사** 형태로 바꿔 형용사를 만든다.

   ❶ **현재분사**(Present Participle): '~을 하고 있는'(진행형)의 의미로 동사 원형에 –ing를 붙인다.
   (☞ 17. 동사의 시제, **C**)
   - 예) sing → sing**ing** (노래하고 있는), go → go**ing** (가고 있는)
     · While I was **going** to grocery, I saw a **singing** bird.

   ❷ **과거분사**(Past Participle): '~하기를 마친'(완료형) 혹은 '~함을 당하는'(수동)의 의미로, 흔히 약자로 p.p.로 표시한다. (☞ 17. 동사의 시제, **B**)
   - 예) love → lov**ed**(사랑했던, 사랑 받는), sing → **sung**(노래했던, 불려지는)

- go → gone(가버린, [자동사이므로 수동의 의미는 못 가짐])
- She has **loved** her son. [완료: 과거부터 사랑해 옴]
- This song was **sung** by Elvis. [수동]
- He is **gone**.(가고 없다) [완료]

4. **전치사구 형용사**: **(전치사)+(명사)** 혹은 **to+(동사)** 형태의 구가 명사를 꾸민다. 전치사구는 늘 한정하는 명사 **뒤**에 온다.
- The *apple* **on the table** is fresh.
- I want a *house* **to live in**. (안에 들어가 살 집)

## B 어미를 통한 품사 전환

1. **명사 + -ful, -some, -en, -ly, -y, -ous, -ed**는 **형용사**가 된다:
   - beauty → beauti**ful**(아름다운)
   - care → care**ful**(조심스러운)
   - trouble → trouble**some**(귀찮은)
   - friend → friend**ly**(친절한)
   - wood → wood**en**(나무로 된)
   - ease → eas**y**(쉬운)
   - glamor → glamor**ous**(매혹적인)
   - long-hair → long-hair**ed**(긴 머리의)
   - joy → joy**ful**(즐거운)
   - labor → labor**some**(힘드는)
   - love → love**ly**(사랑스러운)
   - man → man**ly**(남자다운)
   - gold → gold**en**(황금의)
   - dirt → dirt**y**(더러운)
   - peril → peril**ous**(위험한)

2. **형용사 + ness, 형용사 + dom**은 **명사**가 된다:
   - fit → fit**ness**(적당함, 몸매)
   - round → round**ness**(둥글기)
   - free → free**dom**(자유)
   - busy → busi**ness**(사업)
   - great → great**ness**(위대함)
   - wise → wis**dom**(지혜)

3. **(en) +형용사, or 형용사 +(en)**은 **동사**가 된다:
   - large → **en**large(크게 하다)
   - broad → broad**en**(확장하다)
   - sad → sadd**en**(슬프게 하다)
   - rich → **en**rich(풍요케 하다)
   - wide → wid**en**(넓히다)
   - bright → bright**en**(밝히다)

### 표 15. 중요 접미사

| 접미사 | 의미 | 용례 |
|---|---|---|
| -able | ~할 수 있는 | wash<u>able</u>, eras<u>able</u>(지울 수 있는), read<u>able</u> |
| -age | 집합, 동작, 상태 | bagg<u>age</u>, stor<u>age</u>(창고), us<u>age</u>, marri<u>age</u>(결혼), stopp<u>age</u>(정지) |
| -al | ~적인(형용사) | politic<u>al</u>(정치적인), seri<u>al</u>(일련의), benefici<u>al</u> |
| | 상태(명사) | refus<u>al</u>(거절), arriv<u>al</u>(도착) |
| -an | ~인 사람 | Kore<u>an</u>, Christi<u>an</u>(그리스도인), histori<u>an</u>(역사가) |
| -ance | 성질 | import<u>ance</u>, perform<u>ance</u>(공연), pati<u>ence</u> |
| -ant | ~한 | pleas<u>ant</u>, differ<u>ent</u> |
| | ~하는 사람 | assist<u>ant</u>(조수), serv<u>ant</u>, stud<u>ent</u> |
| -ate | ~한 | affection<u>ate</u>(애정 어린), consider<u>ate</u>(사려 깊은) |
| | ~하게 하다 | anim<u>ate</u>, activ<u>ate</u>(활성화하다), regul<u>ate</u>(규정하다) |
| -ation | 행동, 상태 | declar<u>ation</u>(선언), reform<u>ation</u>(개혁) |
| -ative | ~한 | talk<u>ative</u>(말 많은), imagin<u>ative</u>(상상력 있는) |
| -cide | 죽이다, 죽임 | insecti<u>cide</u>(살충제), pesti<u>cide</u>(구충제) |
| -cy | 성질, 상태 | accura<u>cy</u>(정확성), prophe<u>cy</u>(예언), idio<u>cy</u>(바보짓) |
| -dom | 상태 | king<u>dom</u>(왕국), bore<u>dom</u>(지루함), martyr<u>dom</u>(순교) |
| -ed | ~을 가진 | blue ey<u>ed</u>, hot temper<u>ed</u>(성미 급한) |
| -ee | ~당하는 사람 | employ<u>ee</u>(피고용인), refug<u>ee</u>(피난자), absent<u>ee</u>(결석자) |
| -en | ~로 된 | wool<u>en</u>(모직의), ash<u>en</u>(재가 된) |
| | ~되게 하다[1] | deep<u>en</u>(심화시키다), weak<u>en</u>(약화시키다), dark<u>en</u>, strength<u>en</u> |
| -er, -or | ~하는 사람 | teach<u>er</u>, act<u>or</u>(배우), li<u>ar</u>(거짓말장이), mak<u>er</u> |
| -ery | 성질, 기술 | brav<u>ery</u>(용기), cook<u>ery</u>(요리법), machin<u>ery</u>(기계류) |
| -ette | 작은 | disk<u>ette</u>(작은 판), cigar<u>ette</u>(작은 담배) |
| -fold, -ple | 겹의 | dou<u>ble</u>, tri<u>ple</u>, multi<u>ple</u>, three<u>fold</u>, many<u>fold</u>(여러 겹의) |
| -ful | ~로 가득한 | pain<u>ful</u>, power<u>ful</u>, use<u>ful</u>, skill<u>ful</u>, fear<u>ful</u><br>help<u>ful</u>, harm<u>ful</u>, success<u>ful</u>, doubt<u>ful</u>(의심스런) |
| -fy | ~로 만들다 | simpli<u>fy</u>, justi<u>fy</u>(정당화하다), classi<u>fy</u>, signi<u>fy</u>, puri<u>fy</u> |
| -hood | 상태, 기간 | child<u>hood</u>, adult<u>hood</u>(성년기), brother<u>hood</u>(형제애)<br>false<u>hood</u>, knight<u>hood</u>(기사도), likeli<u>hood</u>(가능성) |
| -ic, ique | ~식의, ~한 | aci<u>dic</u>(산성의), histori<u>c</u>, pictures<u>que</u>(그림 같은), un<u>ique</u>(독특한) |

| 접미사 | 의미 | 예시 |
|---|---|---|
| -ish | ~스러운 | English, Swedish, childish(유치한) |
| -ism | 주의, 사상 | socialism, capitalism(자본주의), egoism(이기주의) |
| -ist | ~하는 사람 | egoist(이기주의자), socialist, pianist, cellist |
| -ite | ~관계자 | Seoulite(서울사람), Israelite |
| -ite | ~한, ~하다 | unite, favorite(호의적인) |
| -ive | ~한 | decisive, explosive, creative, active |
| -ize | ~로 만들다 | realize, civilize, stabilize(안정시키다) apologize(사과하다), nationalize, harmonize |
| -less | ~이 없는 | valueless(가치 없는), endless, useless, helpless worthless, wireless(무선의), priceless(값을 매길 수 없는) |
| -let | 작은 놈 | booklet(소책자), piglet, leaflet(전단지), droplet |
| -like | ~같은 | childlike(순진한), treelike(나무 같은) |
| -ly | ~한, ~하게 | hourly(매시), daily(매일의), truly(진실로) |
| -ment | 행위, 상태 | government, management, development(개발) |
| -ness | ~함 | kindness(친절), goodness, loveliness |
| -ory | ~한 | satisfactory(만족스러운) |
| -ory | ~하는 장소 | laboratory(실험실), observatory(관측소) |
| -ous | ~이 많은 | dangerous, famous, spacious(넓은) |
| -ship | 상태, 기술 | friendship, partnership, scholarship(장학금), membership citizenship, leadership, fellowship(교제), sportsmanship |
| -some | ~을 만드는 | tiresome(피곤한), gamesome(게임을 좋아하는) |
| -t | ~하기 | complaint(불평), pursuit(추구) |
| -ule | 작은 덩이 | granule(과립), globule(혈구) |
| -ure | ~하는 것 | closure(폐쇄), failure(실패) |
| -ward | ~를 향해 | backward(뒤로), toward, forward(앞으로), homeward |
| -ware | ~에 쓰는 것 | hardware, underware(속옷), houseware(가정용품) |
| -wise | ~한 방향으로 | clockwise(시계 방향으로), otherwise(그렇지 않으면) |
| -y | ~한 것 | jealousy(질투), injury(상처), entreaty(간청) |
| -y | ~한 사람, 동물 | granny(할머니), doggy |
| -y | ~한 | cloudy, rainy, yellowy, airy(통풍 잘 되는) |

주: 1. 접두사 en으로 동사를 만드는 경우: enforce(집행하다), enroll, ensure, encourage, enrage, enact(입법하다), enable, entitle(자격을 주다), enclose(둘러싸다)

### 표 16. 중요 접두사

| 접두사 | 의미 | 접두사 | 의미 |
|---|---|---|---|
| ab-, dis-, se-, tele- | away | dia-, trans-, inter- | across, between |
| auto- | self | post-, re- | back, after |
| geo- | earth | ante-, pre-, fore-, pro- | before |
| re-, ana- | again | ex-, extra-, out-, outer- | outside |
| anti-, contra-, unter- | against | un-, dis-, an-, non-, in- | not |
| de-, sub-, under- | down | in-, en-, intra- | inside, into |
| ad-, a- | toward | up-, over-, extra- | up, above |
| ex-, sur-, out-, super- | over | pro- | in favor of |
| multi- | many | mono-, uni- | one, alone |
| bi-, du-, twi- | two | tri- | three |
| per-, up- | thoroughly | en-, be- | make |
| com-, syn- | together | para- | beside |

※ 접두사들은 뒤에 오는 단어의 영향을 받아 형태가 자주 변할 수 있다.
- ad(toward) + price → appreciate(평가하다)
- dis(away) + fer(가다) → differ(다르다)
- con(with) + pan(빵) → company('함께 빵 먹는' 동료, 회사)

※ 접두사는 문법 영역이라기 보단 단어 영역이므로 단어 공부에 활용하면 좋겠다. 이에 관해 더 알고 싶으면 <Word Lord>를 구해 공부하라!

▌**연습문제 31**

괄호 속 단어들 중 알맞은 것에 ○표하라.

1. Tom is (loving, loved) Sarah.
2. This (golden, goldly) watch looks nice.
3. (What, Which) time do you want to meet?
4. Give these candies to (each, all) boy in the room.
5. Do you know the song (singing, sung) by Tom?
6. The teacher is very (friendful, friendly).
7. Please (largen, enlarge) this photograph.
8. This movie is a (saddening, saddened) one.
9. The question is not (ease, easy) for you to solve.
10. I need some water to (drink, drunk).


## C 형용사의 용법

**1 한정적 용법:** 명사 앞이나 뒤에서 **직접적**으로 명사를 꾸미는 역할을 함.
elder, eldest, live(살아있는, 생기 있는) 등은 한정적 용법으로만 쓰인다.

- Jack is a **smart** *boy*.
- She gave me *something* **sweet**.
- Mike is my **elder** *brother*. (형)
- It is a **live** *broadcasting*. (생방송)
- The eel is called a "**living** *fossil*." (살아있는 화석)

**2. 서술적 용법:** 2형식이나 4형식 동사에서 명사를 **간접적**으로 꾸미는 보어 역할을 함. a-로 시작되는 형용사(alive, alone, asleep, awake, alike 등)와 well, glad 등의 일부 형용사는 서술적 용법으로만 쓰인다.

- My grandfather is very **well**. (잘 계시다)
- On Sunday, he was **alone** in the house. (혼자 있었다)
- I am **glad** to meet you.
- The old man is still **alive**.
- It has not **changed** for about 200 million years.

**3. 명사적 용법:** 정관사나 전치사와 함께 명사처럼 사용된다.

the **wellknown**(= wellknown people)  the **rich**(= rich people)
the **deceased**(= the deceased one)  the **accused**(= the accused one)
for **certain**(확실히)  for **good**(영원히),
in **short**(간단히 말해)  in **vain**(헛되이)
in **general**(일반적으로)  in **particular**(특별히)
before **long**(오래지 않아)  on the **whole**(전반적으로)
for **granted**(당연하게)

- You should respect *the* **old**.  [the old = old people]
- I don't know *for* **sure**. (확실히)
- We take the mobile phone **for granted** now. (당연한 것으로 여김)

## D 수량, 정도를 나타내는 부정형용사 및 대명사

막연한 수나 양을 나타내는 부정형용사와 대명사를 정리하면 다음과 같다:

### 표 17. 수량 형용사·대명사

| 수에만 사용 | 공통으로 사용 | 양에만 사용 |
|---|---|---|
| many, few, a few | some(any), a lot of, lots of, all, no, enough, more, plenty of | much, little, a little |

- **A lot of** people were angry at the news.
- **A lot of** milk was sent to the refugee camp.
- He has **few** friends. (거의 없다)　　　　　　　　　　[부정적 의미]
- He has **a few** friends. (약간 있다)　　　　　　　　　[긍정적 의미]
- We have **little** water. (거의 없다)　　　　　　　　　[부정적 의미]
- We have **a little** water. (약간 있다)　　　　　　　　[긍정적 의미]
- I have **enough** money to buy a pizza.
- **Much** of the island was contaminated. (섬의 대부분)
- There were **no** cars in the parking lot.
- **No** salt was left in the box.
- She applied **plenty of** sunscreen on her face.

■ 연습문제 32

괄호 속 단어들 중 알맞은 것에 ○표하라.

1. I feel very (alone, lonely) these days.
2. James is (elder, older) than I.
3. I was (wake, awake) till midnight.
4. The (sleeping, asleep) cat on the roof is Tom's.
5. In (general, generally), Chinese don't like Japanese.
6. She got tired before (long, length).
7. The rich (is, are) not always happy.
8. A lot of sugar (was, were) lost during the flood.
9. Bill has a little (money, books) in his bag.
10. Fortunately, we have (few, a few) cows in the field.
11. We have (many, a lot of) milk in the refrigerator.
12. Bring me (some, a little) books to read.
13. Few people (was, were) rescued in the accident.
14. All the chicken in the freezer (was, were) missing.
15. How (much, many) are these eggs? / Five dollars.

## E 형용사의 위치와 순서

1. **보어**: 형용사가 보어로 사용될 때, 2형식 동사에선 **동사 다음**에, 5형식 동사에선 **목적어 다음**에 위치한다.
   · The girl *seems* **lovely**.           [2형식 동사]
   · I found *the book* **interesting**.    [5형식 동사]

2. **수식어**: 한정 형용사는 원칙적으로 **관사와 명사 사이**에 오는데, **형용사구**는 **명사 뒤**에 온다.
   · It is an **important** *book*.
   · The **tall** *boy* is my brother.
   · I saw a **sleeping** *baby*.
     → I saw a *baby* **sleeping** on the bed.
   · Do you have *friends* **to talk with**? (같이 얘기할 친구)

3. **순서**: 여러 개의 형용사가 한 명사를 꾸밀 때, 순서는 대체로 다음과 같다:
   **관사(or 지시대명사) + 수량(서수-기수) + 성질/상태 + 명사**
   - I cannot forget **these two pretty twin American** *girls*.
   - He showed me **his first two poetry** *books*.

4. **후치**: some-, any-, no-, every- 등과 -thing, -one, -body 등이 결합된 명사를 수식할 때는 그 뒤에 온다.
   - He got *something* **new**.
   - Do you want *anything* **cold**?

5. **관용적으로 명사 뒤에 쓰이는 한정 형용사**:

   a *room* **available** (사용 가능한 방)       a *girl* **upstairs** (위층에 사는 소녀)
   the *people* **outside** (외부인들)           the *members* **present** (참석한 회원들)
   the *art* **proper** (진정한 의미에서의 예술)  the *sum* **total** (총계)
   from *time* **immemorial** (옛적부터)         *Alexander* **the Great** (알렉산더 대왕)
   what *else* (다른 무엇)?                     The World War II (**Two**) = The **Second** World War
   George II (**the Second**)


■ **연습문제 33**

괄호 속 단어들 중 알맞은 것에 ○표하라.

1. It's very hot. Give me (some water, something) cold.
2. Don't you have (anything, something) new?
3. I need a friend to play (at, with).
4. The girls (Chinese, tall, downstairs) are pretty noisy.
5. What (else, other) do you need?
6. I respect (Sejong the Great, the Great Sejong) most.
7. Do you know when the World War (Two, Second) broke out?

# 종합문제 7

## 01 다음 문장에서 어색한 부분을 찾아 바르게 고치라.

1. You have to drink many water for your health.
2. How much children do you have?
3. I found a silveren coin in the cave.
4. We cannot find the tomb of the Alexander Great.
5. Do not drink cold something too much.
6. Please take care of these my two dogs.
7. This book is very funny and interested.
8. Please give me a sheet of paper to write to.
9. Do you have money enough to buy the computer?
10. I searched my lost coin all night in vainly.
11. This is an alive TV show.
12. In particularly, vitamin C is good for preventing colds.
13. The kid went asleepy in the bus.
14. I was exciting with the football game.
15. Mr. Kim introduced two his sons to me.
16. We have few money to spend this week.
17. The deceased were her grandpa.
18. We found this movie bored.
19. There is a cat sleepy on the roof.
20. The noise outside makes me annoying.

## 02 괄호 속에 있는 말을 이용해 다음 우리말을 영작하라.

1. 위층 남자는 매우 쓸쓸해 보인다. (upstairs, seem)

2. 침대 위에서 잠자고 있는 저 아기를 보아라. (sleeping)

3. 그 공원에는 개들이 하나도 남아 있지 않았다. (no, left)

4. 이 두 마리의 커다란 아프리카 코끼리들은 병들었다. (African)

5. 나에게 마실 물과 쓸 모자를 좀 주세요. (drink, hat, put on)

6. 그는 게임에 쓸 돈이 거의 없다. (little, spend)

7. 가난한 사람들이 늘 불행한 건 아니다. (the poor, unhappy)

8. 가방 안에 있는 책은 누구 것이니? (whose, in the bag)

9. 그 모임에 참석한 회원은 모두 한국인이었다. (present)

10. 다른 아무도 그렇게 아름답게 춤출 순 없다. (else)

**접두사/접미사의 중요성:** 영단어를 좀 더 효율적으로 외울 수 있는 방법이 접두사/접미사를 활용하는 것이다. 예전에 <학원>이란 잡지에 embellishment라는 단어가 언급된 적이 있다. 이 엄청 어려워 보이는 단어를 분석해 보면, em-은 "make"라는 의미의 접두사, -lish는 형용사를 만드는 접미사, -ment는 명사를 만드는 접미사이므로, 이것들을 빼내면 달랑 bel(아름다운)이란 어간만 남는다. 잡지 기자는 프랑스 소설 Bel-Ami(아름다운 친구)에서 bel의 뜻을 유추하는데, 우리는 미녀와 야수(Beauty and the Beast)의 아름다운 여 주인공 Belle에서 유추할 수도 있다. 이 어간과 접두사/접미사를 살펴보면 결국 위 단어는 "아름답게 만드는 것" 즉, "장식"이란 뜻이 된다. 이렇게 외우면 오래 기억되겠지?

# Unit 11 부사 (Adverb)

Adverb란 "동사(verb)에 붙는다(ad)"란 뜻으로 본래 동사를 수식하는 말이지만, **형용사**나 다른 **부사, 문장 전체**도 수식할 수 있다. 부사는 문장에서 주어, 목적어, 보어 역할을 못한다. 문장을 잘 이해하려면, 부사들을 발라내고 (S: 주어) (V: 동사) (C: 보어) (O: 목적어)를 찾아낼 필요가 있다.

## A 부사의 형태

### 1. 고유 형태의 부사

예 very, here, soon, often 등
- I will *stay* **here**. [동사 수식]
- He is very fat and eats **very** *quickly*. [형용사, 부사 수식]

### 2. 형용사 + ly

-y로 끝나는 형용사는 -ily로 변화하며, 형용사 끝의 e는 생략되기도 한다.
- easy(쉬운) → easily(쉽게)
- true(진실된) → truly(진실로)
- nice(멋진) → nicely(멋지게)    [nicly는 발음이 '니클리'가 되므로 e를 놔둠]

※ 형용사에 –ly가 붙어 뜻이 달라지는 경우:
- late(늦은, 늦게) → lately(최근에)
- high(높은) → highly(매우)
- hard(어려운) → hardly(거의 ~않는)
- close(가까운) → closely(면밀히)

### 3. 전치사 + 명사구 : 전명구는 명사를 꾸미는 형용사가 될 수도 있다
- He *came* **to school**(학교에) **without his bag**(가방 없이)
- **To my surprise**, he was alive.(놀랍게도)    [문장 전체 수식]

### 4. to+부동사: 목적, 이유, 결과 등으로 사용된다. (☞ 20. 부정사)
- She *entered* the cafeteria **to have** lunch.    [목적]
- I am *glad* **to see** you again. (너를 만나니)    [이유]
- He *studied* hard **only to fail** in exam. (공부했으나 실패)    [결과]

### 5. 명사형 부사: 자주 사용되는 (전치사+명사)구에서 전치사가 생략되는 경우, 형태는 명사지만 실제로는 부사로 쓰인다. (☞ 7. 전치사, D)
- **Yesterday**, on the way **home**, I met a girl who lives **downstairs**.

## 6. 전치사형 부사

up, down, on, off, out, over 등은 종종 부사로도 사용된다. **전치사**는 문장에서 **생략될 수 없는 반면, 부사**는 **생략해도 문장이 되므로** 이를 통해 전치사와 부사를 구별한다. 부사인 경우, **목적어**가 그 앞에 올 수도 있고 뒤에 올 수도 있는데, **대명사 목적어**는 반드시 앞에 온다.

- He looked after the kid.  [전치사, 생략 불가]
  cf He looked the kid after. (×)  [순서 전환 불가]
- He put down the pencil. (= He put the pencil down.)  [부사]
  cf He put it down. (○)   He put down it. (×)

## 7. 형용사와 부사로 모두 쓰이는 단어

fast(빠른, 빨리); high(높은, 높이); long(긴, 오랫동안); hard(딱딱한, 열심히); early(이른, 일찍); enough(충분한, 충분히); tight(꽉 끼는, 단단히) 등.

- He was once a **fast** runner, but cannot run **fast** now.
- Over the **high** mountain, the plane flew **high**.
- Hold **tight** the man who is wearing the **tight** pants.
- **Early** in the morning, I had an **early** breakfast.
- With a **long** neck, she longed for her father all day **long**.
- If I had **enough** food, I could be strong **enough** to win the game.

### ▎연습문제 34

괄호 속 단어들 중 알맞은 것에 ○표하라.

1. John is a (nice, nicely) student.
2. He is (true, truly) honest.
3. It is raining (hard, hardly).
4. He finished the task (good, well).
5. The wind is blowing (strong, strongly).
6. He arrived at the station early (enough, enoughly).
7. Tom got up (late, lately) in the morning.
8. Please speak more (loud, loudly).
9. You shall have to pay (for it, it for) someday.
10. I went (close, closely) to the mirror.

## B 의문부사(Interrogative Adverb)

**1. when(언제):** **시간**을 말할 땐 작은 시간대에서 출발해 넓은 시간대로 간다.
  · When did we meet? / *At six thirty PM, Monday March 6th, 2017*.

**2. where(어디서):** **장소**를 말할 땐 작은 장소에서 출발해 넓은 장소로 간다.
  · Where do you live? / *At 101 Plano Avenue, Dallas, Texas*.

**3. how(어떻게):** 동작을 행하는 **방법, 상태, 정도** 등을 묻는다.
  · How do you go to school? / *By bus*.   [방법]
  · How are you today? / I am *very well*.   [상태]
  · How do you like it?(얼마나 맘에 들어?) / *So, so!*(그저 그래!)   [상태]
  · How do you want(like) your steak? / *Medium*, please!   [정도]
  · How *old* are you? / I am *sixteen* (*years old*).   [정도]
  · How *much* is this book? / It is *two fifty(2.50) (dollars)*.   [정도]
  · How *long* does it take to the school? / *About 20 minutes*.   [정도]
  · I like apples. How(=What) about you?(너는 어때?) / *So do I*.   [정도]

**4. why(왜):** 동작의 **이유**를 묻는 것으로, Because~로 대답한다.
  · Why were you late for school? *Because* I overslept. (늦잠을 자서)
  · I will not go with you. / Why not? (왜 안 가?)

## C 부사의 위치

모든 수식어는 수식하는 말 가까이 오는 게 원칙인데, 부사는 성격과 역할에 따라 다양한 위치를 가질 수 있다.

**1. 빈도 부사:** always, usually, sometimes, often, hardly, never, frequently, still, once 등은 **조동사나 be 동사 뒤에, 일반 동사 앞에** 둔다.

  · He *is* **always** honest and *will* **never** be a liar.
  · She **often** *goes* swimming.
  · He was **once** a popular singer. (한 때)

2. **시간 부사:** 문장 맨 뒤 혹은 맨 앞(강조적 의미)에 올 수 있다.
   - Last night, I went to the K-mart. = I went to the K-mart last night.
   - (On) Saturday, we will have a party.

3. **문장 전체를 꾸미는 부사:** 문장 맨 앞에 올 수 있다.
   - Fortunately, he came back home safe. (다행히도)
   - To my surprise, she passed the exam. (놀랍게도)

4. **일반 부사:** 대개 동사 다음에 오며, 목적어가 있으면 목적어 다음에 온다.
   - They ran *fast* and *took* the food *quickly*.
   - I *sat* there and *read* the book *happily*.

5. **형용사를 수식하는 부사:** 대개 그 **형용사 앞**에 온다.
   - This rock was **pretty** *heavy*.
   - I am **so** *tired*.

6. **타동사와 부사로 이뤄진 동사구:** turn on, take off, throw away 등의 경우, **일반 명사 목적어**는 동사와 부사 사이 혹은 부사 뒤에 오지만, **대명사 목적어**는 반드시 **동사와 부사 사이**에 온다.
   - I **turned on** *the computer*. (○)   · I **turned** *the computer* **on**. (○)
   - I **turned on** *it*. (✗)   · I **turned** *it* **on**. (○)

7. **순서:** 부사들이 여러 개 겹치는 경우, **전하고 싶은 내용부터** 말하거나 **간단한** 말부터 하되, 대개 **장소(좁은 곳 → 넓은 곳) → 상태 → 시간(작은 단위 → 큰 단위)** 순으로 한다.
   - He went **to the bank in the town early in the morning last Monday**.
   - I will meet her **at 2 PM in the park near the lake**.

8. **특별한 위치를 갖는 부사**

   ❶ enough이 형용사를 수식하는 부사로 쓰일 때는 그 형용사의 **뒤**에 온다.
   - He has **enough** *money* to buy the house.  [형용사]
   - He is *rich* **enough** to buy the house.  [부사]

   ❷ only는 원칙적으로 수식하는 말 앞에 둔다.
   - He is an **only** *child*. (그는 외동아들이다)  [형용사]
   - He is **only** *a child*. (그는 단지 어린이일 뿐이다)  [부사]
   - **Only** *he is a child*. (오직 그만이 어린이다)  [부사]

❸ however와 though: "그러나"라는 뜻을 갖는데, however는 문두나 첫 어귀 뒤에 오는 반면, though는 첫 어귀 뒤나 문장 맨 끝에 온다.
- Mom was hungry. **However**, she didn't eat chicken.
  = She, **however**, didn't eat chicken.
- I bought a watch. It was expensive, **though**. (그게 비싸긴 했지만)

■ 연습문제 35
괄호 속 단어들 중 알맞은 것에 ○표하라.
1. (What, How) do you want for lunch?
2. (What, Why) the long face?  /  I failed in math.
3. (How, Where) long did you wait for me?
4. (Lucky, Luckily), I won the game.
5. Tom got on the bus and got (off it, it off) after 10 minutes.
6. Without any brothers and sisters, Mike is (an only, only a) son.

## D 주의할 부사의 용법

### 1. 동조하는 too 와 not ~ either
긍정문에 대해 동조할 때는 too, 부정문에 동조할 때는 not ~ either를 쓴다.

- He is an actor.  /  I am an actor, **too**. (= I am also an actor.)
- He is not a teacher.  /  I am **not** a teacher, **either**.

※ 미국 구어체에선 위의 각 경우 **Me, too!** 와 **Me, neither!** 라고 대답한다.

### 2. 동조하는 so 와 neither
**대동사**를 이용해 긍정문에 대해 동조할 때는 so, 부정문에는 neither를 쓴다.

- He likes coffee.  /  **So** do I. (= I like coffee, too.)
- He doesn't like tea.  /  **Neither** do I. (= I don't like it, either.)
- I am tired.  /  **So** am I. (= Me, too.)

### 3. already와 yet
**already는 긍정문, yet은 부정문, 의문문**에 쓰이는데, already가 의문문에 오면 **놀라움**의 표시가 된다.
- I am **already** full.  /  Are you **already** full? (벌써 배불러?)
- I am not satisfied **yet**.
- Are you watching TV **yet**?

### 4. cannot ~ too
"너무 ~할 수는 없다"는 말에서 "아무리 ~해도 괜찮다"는 뜻이 된다.
- You **cannot** be **too** careful of snakes. (뱀들을 정말 조심해라.)
- Holidays **cannot** be **too** many. (휴일은 아무리 많아도 괜찮다.)

### 5. ago와 before
ago는 특정 기간과 함께 **과거형**에 쓰이며, 완료형과는 잘 사용되지 않는다.
- Jack *died* two weeks **ago**.
- I *helped* him **before**.
  - cf I helped him ago. (×)
- I think we *have met* somewhere **before**.
  - cf I think we *met* long **ago**.

### 6. there와 here
here is(are)는 "여기에 ~이 있다"는 뜻이지만, there is(are)엔 "거기에"란 의미가 없이 다만 "~이 있다"를 뜻한다. **대명사 주어**는 도치되지 않는다.
- **There** is a book **here**. (여기에 책 한 권이 있다)　　　　　　　　[there에 강세 없음]
- **Here** is the book. ([찾고 있던] 그 책이 여기 있다)　　　　　　　　[here에 강세]
- Where is my book?  /  **Here** it is. (여기 있어)　　　　　　　　[here에 강세]
- **There** you are! (너 거기 있구나!)　　　　　　　　[there에 강세]

### 7. very(진실로) 와 much(훨씬)
very는 절대적 의미를 갖는 반면, much는 "차이가 크게"라는 함축적 의미를 가지므로 비교 대상(설사 표현되지 않아도)을 염두에 두고 있다.
- That book is **very** *easy* but this is **much** *easier*. (훨씬 더 쉬운)
- Today, he eats too **much**. (평소보다 혹은 다른 사람보다 훨씬 더)

## 8. 부사를 포함하는 중요 관용 동사구

**❶ bring up**(키우다, 양육하다)
 · Sally **brought up** two children.

**❷ call up**(~을 소환하다, 전화로 불러내다)
 · The general **called up** the reserves. (예비군을 소집했다)

**❸ cut off**(~을 잘라내다)
 · He **cut off** the branches from the tree.

**❹ find out**(~을 발견하다)
 · They **found out** that the house was empty.

**❺ get on** (~에 타다) ↔ **get off** (~에서 내리다)
 · Jane **got on** the taxi and **got** *it* **off** after 5 blocks.

**❻ give up** (~을 포기하다)
 · He kept climbing until he **gave** *it* **up** because of an accident.

**❼ hold up** (~을 지탱하다, 쳐들다, 지연시키다)
 · The blocks could not **hold up** the wall.
 · This morning, I was **held up** in the traffic.

**❽ make up** (~을 지어내다, 구성하다, 화장하다, 화해하다, 보상하다)
 · Who **made up** this silly story? (누가 이 어리석은 얘길 꾸며냈니?)
 · The crown was **made up** of 200 jewels. (2백 개의 보석으로 만들어졌다)
 · They fight and **make up** quite often. (자주 싸우고 화해한다)
 · I work overtime to **make up** the loss. (손해를 보상하려 초과 근무한다)
 · She is busy **making up** her dog. (개 화장시키느라 바쁘다)

**❾ pick up** (~을 주워들다, 뽑다, 나가서 차에 태워주다)
 · Please **picked** *me* **up** at the bus stop at 9.

❿ point out (~을 지적해 내다)
· Henry **pointed out** that the answer was wrong.

⓫ put off (~을 연기하다, 미루다)
· Don't **put** *it* **off** till tomorrow.

⓬ put on(~을 입다) ↔ take off(~을 벗다)
· He **took off** the jeans and **put on** the shorts.

⓭ set out(시작하다, 출발하다)
· We **set out** the program to develop the country.

⓮ turn over(뒤집다, 양도하다)
· They **turned over** the losing game. (지고 있던 경기를 뒤집었다)

⓯ turn on(전원을 켜다) ↔ turn off(전원을 끄다)
· **Turn on** the TV and **turn off** the light. (TV를 켜고 불을 꺼라)


■ **연습문제 36**

괄호 속 단어들 중 알맞은 것에 ○표하라.

1. This bug moves (very, much) quickly.
2. Mary was (so, very) pretty that everyone loved her.
3. She (set, pointed) out her first business with her sister.
4. Are you ready (already, yet)?
5. As he failed the test, he has to make (up it, it up).
6. I am not thirsty.  /  Me, (too, neither).
7. We can't be (very, too) careful about our health.
8. Our family lived here (ago, before).
9. John (put, took) off the wet shirt and put on the new one.
10. Bill (gave, made) up smoking because of his new born baby.

## 종합문제 8

**01 다음 문장에서 어색한 부분을 찾아 바르게 고치라.**

1. Mary was enough kind to lend me a lot of money.
2. You may watch TV, but please turn off it when leaving the room.
3. He looks awfully with those glasses.
4. In last year, he entered Boston University for a Ph.D. degree.
5. Jack goes often fishing with his cousin.
6. To our surprised, he was accepted to Duke University.
7. There was a lot of children in the play ground.
8. I am glad to meeting you again.
9. Yesterday, Mary came back home very lately.
10. I can hard believe he attended high school in Canada.
11. She showed me the way to the subway station very kind.
12. Tom sat on the chair and ate the ice cream happy.
13. Dr. Johnson passed away ago seven years.
14. I don't like pineapples.  /  Me, too.
15. Wow, how could you arrive yet?  /  The traffic was not so heavy.
16. Don't throw away it on the road.
17. I am terrible sorry for being late.
18. I can't hear you well. Please speak more loud.
19. Cindy looked close at the stamp on the letter.
20. These melons are very cheaper than those ones.

**02 괄호 속에 있는 말을 이용해 다음 우리말을 영작하라.**

1. 나는 한 때 이 학교의 학생이었다. (once)

2. 토요일마다, 그는 양로원을 방문한다. (every, nursing home)

3. 우리는 지난 월요일 오후 2시에 서울에 있는 도서관에서 그를 만났다. (2PM)

4. 그는 혼자 살고 있지만 외로움을 느끼지 않는다. (alone, lonely)

5. Tom은 더 이상 여기 없지만 Mary는 여전히 있다. (no longer, still)

6. 아직 내 컴퓨터를 수리하지 않았습니까? (fix)

7. 내가 공항에 도착했을 때 엄마가 나를 데리러 오셨다. (arrive, pick up)

8. 우리는 나쁜 시력을 보완하려고 안경을 쓴다. (make up, bad eyesight)

9. 나는 인천 남구 수봉로 6-11 제물포 아파트 A-308에 산다. (at)

10. 만약 네가 포기하지 않는다면, 나도 포기하지 않겠다. (if, give up, either)

---

**on earth와 the hell:** "도대체"라는 의미의 on earth와 the hell은 의문사를 가진 의문문에 주로 사용되는데, 항상 의문사 바로 뒤에 위치한다. 단, the hell은 약간 비속어적 느낌을 갖는다.
- Why on earth did he call the police? (걔는 도대체 왜 경찰을 부른 거야?)
- Who the hell's out there? (그 바깥에 도대체 누구야?)

# Unit 12 접속사 (Conjunction)

접속사는 단어와 단어, 구와 구, 절과 절을 연결하는 말로, 둘을 대등하게 연결하는 **등위접속사**와 하나를 다른 것의 일부분으로 만드는 **종속접속사**가 있다. 두 절이 등위접속사로 연결되면 그 문장을 **중문**(compound sentence), 종속접속사로 연결되면 **복문**(complex sentence)이라 한다.

## A 등위접속사(Coordinate Conjunction)

### 1. and(~와, 그리고)

첨가에 사용되며, 여러 개를 나열할 때는 맨 마지막에만 and를 쓴다.

- I need *an apple, a banana* and *two oranges*.    [and는 마지막에만]
- In the morning, he watches TV **and** I read newspaper.
- I like this *black* and white dog. (얼룩 강아지 한 마리)
  - **cf** Come *help* me! (= Come and *help* me! = Come to *help* me!)    [구어체]

❶ **동시성**: '~이면서 동시에 ~'이란 뜻
- He is my *uncle* and *guardian*. (나의 보호자이자 삼촌)

❷ **더하기** 의미의 and: 수학식에서 and는 plus 의미를 갖는다.
- 2 and 3 equal(s) 5.    • 2 and 3 is(are) 5.

❸ **명령문** + and(그러면): and = then
- Study hard, **and** you will pass the exam.

❹ **and 포함 관용구**:
both A and B (A와 B 둘 다); on **and** on (계속해서); bread **and** butter (버터 바른 빵, 생계수단); by **and** by (점차적으로)

- I can **both** *ski* **and** *skate*.
- This *bread* and *butter* tastes good. (버터 바른 빵)    [단수 취급]
- My *bread* and *butter* is drawing. (내 생계수단은 그림그리기이다)
- They met each other *on* **and** *on* and got closer *by* **and** *by*.

## 2. or(혹은)
선택에 사용되며. 여러 개를 나열할 때는 맨 마지막에만 or를 쓴다.

- You can come here *by car, by bus* **or** *by train*.

**❶ 동격**: '혹은 다른 말로'라는 뜻인데, 앞뒤에 콤마(,)를 놓는다.
- *Siam,* **or** *Thailand,* was once a big country. (시암 곧 태국)

**❷ 명령문 + or**(그러지 않으면): or = otherwise
- Study hard, **or** you will fail the exam.                                    [중문]

**❸ or를 포함한 관용구**:
either A or B(A, B 둘 중 하나); neither A nor B(A, B 둘 다 아닌)

- **Either** you **or** he *has* to go.                              [동사는 뒤 단어에 맞추어 활용]
- **Neither** you **nor** I *am* welcomed here. (둘 다 환영받지 못한다)

## 3. but(그러나)
- He is *rich* but I am *poor*.                                                [중문]

**❶ but 포함 관용구**:
not A but B (A가 아니라 B); not only A but (also) B (A뿐 아니라 B도)

- He is **not** *a lawyer* **but** *a writer*. (변호사가 아니라 작가)
- He is **not only** *a lawyer* **but (also)** a poet. (변호사일 뿐 아니라 시인)
  = He is *a poet* **as well as** *a lawyer*.                    [강조하고 싶은 것은 '시인']

**❷ 전치사적 용법**: '~을 예외하고(except)'의 의미로 쓰임
- No one **but** me knew her. (나 이외엔 아무도 그녀를 몰랐다)

## 4. yet(그러나)
종종 종속절의 although, though와 함께 쓰인다.

- Jack was hungry, **yet** he didn't eat the hamburger.
- **Yet,** the president was hiding it from the public.
- Though we have lost a lot, **yet** we must survive.

## ■ 연습문제 37
괄호 속 단어들 중 알맞은 것에 ○표하라.

1. Three (and, or) five makes eight.
2. Hurry up, (and, or) you will miss the bus.
3. He was not only angry (but, and) also disappointed.
4. Jane was sad. She, (but, however), didn't cry.
5. Mr. Kim, (and, or) my homeroom teacher, lives in this apartment.

## B 종속 접속사(Subordinate Conjunction)

### 1. 명사절을 이끄는 종속접속사

❶ **that(~라는 것)**: that은 **목적어절, 보어절, 동격절**에서 종종 생략

- *It* is certain **that** he is honest.　　　　　　　　[it~that의 용법]
- I know (**that**) he is honest.　　　　　　　　[목적어절에선 that 생략 가능]
- My point is (**that**) he is honest.　　　　　　　　　　　　[보어절]
- I know the *fact* (**that**) he stole the money. (~라는 사실)　　[동격]

❷ **의문접속사**: who(누구인지); when(언제인지); where(어디인지); how(어떻게인지); why(왜인지); what, which(무엇인지)

- It is important **who** he is.　　　　　　　　　　[who 이하가 진주어]
- They wonder **where** he lives.
- I want to see **why** he did it.
- Did you find **what(which)** they want?
- The problem is **how** we cross the river.

❸ **whether와 if(~인지)**: **의문사가 없는 의문문**을 절로 만들 때 쓴다.
- It is not certain **whether(if)** he is honest. (← Is he honest?)
- I don't know **whether(if)** he is honest.

## 2. 부사절을 이끄는 종속 접속사

❶ **시간접속사**: after(~후에); before(~전에); as(~하면서); since(이후로); till(until)(~때까지); when(~때); whenever(~할 때마다); while(~동안); as long as(~하는 한); as soon as(~하자마자) 등

- I played soccer **after** the class was over.
- **As** we walked along the river, we saw many boats.
- It is(has been) 5 years **since** he died.
- I was happy **when** I met her.   [의문접속사와 구별!]
- We played soccer **until** the sun set.
- Don't talk **while** you are eating.
- You may stay here **as long as** you want.
- It began to snow **as soon as** I came home.

❷ **장소접속사**: where(~에), wherever(~한 곳마다)
- The car is not **where** I parked it. (내가 주차했던 곳에 차가 없다.)
- They stayed **wherever** there was water. (물이 있는 곳에서마다)

❸ **조건접속사**: if(만약); unless(만약 ~아니라면); once(일단 ~하면)
- We will play soccer **if** it is fine tomorrow.
- I will not work for you **unless** you pay me. (만약 돈을 안주면)
- **Once** you are addicted to gambling, it's too late. (일단 중독되면)

❹ **원인접속사**: because; since; as(~ 때문에); for(왜냐하면)
- He went to bed **because(since)** he was very tired.
- **As** I was too young, I could not enter school. (~ 때문에)
- I looked at Mary, **for** she was so pretty. (왜냐하면)
※ for는 항상 문장 뒤에 오며, 그 앞에 콤마(,)나 세미콜론(;)을 둔다.

❺ **양보접속사 1**: though(although); even if(though); whether ~ or not
- **Though** he was tired, he went to work. (~할지라도)
  = (As) Tired **as** he was, he went to work.
- **Even if** I am poor, I will never go begging.
- I will go **whether** you like it **or not**. (~하든 안 하든)

❻ **양보접속사 2**: no matter + (의문접속사) = 의문접속사 + ever
no matter who = whoever(누구든); no matter when = whenever(언제든)
no matter where = wherever(어디든); no matter which = whichever
no matter how = however(어찌하든); no matter what = whatever

- **Whoever**(=No matter who) asks you, don't answer.
- We eat pizza **whenever**(=no matter when) we meet.
- I will follow you **wherever**(=no matter where) you go.
- **However**(=No matter how) sad you are, never cry.
- **Whichever**(or **Whatever**) I want, he gives it to me. (원하는 건 뭐든)

❼ **비교접속사**: as(~같이); than(~보다)
- Tom made a box *just* **as** I asked him. (내가 부탁한 그대로)
- I am *as* tall **as** she. (그녀만큼)
- Seoul is *bigger* **than** Busan. (부산보다)

## 3. 그 외 중요 접속사

❶ **next time**(다음번에), **every time**(매번) : 뒤에 when이 생략된 형태
- **Next time** you come here, I will show you my store.
- **Every time** they meet together, they have a quarrel.

❷ **now that** (이제 ~했으니): that은 생략 가능
- **Now (that)** the ground is dry, let's play soccer. (이제 땅이 말랐으니)

❸ **so** (형용사) **that**; **such** (명사) **that** (너무 ~해서 ~하다)
- It is **so** *cold* **that** we cannot go outside. (너무 추워 나갈 수 없다)
  = It is **such** *a cold weather* **that** we cannot go outside.
  = It is **so** *cold a weather* **that** we cannot go outside.

❹ **so that ~ may(can)** = **in order that ~ may(can)** (~하기 위해)
- She works hard **so that** she **may** become rich. (부자가 되기 위해)
  = She works hard **in order that** she **may** become rich.

❺ lest ~ (should) = in order that ~ should not (혹시나 ~ 않기 위해)
· He works hard **lest** he (should) become poor.
 = He works hard **in order that** he **should not** become poor.

❻ as if (마치 ~인 것처럼): 대개 가정법과 함께 사용. (☞ 20. 가정법)
· She talks **as if** she *were* a princess. (마치 공주라도 되는 것처럼)

❼ (just) as ~, so (~인 것처럼, 그렇게~하다)
· **As** humans love their children, **so** do bears their cubs.
(인간이 자녀들을 사랑하듯이, 곰도 그 새끼들을 사랑한다)

❽ so (그래서): and so의 준말
· It was cold, (and) so I stayed in the house.

❾ that I know of (내가 아는 한) = as far as I know
· Is he honest?  /  Not that I know of. (= No, as far as I know.)

❿ in that (~한 면에서): that은 생략 불가
· He is useful **in that** he can speak Chinese.

⓫ There is no doubt that (~에 대해 의심의 여지가 없다):
· There is no doubt (that) he is honest.

※ 접속사를 대신하는 구두점: 콜론(:), 세미콜론(;)
  **콜론**은 **부연설명**을 위한 것이고, 세미콜론은 **and의 축약형**으로 보면 된다.
 · Take followings with you: lantern, knife, and goggle.
 · Read the verses in the Bible: John 3:16, 17; Rom 1:17, 20; 5:1, 2

■ 연습문제 38

괄호 속 단어들 중 알맞은 것에 ○표하라.

1. John felt a little tired, (for, so) he took a break.
2. It is doubtful (that, what) he graduated from the college.
3. Do you know (when, while) she will come?
4. I don't know (which, whether) I can pass the exam or not.
5. (When, Whether) she comes back, please let her call me.
6. Do you know (what, why) they want it?
7. You must arrive at the station (before, after) your train leaves.
8. I didn't go to school (why, because) I was sick.
9. (As, Though) Jim was not rich, he bought a luxurious car.
10. Fasting, (and, or) not eating, is encouraged as well.
11. (If, Whether) it is fine tomorrow, let's go on a picnic.
12. (If, Unless) you make haste, you will be late for school.
13. Either he or I (is, am, are) in charge of this problem.
14. (Whenever, Whatever) Tom sees me, he waves his hand.
15. I have known her (since, until) she was a baby.
16. I will never forgive him as (far, long) as I live.
17. Mary began to cry (as soon as, till) I entered the room.
18. It was (so, such) hot a weather that we had to take a shower.
19. (Whoever, Whatever) buys it, he or she will be satisfied.
20. Jack is far much taller (than, that) me.
21. Sally studies hard (so that, lest) she should fail the test.
22. (As, Even) if they were rich, the Christians lived frugally.
23. Tom was hurt so badly (that, because) he went to see a doctor.
24. Jane is useful in (this, that) she can speak Japanese.
25. Is Jack smart?  /  No, not (as, that) I know of.

# 종합문제 9

**01 다음 문장에서 어색한 부분을 찾아 바르게 고치라.**

1. Be careful, and you will fall off the tree.
2. Practice hard, or you will pass the physical test.
3. Bill fell asleep where he was watching the TV.
4. In the clinic, there were a doctor, and a nurse, a patient.
5. Cindy is not only pretty and also smart.
6. When everytime it rains hard, this area is flooded.
7. It is so a fine weather that we'd better go on a picnic.
8. Which is bigger, elephant and whale?
9. Neither you nor I were correct in the problem.
10. For your partner, you may choose Mike, or Tom, Jerry.
11. John tried to find his gloves, so he couldn't.
12. Whatever cold it is, he always goes swimming.

**02 다음 문장을 괄호 속의 말을 이용해 고치라. (밑줄 부분만)**

1. He was <u>too short to</u> ride the horse. (so ~ that) ⇒
2. I studied hard <u>in order to</u> pass the exam. (so that ~may) ⇒
3. <u>Read my letter, and</u> you will understand why I left you. (if) ⇒
4. <u>I was fishing in the river, and then</u> I saw a crocodile. (while) ⇒
5. <u>As it was a very cold day,</u> she could not go shopping. (such) ⇒

**03 괄호 속에 있는 말을 이용해 다음 우리말을 영작하라.**

1. Mary는 간호사가 아니라 의사이다. (not, but)

2. 엄마가 설거지를 하시는 동안 아빠는 신문을 읽으셨다. (while)

3. 내 눈으로 보기 전까진 믿지 않겠다. (until, with my own eyes)

4. 누구를 만나든, 그에게 친절하게 하라. (whoever)

5. 이제 비가 그쳤으니, 밖으로 나가 농구를 하자. (now)

6. 시간이 지났지만, 기차는 출발하지 않았다. (though, over)

7. 내가 아는 한, 그는 부자가 아니다. (as far as)

8. 네가 어딜 가든지 나는 찾아낼 수 있다. (wherever)

9. 나는 너무나 바빠서 점심을 먹을 수 없었다. (so, that)

10. 이 과일은 맛있을 뿐 아니라 보기도 좋다. (not only, but, look)

---

**고대 로마와 관련된 Tri:** 숫자 3을 뜻하는 tri는 고대 로마 왕국과 관련이 있다. 초기 로마의 집정부는 3부로 나뉘어 있었는데, 그 부는 세 tribe(종족)들에 의해 관장되었고 그 세 부족에게 바치는 세금이 tribute(조공)이었다. 고대 로마의 3거리에는 종종 장터가 열렸는데, 거기서 일어나는 사건들은 trivial(사소한, tri[3]+via[way])한 것들이었다.

# Unit 13 관계대명사 (Relative Pronoun)

**접속사와 대명사 역할**을 동시에 하는 말이 관계대명사이다. 관계대명사가 대신하는 원래 명사를 **선행사**라 부르는데, 관계대명사에는 who, which, that, what 이외에 유사 관계대명사(as, than, but 등)도 있다.

## A 관계대명사의 한정적 용법

### 1. who: 선행사가 사람일 때

❶ **주격**: who
- I love *Jane* and she lived in the house.
  ⇒ I love *Jane* who lived in the house.   [선행사: Jane]

❷ **소유격**: whose (*or* of whom)
- I love *Jane* and her father built that house.
  ⇒ I love *Jane* whose father built that house.
- I have two brothers and both of them live in Busan.
  ⇒ I have two brothers, both of whom live in Busan.   [콤마(,) 주의]

❸ **목적격**: whom (구어에선 간편함을 위해 종종 who로 쓰기도 한다)
- I love Jane and I met her in the summer festival.
  ⇒ I love Jane whom I met in the summer festival.

### 2. which: 선행사가 사물일 때

❶ **주격**: which
- I live in *the house* and it was built in the 1960s.
  ⇒ I live in *the house* which was built in the 1960s.

❷ **소유격**: of which (구어체에선 주로 whose를 쓴다)
- I live in *the house* and its *roof* is red.
  ⇒ I live *in the house* whose *roof* is red.
  = I live in *the house* of which the *roof* is red.   [관사 주의]
  = I live in *the house*, the *roof* of which is red.   [콤마, 관사 주의]

❸ **목적격**: which
- I live in *the house* and my dad built **it**.
  ⇒ I live in *the house* **which** my dad built.

3. **that**: 사람과 사물 선행사에 모두 쓸 수 있음
   주격과 목적격의 형태가 같고, 소유격은 없으므로 whose를 전용해 쓴다. 전치사의 목적어로는 쓸 수 없다.

   ❶ **사람과 사물을 한꺼번에 지칭할 때 사용**
   - I know a man and his dog **and they** live in a cave.
     = I know a man and his dog **that** live in a cave.
   - I know a man and his dog **and their** friendship is very deep.
     = I know a man and his dog **whose** friendship is very deep.
   - I know a man and his dog **and** Tom gave **them** a shelter.
     = I know a man and his dog **that** Tom gave a shelter.

   ❷ **하나뿐인 것 혹은 특정된 것**(최상급, the only, all, no, the same 등)을 받을 때 who나 which 대신 주로 that을 쓴다. who나 which가 앞에서 이미 사용된 경우엔 반복을 피하기 위해 that을 쓴다.
   - Jesus healed *all* **that** were sick.
   - You are *the first* **that** solved this problem.
   - It is *the same* pen **that** I lost. (내가 잃어버린 바로 그 펜)
     ▣ It is the *same* pen **as** I lost. (내가 잃어버린 것과 같은 종류의 펜)
   - *Who* is the girl **that** is standing there?[who의 반복을 피하기 위해]

4. **what**(= the thing that, the thing which): 선행사를 자체에 포함
   what 속에 이미 선행사를 포함하고 있으므로 선행사를 필요로 하지 않는다. 주격과 목적격의 형태가 같고, 소유격은 존재하지 않는다. 때때로 의문대명사 what과의 구별이 쉽지 않다.
   - This is **what** happened last night. (어젯밤에 일어난 일)           [관계대명사]
   - **What** he said is not true.                                    [관계대명사]
   - Tell me **what** you want. (네가 **원하는 것을**, or 네가 **무엇을** 원하는지)
     ▣ Tell me **what** is true. (**무엇이** 진실인지)                    [의문대명사]

## 5. 유사 관계대명사

**❶ as**: such, the same, as, so 등과 호응하여 사용
- Find *such* friends **as** will do good to you.(네게 유익이 될 친구)
- Jack bought a *same* bike **as** I have. (같은 종류의 자전거)
- **As** is usual, he fell asleep after lunch.(늘 그랬듯이)

**❷ than**: more와 함께 사용
- You should not take *more* food **than** is necessary.(필요 이상의 음식)
- We had *more* guests **than** we expected.(기대 이상으로 많은 손님)

**❸ but** (= that ~not)
- There is *no one* **but** knows her. (모르는 이가 없다)
  = that does not know her

### ■ 연습문제 39

**01. 괄호 속 단어들 중 알맞은 것에 ○표하라.**

1. Tom has a brother (who, whose) name is Bill.
2. I know a girl (who, whom) can speak French.
3. Jane lives in the house (which, what) was built 30 years ago.
4. That is the girl (whom, whose) bag was stolen yesterday.
5. Who is the guy (who, that) bought you this ring?
6. I gave you all the money (which, that) I had.
7. That is the house in (that, which) the bread is made.
8. Mary bought a house, the yard (of which, whose) is very wide.
9. This is a same dog (that, as) I used to keep in my youth.
10. Bill spends more money (that, than) he earns.

**02. 주어진 관계대명사를 이용해 두 문장을 한 문장으로 만들라.**

1. I have a friend. He has five bulldogs. (who)

2. We visited Jane. Her mother was a cook. (whose)

3. Look at the house. Its wall is painted in red. (of which)
_____

4. There was a queen in England. All the people loved her. (whom)
_____

5. Do you know the thing? Tom gave me it last night. (what)
_____

6. I know them all. They came from China. (that)
_____

## B 관계대명사의 특별 용법

### 1. 계속적 용법(Continuative Use)
관계대명사 앞에 콤마(,)를 붙여 순서적 상황을 나타낼 수 있다. that과 what은 계속적 용법을 쓰지 않는다.
- She had a son, **who** became a doctor. (그는 후에 의사가 되었다)
  = She had a son **and then he** became a doctor.
- I planted a seed, **which** grew a big tree. (씨는 자라 큰 나무가 됐다)
  = I planted a seed **and then it** grew a big tree.

2. 관계대명사 which 앞에 콤마를 붙여 **앞의 절 전부**를 받을 수 있다.
- He said *she was ill*, **which** was a lie.　　　　　[which의 선행사는 앞 절 전부]

3. 관계 절 앞뒤에 콤마를 넣어 **삽입절**을 만드는데, 콤마는 생략할 수도 있다. 콤마를 넣을 때는 관계대명사 that을 쓰지 않는다.
- Tom, **whom** I thought an American, was a Canadian.

4. **전치사 + 관계대명사**: 관계절에서 관계대명사가 **전치사의 목적어**일 때, 전치사는 제 자리에 남겨두고 관계대명사만 앞으로 보낼 수도 있다.
- I need *a man* **whom** I can work **with**.
- = I need *a man* **with whom** I can work.　　　　　[with who는 쓰지 않음]

❶ 전치사와 목적어가 **너무 멀리 떨어지면** 함께 내보내는 게 좋다.
- It is the room **in which** Mary gave birth to her son in pain. (○)
  - **cf** It is the room **which** Mary gave birth to her son in pain **in**. (×)
- I held a meeting **during which** Jim made a presentation. (○)
  - **cf** I held a meeting **which** Jim made a presentation **during**. (×)

❷ 전치사가 **동사와 관용구**를 이루면(look at, ask for, be fond of, look for, put up with 등), 전치사는 오해를 피하기 위해 앞으로 내보내지 않는다.
- It is the dog **which** I have *looked* **after** at the door. (○)
  - **cf** This is the dog **after which** I have *looked* at the door. (×)
- It is the game **which** I *was* very *fond* **of** in my school days. (○)
  - **cf** It is the game **of which** I *was* very *fond* in my school days. (×)

## 5. 관계대명사의 생략: (오해의 여지가 없는 한)

❶ 관계대명사의 **목적격**은 생략될 수 있다: what은 예외
- This is the girl **(whom)** I met in the park yesterday.
- I lost the ball **(which)** you gave me before.

❷ (**전치사+관계대명사**) 경우엔 관계대명사를 생략할 수 없다.
- This is the house **(which)** I lived in. (○)
  - **cf** This is the house **in (which)** I lived. (×)

❸ (**주격 관계대명사**+be)는 뒤에 **형용사**나 **부사**가 오는 경우 생략 가능하다.
- I called the man **(who was)** sitting on the chair. (남자를 불렀다)
- I called the man **(who was)** with a dog.
  - **cf** I called the man **who was** a singer.         [who was는 생략 불가]
  만약 생략하면, I called the man a singer. (그 남자를 가수라고 불렀다?)

❹ 주격 관계대명사는 생략할 수 없으나 다음 경우는 예외이다.
- There was someone **(who)** made me crazy.         [there 문]
- It was Tom **(that)** drew the picture on the hall.     [It ~ that 강조문]
- Mary was not the girl **(who)** she used to be.         [주격 보어]

■ 연습문제 40

괄호 속 단어들 중 알맞은 것에 ○표하라.

1. Jack has two friends, (that, who) came here with him.
2. I sold a car to Bill last year, (who, which) was totally broken now.
3. I went to the park, (in which, which) I saw Jane.
4. I heard Tom was ill, (what, which) was not true.
5. Jane, (who, whom) I thought was weak, was actually an athlete.
6. I want a friend with (who, whom) I can play tennis.
7. This is the chair (which, on which) Mozart used to sit.
8. The bears which I looked (at, like) in the park were from China.
9. I saw a boy in the library, (which, who) slept there all day long.
10. It is the pen (which I looked for, for which I looked) after school.
11. I passed by the house, (in that, in which) my father was born.
12. I met Jane in the church, (who, which) was built 10 years ago.

**문법의 핵심**: 속담에 "바로 가나 모로 가나 서울만 가면 된다"는 말이 있다. 영어에서도 마찬가지이다. 상대가 제대로 이해만 하면 조금 문법적으로 어색해도 괜찮다. 특히 구어체에선 그렇다. "Go get him!(가서 걔 데려와)"이란 말은 문법적으로 틀렸지만 많이 쓴다. Go and get him 혹은 Go to get him 이라 해야 맞지만, 사람들이 알아듣기 때문에 상관치 않는다. 물론 영어는 상당히 과학적인 말이라 주어, 동사, 목적어, 보어 등은 물론이요. 전치사들도 제대로 챙겨서 말하는 게 원칙이지만, 이를 엄격하게 지키기 위해 접속사와 to be, 전치사 등을 남발하는 건 좋지 않다. 우리가 중요 단어들만 열거해도 상대가 알아들을 수 있는 만큼, 오해를 사지 않는 수준에서 간단히 말하는 방법을 연습할 필요가 있다.

# 종합문제 10

**01** 다음 문장에서 어색한 부분을 찾아 바르게 고치라.

1. I don't know the girl whom is standing at the door.
2. Look at the church which windows are so beautiful.
3. I saw a nurse, the bike of which was red.
4. It is all what I know of about the girl.
5. This is the dog whom I bought yesterday.
6. I entered the Johnson College, who became famous later.
7. We found which we had never expected before.
8. This is the only book what he wrote during the war.
9. She has more dogs that she can take care of.
10. Do you have the pen that I gave it to you yesterday?
11. I want a girl can take care of puppies.
12. On the way home, Bill saw a snake of which he is very afraid.
13. I found a book, in which my dad was very interested.
14. This is the ball for which I have looked for a week.
15. We reached the point which we had never been beyond before.

**02** 다음 중 생략 가능한 부분을 찾으라. (생략할 부분이 없으면 그냥 둔다.)

1. Do you know the boy who is standing there?
2. We want friends with whom we can play soccer.
3. You'd better forget the boy that I used to be.
4. We could not find the girl who Tom wanted to talk with.
5. There was some secret that made him worried.

**03** 괄호 속에 있는 말을 이용해 다음 우리말을 영작하라.

1. 누가 문 앞에 서 있는 저 남자를 아는가? (who knows)

2. 나는 저 노인을 아는데, 그의 두 아들은 일본에 살고 있다. (whose)

3. 지붕이 눈으로 덮여 있는 저 집이 보이느냐? (covered with)

4. 네가 어제 공원에서 쳐다봤던 소녀는 내 여동생이다. (look at)

5. 이것이 내가 졸업한 중학교이다. (graduate, from)

6. 그는 그가 갖고 있던 모든 돈을 나에게 주었다. (all)

7. 그가 정말 필요로 하는 것은 사랑이다. (what)

8. 그녀를 사랑하지 않는 이는 아무도 없다. (but)

---

**두문자어(Acronym):** 희랍어 acro(highest)+nym(name)이 합쳐진 말로, 단어의 머리글자로 만든 말이다. 우리가 흔히 보는 두문자어는 다음과 같다:
AIDS: acquired immune deficiency syndrome(후천성 면역 결핍증)
UN: united nations(국제 연합)
DIY: do it yourself(스스로 만들기)
FAQ: frequently asked questions(자주 제기되는 질문)
SARS: severe acute respiratory syndrome(중증 급성 호흡기증후군)

# Unit 14 관계부사 (Relative Adverb)

관계부사는 접속사와 부사의 역할을 동시에 하는데, 관계대명사처럼 선행사를 가지나 격변화는 없다. 장소에 대해선 where, 시간에 대해선 when을 쓴다. 방법에 대해 how, 이유에 대해 why를 쓰지만, 이 둘은 거의 생략된다.

## A 관계부사의 한정적 용법

1. **where**: **장소**를 나타내며, in(or at) which로 바꿔 쓸 수 있다.
    - This is *the house* and **there** I was born.
        ⇒ This is *the house* **where** I was born.      [where의 선행사는 house]
        = This is *the house* **in which** I was born.
        = This is *the house* **(which)** I was born **in**.

2. **when**: **시간**을 나타내며, on(or in) which로 바꿀 수 있다.(생략 가능)
    - This is *the day* and **then** we met first.
        ⇒ This is *the day* **when** we met first.      [when의 선행사는 day]
        = This is *the day* **on which** we met first.

3. **why**: **이유**를 나타내며, the reason why 형태로 쓰되 대개 둘 중 하나만 쓴다. why 대신 that을 쓰기도 한다.
    - I know *the reason* and **for it** he cried.
        ⇒ I know the reason **(why)** he cried.
        = I know **why** he cried. (왜 울었는지)      [why는 의문대명사]
        = I know *the reason* **for which** he cried.
        = I know the reason **that** he cried.      [동격을 나타내는 that]

4. **how**: **방법**을 나타내며, the way how 형태로 쓰되 보통은 둘 중 하나만 쓴다. how 대신 that을 쓰기도 한다.
    - I know *the way* and **in that way** he escaped the prison.
        ⇒ I know *the way* **(how)** he escaped the prison.
        = I know **how** he escaped the prison. (어떻게 탈출했는지)      [의문대명사]
        = I know *the way* **(in which)** he escaped the prison.
        = I know *the way* **(that)** he escaped the prison      [동격의 that]

## B 관계부사의 계속적 용법

관계부사 앞에 콤마(,)를 두며, 일의 순서적 상황을 나타낸다. 계속적 용법의 관계부사는 생략할 수 없으며, why와 how는 계속적 용법에 사용하지 않는다.

· I went to L.A., and there I met Mary.
  = I went to L.A., where I met Mary. (LA에 갔는데, 거기서)
· I went to L.A. last Sunday, and then there was a festival there.
  = I went to L.A. last Sunday, when there was a festival there. (그때)

### ▌연습문제 41

괄호 속 단어 중 알맞은 것에 ○표하라.

1. Do you know (why, how) she cried so hard in the room?
2. This is the factory (which, where) my dad works.
3. I still remember the day (which, when) I took the entrance exam.
4. She left the small town (which, where) she grew up.
5. I visited the store (which, where) my aunt works in.
6. Workers have to know the (way, reason) this machine works.
7. I went to Busan last Sunday, (where, when) it was my birthday.
8. I visited a shop yesterday, (where, when) many toys were displayed.
9. Please find out the reason (that, how) the train stopped.
10. This trick is (how, why) he could solve the puzzle so fast..

# Unit 15 감탄사 (Interjection)

기쁨, 놀라움, 슬픔 등의 감정을 표현하는 말로, 주로 독립적으로 사용된다.

- Oh, look at that girl!
- Oops, I am sorry! (아이쿠)
- Hurray, we won! (만세)
- Alas, we lost! (오호라) [슬픔]
- Phew, I'm lost! (휴, 졌다.)
- Oh, boy! (아, 저런!)
- Come on! (얼른!) [재촉]
- Wow, it looks great! (와)
- Ouch, I cut my finger! (아야)
- Yippee! (야호!) [기쁨]
- Well, I don't know. (글쎄요)
- Oh, my God! (하나님 맙소사!)
- Hallelujah! (하나님 찬양!)
- Shit! (젠장!)

## 종합문제 11

**01 다음 문장에서 어색한 부분을 찾아 바르게 고치라.**

1. Summer is the season when I like best.
2. This is the house which Mozart was born.
3. Can you tell me the reason, why you left Seoul?
4. I went to the concert last year, when I had a great time.
5. Tom told me he met Jane last week, when was a lie.
6. We went on a picnic, which I lost my wallet.
7. Let's find out the way why he could solve the problem.
8. Roy visited New York, while he heard about Mary.
9. Show me the way to the plaza how the concert is held.
10. Hurray, we lost the game at last!

## 02 주어진 두 문장을 관계부사를 이용해 한 문장으로 만들라.

1. This is the garden. Jack planted the magic bean in it.
2. Bill died in 2016. There was a great famine then.
3. She survived the cold winter in some way. Do you know the way?
4. Mary does not answer my phone. I don't know the reason.
5. I arrived in Busan at 2 PM. Then, it began to rain.

## 03 괄호 속에 있는 말을 이용해 다음 우리말을 영작하라.

1. 오늘 공원에 갔는데, 거기서 Tom을 만났다. (where)

2. 그가 왜 오늘 학교에 결석했는지 말해 주렴. (why)

3. 비가 몹시 내리던 오후에 그가 나를 방문했다. (when)

4. 그가 한 때 살았던 집은 이제 호텔이 되었다. (where)

5. 어제 오후 4시에 집에 왔는데, 그때 Jane이 내게 전화를 했다. (when)

6. Tom은 그가 어떻게 문을 열었는지 나에게 말해 주셨다. (how)

7. 우리는 그가 언제 어디서 태어났는지 모른다. (when and where)

8. 하나님 맙소사, 타이어가 펑크 났어! (flat tire)

9. 아야, 발이 문틈에 끼었어! (caught in the door)

10. 어이쿠, 죄송합니다. / 괜찮습니다. (Oops, OK)

# 활용
(Conjugation)

# 03

Mentoring English Grammar

# 제 3 장
# 활용(Conjugation)

활용이란 단순히 "사용(use)"이나 "적용(application)"을 뜻하는 것이 아니라, 상황에 따라 어미 등의 첨가로 단어 자체의 형태가 바뀌거나 문장에서 단어의 배열 등이 변하는 것을 가리킨다.

영어에서는 **명사와 대명사의 활용**, 즉 **성**(gender: **남성, 여성, 중성**), **수**(number: **단수, 복수**), **격**(case: **주격, 소유격, 목적격**)**의 변화**가 미미하다. 인칭대명사에서만 조금 존재하는데, 이에 대해선 품사 편에서 이미 다루었다. 따라서 이 장에선 동사의 활용을 주로 다룬다.

앞서 언급하였듯이, 고대 언어에선 동작 주체 곧 주어의 인칭(person: 1인칭·2인칭·3인칭)과 수(number: 단수·복수)에 따라 모든 동사의 활용형태가 달랐는데, 동사의 법(mode: 직설법·명령법·가정법), 시제(tense: 현재·과거·미래·완료·미완료), 태(voice: 능동태·수동태·중간태)가 바뀔 때마다 인칭·수에 따른 동사의 형태가 죄다 바뀌었으니 얼마나 복잡했겠는가!

본 장에서는 **법(직설법·명령법·가정법), 시제(현재·과거·완료), 태(능동태·수동태)**에 따른 동사의 활용법과 **동사의 전용(to부정사·동명사), 형용사·부사의 비교 형태**를 공부하고 마지막으로 **일치와 화법, 특수 구문** 등을 다룬다.

# Unit 16 동사의 법 (Mood)

동사의 용법은 말하는 자의 의도에 따라 달라진다. 있는 사실을 그대로 표현할 때는 **직설법**, 상대에게 행위를 시킬 때는 **명령법**, 이뤄질 수 없는 소원 등을 표현할 때는 **가정법**을 쓰는데, 고대 언어에서는 각 법에서의 활용이 모두 달랐지만 영어에선 별 차이가 없다. 가정법은 뒤에서 다루기로 하고, 여기서는 직설법과 명령법을 다룬다. 각 법의 핵심은 **동사의 형태**에 있음을 잊지 말자.

## A 직설법(Indicative Mood)

동사 활용의 기본형으로 사실이나 상황을 그대로 표현할 때 쓰는데, 평서문과 의문문이 있다. 특이한 활용은 일반 동사의 현재형 3인칭 단수에서만 일어난다.

### 1. 일반 동사의 직설법 현재: 3인칭 단수

be동사(표 13 참조)를 제외한 모든 동사는 3인칭 단수의 경우 외에는 인칭·수에 따른 변화를 하지 않는다.

❶ **3인칭 단수** 현재형을 만들 때는, 동사 원형 뒤에 -s를 붙인다. 예외적으로 have는 현재 3인칭 단수에서 has가 된다.
- I **like** apples but Mary **likes** melons.
- You **have** a dog and Bill **has** a cat.

❷ 동사가 **-o, -x, -s, -sh, -ch**로 끝나면 -s 대신 –es를 붙인다.
- He **fixes** the PC and **touches** it.

❸ 동사가 **(자음)+y**로 끝나면 -y 대신 –ies를 쓴다. [**(모음)+y**는 –s만 붙임]
- She **buys** apples and **carries** them home.

❹ 모든 **조동사**(can, will, may, must 등)는 do → does, have → has 를 예외하곤 현재 3인칭 단수형에 -s를 붙이지 않는다. have는 조동사처럼 보이지만 (다른 조동사와 겹쳐 쓸 수 있고, 다음에 동사 원형을 쓰지 않는다는 면에서) 조동사가 아닌 특수동사이다.
- He **can** play the guitar but **does not** want to play it now.
- Jina **has** to go home but her teacher **will** not allow her.

## 2. 평서문(Declarative Sentence): 사실·느낌을 전달하는 말

**❶ 긍정문(Affirmative):** not을 포함하지 않는 문장
- I **am** a student, and you **are** a teacher.
- She **was** sad, but we **were** happy.
- I **run** slowly but he **runs** fast.
- She **has** a dog.
- I **cried** and he **cried**, too.
- She **will take** him out.

**❷ 부정문(Negative):** not을 포함하는 문장. not은 be**동사**·**조동사 뒤**에 둔다. 일반동사의 경우, 조동사 do(does)를 첨가해 부정문을 만든다. (대명사 다음에 be+not이 오면 be는 not과 축약형을 만들기 보다 대명사와 축약형을 만든다)
- I *am* **not** a student, and you *are* **not** a teacher.　　　　　　[be동사+not]
- She *was* **not** sad, but they *were* **not** happy.
- She **doesn't** have a dog.
- He **can't** speak English.
- she isn't a nurse.(X) ⇒ she's not a nurse.(O)

## 3. 의문문(Question): 상대에게 사실이나 의향을 묻는 말.

**❶ 의문사 없는 의문문(Yes-No Question):** Yes나 No로 대답하는 의문문으로, 동사를 주어 앞에 도치시킨다. be**동사**나 **조동사**는 자신이 도치되지만, **일반 동사**는 조동사 do(does, did)를 앞에 내놓는다. 끝을 올려 말하고, 대답은 질문에 사용된 동사의 종류로 답한다.

- This **is** a book. ⇒ **Is** this a book↗? / Yes, it **is**.
　　　　　　　　　　　　　　　　　　 / No, it **isn't**.
- I **can** play tennis. ⇒ **Can** you **play** tennis↗? / Yes, I **can**.
　　　　　　　　　　　　　　　　　　　　　　　　 / No, I **can't**.
- She **has** a dog. ⇒ **Does** she **have** a dog↗? / Yes, she **does**.
　　　　　　　　　　　　　　　　　　　　　　　　 / No, she **doesn't**.
- You **went** to school. ⇒ **Did** you go to school↗? / Yes, I **did**.
　　　　　　　　　　　　　　　　　　　　　　　　　 / No, I **didn't**.
- **Is** *there* a cat at the door↗? / Yes, *there* **is**.
　　　　　　　　　　　　　　　　　 / No, *there* **isn't**.

※ not 포함 의문문은 일종의 기교 어법인데, 대답은 not **없는** 의문문과 **동일**하게 한다.
- Isn't this a book↗? / Yes, it is. [책인 경우]
  / No, it isn't. [책이 아닌 경우]
- Can't he play the violin↗? / Yes, he can. [연주할 수 있는 경우]
  / No, he can't. [연주할 수 없는 경우]

❷ **의문사 있는 의문문**(WH-Question): 끝을 올리지 않으며, Yes / No로 대답하지 않는다. 의문사가 주어이면 동사를 도치시키지 않는다.
- **Who** *is* the girl↘? / She is my sister.
- **Who** *broke* the window↘? / Tom did.
- **What** *made* you happy↘? / I won the prize.
- **How** *could* you pass the exam↘? / I studied hard.
- **What** *does* she do↘? / She is a nurse. [직업]

❸ **선택 의문문**(Alternative Question): 둘 중 선택을 묻는 말로, Yes나 No로 대답하지 않는다. 대개 or 앞은 올려 말하고 뒤는 내린다.
- Do you want beef↗or chicken↘? / Chicken, please.
- Which bag do you like better, this↗or that↘? / This (one).

❹ **간접 의문문**(Indirect Question)

① 의문문이 문장 성분이 되면, **(의문사)+(주어)+(동사)**의 순으로 놓되, 의문사가 없으면 의문사 자리에 if나 whether를 첨가한다.
- Do you know? + *Who is he*? ⇒ Do you know **who** *he is*↗?
- Do you know? + *Is she rich*? ⇒ Do you know **if** *she is rich*↗?
- Tom wouldn't tell me **where** *he went* last night.
- *It* is important **when** *the train comes* here.
- Tell me **whether** *John is married*.

② Do you **think** (believe, imagine, guess, suppose)를 포함하는 구절: **삽입구**처럼 사용되므로 **의문사**가 있으면 그것이 **맨 앞**으로 나오고 의문사가 없으면 그냥 쓴다.
[Do you know… 구문과 차이점을 확인할 것!]
- Do you think? + *Who is he*? ⇒ **Who** do you think *he is*↘?
- Do you think? + *Is he honest*? ⇒ **Do you think** *he is honest*↗?

❺ **반문**(Cross Question): **도치 없이** 끝만 올려 묻는데, 구어체에 주로 쓴다.
- He **lives** in America. / He **lives** in America↗? (미국에 산다고?)
- He likes porcupines. / He likes **what**?↗ (뭘 좋아 한다고?)
- Excuse me↗? (뭐라고?)　　　　　　　　　　　　[끝을 내리면 '실례합니다'의 뜻]
  = Pardon me↗? ([못 알아들은] 날 용서해 주겠니?)
  = (May I) Beg your pardon↗?
  = (Can you) Come again↗?

## ▌연습문제 42

괄호 속 단어들 중 알맞은 것에 ○표하라.

1. Every student in my class (was, were) diligent.
2. She (don't, doesn't) eat pork at all.
3. Mary (haves, has) a dog in her house.
4. (He isn't, He's not) a student but a teacher.
5. Tom (can, cans) run fast.
6. Is there a book on the desk? / No, (it, there) isn't.
7. Don't you like tea? / (Yes, No), I don't.
8. (What, Who) is the boy? / He is my brother.
9. Who (did play, played) the guitar last night?
10. What (did you make, made you) angry? / We lost the game.
11. Do you want coffee (and, or) tea? / Coffee, please.
12. Do you know who (she is, is she)?
13. (Do you think who, Who do you think) I am?
14. Please tell me what (did you do, you did) last night.
15. You should go now. / Pardon (me, you)?

### 4. 부가 의문문(Tag Question): 평서문 뒤에 첨가되는 단축 의문문으로, 사실을 이미 알고 상대의 동의를 구할 땐 끝을 내려 말하고, 확인을 할 땐 끝을 올린다.

**❶ 일반 원칙**

① 긍정문 뒤엔 부정문, 부정문 뒤엔 긍정문으로 물음.
  · Mary *is* a nurse, **isn't** she?
  · Mary *is* **not** a nurse, **is** she?

② be동사는 be동사로, 일반동사는 do(does)로, 조동사는 조동사로 받음.
  · Your family *are not* in Korea, **are** they?
  · Sandy *likes* fish, **doesn't** she?
  · Your brother *didn't* go to church, **did** he?
  · You *can* play the piano, **can't** you?
  · You *have* finished shopping, **haven't** you?          [have는 조동사 취급]
    cf She *has* a boat, **hasn't** she?

③ 부가 의문문의 **주어**는 반드시 **인칭대명사**여야 한다.
  · This is yours, isn't **this**? (×) ⇒ This is yours, isn't **it**? (○)

④ not을 붙일 때는 반드시 **축약형**을 쓴다.
  · *You will* never let her go, **won't** you?          [won't = will not]
  · *I am your* boss, **ain't** I?                      [ain't = am not]
  · That *must* be a camera, **mustn't** it?

**❷ 특별 부가의문문**

① There is(are)로 시작하는 문장에선 **주어 자리**에 there를 쓴다.
  · *There were* books on the table, **weren't** there?

② I think, I believe 등은 일종의 **삽입구**이므로, 부가의문문은 이를 뺀 **나머지 문장에 대해** 만든다.
  · I *think* Mary loves me, **doesn't** she?
  · I *don't* think Mary loves me, **does** she?
    cf I *don't* think Mary loves me = I think Mary doesn't love me.

③ **명령문**에서의 부가의문문은 will you?로, let's로 시작하는 **청유문**에선 shall we?로 부가의문문을 만든다.
- Go at once, **will** you?
- Let's go to school, **shall** we?

④ 이것저것 다 귀찮으면, 그냥 **right**?(사실 확인) 혹은 OK?(명령문, 청유문)로 하자!
- You got tickets, **right**?
- Come to the park at eight, **OK**?

### ▌연습문제 43
괄호 속 단어들 중 알맞은 것에 ○표하라.

1. Jane is uncareful, (is, isn't) she?
2. It tastes nice, (isn't, doesn't) it?
3. Dad will buy me a bike, (will not, won't) he?
4. I am going to inherit this house, (am not, ain't) I?
5. You were present at the meeting, (aren't, weren't) you?
6. That is your notebook, isn't (that, it)?
7. Let's dance together, (won't, shall) we?
8. I don't think Jack can pass the exam, (do I, can he)?
9. Don't be late for school, (will, do) you?
10. There was nothing in this room, wasn't (it, there)?

## 5. 감탄문(Exclamatory Sentence)
감탄문은 강한 감정을 나타낼 때 쓰며, 감탄부호로 문장을 마친다. What+(명사) 혹은 How +(형용사, 부사) 형태로 시작하며 **주어 - 동사 위치는 바꾸지 않는다**. 직설법 동사를 그대로 사용하므로 **직설법**의 일종인데, 강조하는 내용이 문장 맨 앞으로 나간다는 점에 주의하자.

❶ What + 명사
- She is a *very* pretty girl. ⇒ What *a pretty* girl she is!
  = How *pretty* a girl she is!

❷ How + 형용사, 부사
- He studies *very* hard. ⇒ How *hard* he studies!
- This picture is *really nice*. ⇒ How *nice* this picture is!

❸ 여러 가지 감탄 표현(구어체)
- **How** it snows! (눈이 엄청 오는구나!)
- **What** *a girl!* (대단한 소녀다!)
- *Two thumbs up!* (최고!)
- *Unbelievable!* (믿을 수가 없군!)
- *Kids!* (애들이란!)
- *Wonderful!* (놀라워요!)
- *No kidding!* (농담하지 마!)

## B 명령법(Imperative Mood)

상대에게 어떤 행동을 하도록 명령할 때 사용하는 방법이다. 행동의 주체는 항상 you(너, 너희)로 한정되어 있으므로 강조 때 이외엔 **주어를 생략한다.** 동사는 **원형**을 사용하고 **be 동사의 금지적 명령**을 만들 때 **don't**를 쓴다는 점에서 **직설법**과 차이가 난다.

### 1. 직접 명령문
- **Close** the window, John.  /  *You* **close** the window, Mike. (네가 닫아)    [강조]
- **Don't close** the window.
- **Be** quiet.
- **Don't be** noisy.                                               [직설법과의 차이]
  - cf Be not noisy. (×)

### 2. 청유문
상대에게 어떤 행동을 함께하자고 권할 때는, let's를 이용해 청유문을 만든다. let's의 부정형은 let's not이다.
- **Let's** go. (가자)                                    [상대방이 us에 포함될 때 us를 약하게]
  - cf **Let** us go. (우릴 놓아 줘)                 [상대방이 us에 포함되지 않으면 us에 강세]
- **Let's not** forget God's grace.

※ 부탁조로 약하게 명령할 때는 why don't you~? 형을 쓴다.
- **Why don't you** join us? = **Please,** join us. (우리랑 합류하지 그래.)

## 3. 명령문의 특별 용법

**❶ 명령문, and (then)~: ~하라, 그러면 ~**

· *Start now*, **and** you will get the train. (그러면 기차를 탈 것이다.)
= *Start now*. **Then**, you will get the train.
= *If* you start now, you will get the train.

**❷ 명령문, or (otherwise)~: ~하라, 그렇지 않으면 ~**

· *Start now*, **or** you will miss the train. (안 그러면 기차를 놓친다.)
= *Start now*. **Otherwise**, you will miss the train.
= *Unless* you start now, you will miss the train.

### ▌연습문제 44

**01.** 괄호 속 단어들 중 알맞은 것에 ○표하라.

1. What a nice car (is it, it is)!
2. (Who, What) a woman!
3. (How, What) pretty a flower it is!
4. (Be not, Don't be) stupid in this emergency situation.
5. Officer, we don't know anything about the accident, so (let us, let's) go.
6. (How, Why) don't you come here?   /   Sure I will.
7. Stop smoking, (and, or) your health will get better.
8. She is beautiful.   /   Yes, (awesome, awful)!

**02.** 다음 문장을 감탄문으로 바꾸라.

1. This stone is very heavy. (how를 이용하여)
   ⇒ _____

2. It is a very tall building. (what을 이용하여)
   ⇒ _____

3. Kim runs very fast. (what을 이용하여)
   ⇒ _____

## 종합문제 12

**01 다음 문장에서 어색한 부분을 찾아 바르게 고치라.**

1. What a flower pretty it is!
2. Who do you know the boy is?
3. I ain't the kind of girl. Do you understand?
4. What on earth you are thinking about?
5. Does he has a computer in his room?
6. You have finished your homework, didn't you?
7. Pick up the phone for me, won't you?
8. Tell me where did you go last weekend.
9. This is what did he during the vacation.
10. What do you know happened in the school yesterday?

**02 다음 빈칸을 채워 부가 의문문을 만들라.**

1. Please let us go to the concert, _____?
2. It is not very hot today, _____?
3. You have been to New York, _____?
4. This is your phone, _____?
5. Let's play tennis together, _____?
6. Mary goes to church on Sundays, _____?
7. I don't think Tom is taller than you, _____?
8. There are many pretty girls in your class, _____?
9. Jane will come to the party, _____?
10. I am going to be sent to Busan, _____?

**03 괄호 속에 있는 말을 이용해 다음 우리말을 영작하라.**

1. 돈 때문에 나한테 화 내지 마라. (angry at)

2. 오늘은 정말 춥군! (how)

3. Tom은 정말 영리한 학생이군! (what)

4. Mary가 지금 어디 있다고 생각하니? (think, where)

5. Mary가 언제 이 책을 샀는지 아니? (know, when)

6. 우리랑 수영하러 가지 그래? (why)

7. 그녀는 아픈 게 틀림없어, 그렇지 않나? (must, sick)

8. 빨리 날 따라와, 안 그러면 길을 잃을 거야. (quickly, or, lost)

> **Be 동사의 축약**: be 동사가 not과 결합하면 am not = ain't, are not = aren't, is not = isn't, was not = wasn't, were not = weren't 로 바뀐다. 그런데 대명사가 쓰이는 현재형에서 I ain't 보다는 I'm not으로, You aren't 보다는 You're not으로, He isn't 보다는 He's not으로 축약된다. (과거형에선 wasn't, weren't가 사용됨) it was는 노래 등에서 'twas 로 축약되곤 한다.

## 표 18. 불규칙 동사표

| 현재(원형) | 과거 | 과거분사 | 뜻 | 현재(원형) | 과거 | 과거분사 | 뜻 |
|---|---|---|---|---|---|---|---|
| be | was, were | been | 이다, 있다 | feel | felt | felt | 느끼다 |
| begin | began | begun | 시작하다 | fight | fought | fought | 싸우다 |
| bite | bit | bitten | 물다 | find | found | found | 발견하다 |
| blow | blew | blown | 불다 | have | had | had | 가지다 |
| break | broke | broken | 깨뜨리다 | hear | heard | heard | 듣다 |
| choose | chose | chosen | 선택하다 | hold | held | held | 붙잡다 |
| do | did | done | 하다 | keep | kept | kept | 지키다 |
| draw | drew | drawn | 그리다 | lay | laid | laid | 놓다 |
| drink | drank | drunk | 마시다 | leave | left | left | 남겨두다 |
| drive | drove | driven | 운전하다 | lend | lent | lent | 빌려주다 |
| eat | ate | eaten | 먹다 | lose | lost | lost | 잃다 |
| fall | fell | fallen | 떨어지다 | make | made | made | 만들다 |
| fly | flew | flown | 날다 | meet | met | met | 만나다 |
| forget | forgot | forgotten | 잊다 | pay | paid | paid | 지불하다 |
| forgive | forgave | forgiven | 용서하다 | say | said | said | 말하다 |
| get | got | got, gotten | 얻다 | sell | sold | sold | 팔다 |
| give | gave | given | 주다 | send | sent | sent | 보내다 |
| go | went | gone | 가다 | sit | sat | sat | 앉다 |
| grow | grew | grown | 자라다 | sleep | slept | slept | 자다 |
| hide | hid | hidden | 숨기다 | spend | spent | spent | 써버리다 |
| know | knew | known | 알다 | stand | stood | stood | 서다 |
| lie | lay | lain | 눕다 | teach | taught | taught | 가르치다 |
| ride | rode | ridden | 타다 | tell | told | told | 말하다 |
| ring | rang | rung | (종)울리다 | think | thought | thought | 생각하다 |
| see | saw | seen | 보다 | become | became | become | 되다 |
| show | showed | shown | 보여주다 | come | came | come | 오다 |
| sing | sang | sung | 노래하다 | run | ran | run | 달리다 |
| speak | spoke | spoken | 말하다 | beat | beat | beat, beaten | 때리다 |
| swim | swam | swum | 수영하다 | burst | burst | burst | 터지다 |
| take | took | taken | 취하다 | cut | cut | cut | 자르다 |
| tear[tɛər] | tore | torn | 찢다 | hit | hit | hit | 때리다 |
| throw | threw | thrown | 던지다 | hurt | hurt | hurt | 상처주다 |
| wake | woke | woken | (잠)깨다 | let | let | let | 하게하다 |
| wear | wore | worn | 입다, 닳다 | put | put | put | 놓다 |
| write | wrote | written | 쓰다 | read[riːd] | read[red] | read[red] | 읽다 |
| bring | brought | brought | 가져오다 | set | set | set | 설정하다 |
| build | built | built | 세우다 | shut | shut | shut | 닫다 |
| buy | bought | bought | 사다 | spread | spread | spread | 펼치다 |
| catch | caught | caught | 잡다 | quit | quit | quit | 그만두다 |

# Unit 17 동사의 시제 (Tense)

영어에서 시제에 따른 동사의 활용형은 **현재**, **과거**뿐이며, **분사**들을 이용해 각각 **진행형**과 **완료형**을 추가로 만든다. 고대 언어에는 **미래형**도 있었지만 영어엔 존재하지 않고, **현재형 혹은 조동사**를 통해 이를 표현한다.

## A 단순 현재형(Simple Present)

동사의 원형을 쓰며, 그 용법은 다음과 같다. (동사 활용에 대해선 ☞ 16. A. 1)

### 1. 현재의 사실, 동작, 상태를 나타낼 때
· He **works** hard hard and **feels** very happy now.   [현재 사실]

### 2. 현재의 습관, 반복적 동작을 나타낼 때 (종종 빈도 부사와 함께 쓰인다)
· I *always* **brush** my teeth after meal.   [현재 습관]

### 3. 불변의 진리, 사실, 격언 등을 말할 때
· *Did* you hear the proverb, "A barking dog never **bites**"?   [속담]

## B 단순 과거형(Simple Past)

### 1. 과거형(및 과거분사) 만드는 법(규칙동사): 불규칙 변화는 표 18 참조

❶ 기본형: (원형)+ed
  call → call**ed**,  play → play**ed**

❷ e로 끝나는 동사: (원형)+d
  love → lov**ed**,  dive → div**ed**

❸ 끝이 (자음)+y인 동사: -y 대신 –ied
  study → stud**ied**,  dry → dr**ied**

❹ 끝이 (단모음)+(단자음)인 동사: 끝 자음을 겹쳐 쓰고 –ed
  stop → stop**ped**   (예외) visit – visit**ed**

❺ c로 끝나는 동사: 발음상 k를 덧붙인 후 –ed(-ing도 동일).
   picnic → picnicked(picnicking),  mimic → mimicked

2. -(e)d의 발음

   ❶ 무성음 [p], [k], [f], [s], [ʃ], [tʃ]로 끝나는 동사에선 [t]로 발음:
      walked(웍트),  stopped(스탑트)

   ❷ [d], [t]로 끝나면 [id]로 발음:
      waited(웨이티드),  handed(핸디드)

   ❸ 그 외 유성음으로 끝나면 [d]로 발음:
      loved(럽드),  hanged(행드)   **cf** beloved(빌러비드)

3. **용법:** 과거의 사실, 동작, 경험, 상태 등을 나타낼 때 쓴다.
   · She **lived** here in the 1990s.                    [과거 사실]
   · She **cried** out when I **left** her.              [과거 동작]
   · She **was** so sad at that time.                    [과거 상태]
   · **Did** you ever hear about her?                    [경험]

※ **used to (동사원형):** 과거의 습성. 과거의 습성으로 현재는 그렇지 않음.
   · He **used to** *live* in Incheon. (한때 인천에 살았었다)
   · She *didn't* use to *brush* her teeth. (양치질을 안 하곤 했다)
      **cf** He **was(got) used to** *speaking* English. (영어 말하는 데 익숙해 있었다)


## C 진행형(Progressive)

행위의 진행을 표현할 때 **be+(현재분사)**를 쓴다.

1. 현재분사 만드는 법: (동사원형)+ing

   ❶ **(자음)+e**로 끝나는 동사: e를 빼고 –ing
      (예) move → moving    (예외) dye(염색) → dyeing

❷ -ie로 끝나는 동사: -ying
  예 die → dying    cf study → studying

❸ (단모음)+(단자음)으로 끝나는 동사: 단자음을 하나 덧붙이고 -ing
  예 run → running    cf assume → assuming

2. **현재진행:** be 동사의 현재형(am, are, is)+현재분사(**원형+ing**)
  · I am readin g a book. (책을 읽고 있다.)

3. **과거진행:** be 동사의 과거형(was, were)+현재분사(**원형+ing**)
  · I was reading a book. (책을 읽고 있었다.)

4. **진행형을 잘 쓰지 않는 동사**

  ❶ 인식: think, believe, know, remember, understand, doubt 등
    · I think he is honest.  ⇏  I *am thinking* he is honest. (×)
    cf I am thinking about this problem. (○)     [특정 대상에 대한 생각]

  ❷ 감정, 심리: love, want(원하다), like, hate, prefer(선호하다) 등
    · I want to be a doctor.  ⇏  I *am wanting* to be a doctor. (×)
    cf We *are* wanting a new business item. (○)    [결여에 중점을 둘 때]

  ❸ 소속·소유: have(갖고 있다), belong, consist(구성되다), contain 등
    · I have two books.  ⇏  I *am having* two books. (×)
    cf I am having dinner now. (○)    [식사하는 중]

  ❹ 2형식 자동사: be, feel(느껴지다), sound(들린다), taste(맛 난다) 등
    · It feels soft. (부드럽게 느껴진다.)  ⇏  It *is feeling* soft. (×)
    cf I am feeling love with her. (○)    [feel은 3형식 동사]

  ❺ 상태: differ(다르다), resemble(닮다), lack(부족하다) 등.
    · She resembles her mother.  ⇏  She is *resembling* her mother. (×)
    cf She *is resembling* her mother *day by day*. (○) (나날이 닮아간다)

### 연습문제 45

**01.** 보기와 같이 다음 동사들의 3인칭 단수 현재, 과거, 현재분사 활용형을 쓰라.

[보기] drink – drinks(3단현) – drank(과) – drinking(현분)

1. play -
2. have -
3. get -
4. arrive -
5. marry -
6. lie(거짓말하다) -
7. visit -
8. fall-
9. run -
10. set -

**02.** 괄호 속 단어들 중 알맞은 것에 ○표하라.

1. I (played, plaied) tennis with Jack.
2. She (wrote, written) a letter to my teacher.
3. Dad (stoped, stopped) smoking because of health.
4. I am (dying, dyeing) for hunger.
5. When I came back home, mom (is, was) cleaning the room.
6. Tom (spread, spreads) the news as soon as he heard it.
7. She (hurt, hurted) herself while crossing the valley.
8. This book (belongs, is belonging) to me.
9. This cloth (is feeling, feels) soft.
10. She (had, was having) lunch when I visited her house.
11. I used to (catch, catching) frogs in this pond.
12. Koreans are used to (eat, eating) hot foods.
13. Joan (lay, lied) down on the floor after work.
14. Kim (studies, studys) English very hard.
15. He (is used, used) to this new cell phone.

## D 미래의 표현(Future Expressions)

영어 동사엔 미래형이 없어 **현재형** 및 **조동사** 등을 이용해 미래를 표시한다.

### 1. 단순 현재형: 시간 부사, 조건 부사 등으로 미래 사실이 확실할 때
- I **go** to Busan tomorrow. (나 내일 부산 간다.)
- This project **sets out** next year. (그 사업은 내년에 시작한다.)
- This train **can start** if the problem is fixed. (문제가 해결되면)

### 2. 현재 진행형: 상황이 어떤 방향으로 나아가고 있음을 의미
- We **are giving** a party this Saturday.
- **Are** you **coming** back soon? (곧 돌아올 건가요?)

### 3. 조동사(의지, 의무, 예정 등)를 쓰는 방법

**❶ will**: 본래 주어의 **의지**로 일을 추진하겠다는 뜻인데, 미래 의미로 전용됨
- He **will** move to New York. (그는 뉴욕으로 이사 갈 거야.)     [의지]
- This rain **will** stop soon.     [단순미래]

※ 시간과 조건의 부사절에는 will을 사용치 않고 그냥 현재형을 쓴다.
- Please wake me up *when* the train **arrives** in Seoul.     [부사절]
- **cf** Please tell me *when* she **will arrive**. (언제 도착할지)     [명사절]

**❷ shall**(의무): **의무**에 따라 앞으로 어떤 일을 행해야 한다는 뜻
- Chef **shall** prepare food for customers. (음식 준비를 할지라)
- You **shall** be punished before God. (벌을 받아야 하리라)
- **Shall** I go now?     [1인칭에서 will 대신 사용]

**❸ be going to**(예정): 어떤 일이 정해진 방향으로 가고 있음을 뜻함
- It **is going to** be dark soon. (날이 어두워져 간다)
- = It **will** be dark soon.     [편의 상 will과 구별 없이 사용]

**❹ be about to**(긴박): '~의 근처에 있다'는 뜻으로 가까운 미래를 의미
- Jack **is about to** die. (죽기 직전이다.)

❺ **be planning to**: '~하려고 계획 중이다'
  · We **are planning to** hold a concert next month.

## E 완료형(Perfect)

현재·과거를 기준으로 어떤 일의 **완료·경험·지속·결과** 등을 나타낸다.

### 1. 현재완료(Present Perfect): have(has)+p.p(과거분사)

❶ **완료**: 하던 일이 완료되어 현재 **더는 그 일이 진행되지 않을 때**
  · I **have done** my work. (내 일을 다 마쳤다)
    cf I **did** my work yesterday.                    [완료여부는 모름]

❷ **경험**: '~한 적이 있다'는 뜻으로, ever, never, before, once 등과 쓰임
  · **Have** you *ever* **been** to LA? / Yes, I **have** twice.

❸ **지속**: for (기간) 혹은 since (시점) 등과 함께 현재까지의 지속을 나타냄.
  · It **has rained** *for* three days. (3일간 비가 왔고 지금도 오고 있다.)
  · It **has been** 2 years since he died. (죽은 지 2년 되었다)
   = 2 years have passed since he died."

❹ **결과**: '~해 버렸다'는 뜻으로, 그 일의 **결과를 강조**한다.
  · She **has gone** to Busan. (부산으로 가버렸고, 지금은 여기 없다.)

※ 현재완료는 last night, two days ago, just now 등 **명백한 과거**를 나타내는 부사와는 같이 사용되지 않고, lately, before 등과는 같이 쓰인다.
lately는 과거형과는 함께 쓰지만 현재형과는 쓰지 않는다.

  · He **has come** *just now*. (×) ⇒ He **came** *just now*. (○)
  · I **am** *sick lately*. (×) ⇒ I **have been** sick *lately*. (○)

## 2. 과거완료(Past Perfect): had+p.p(과거분사)
**완료·경험·지속·결과** 외에 과거에 **먼저 일어난 사건(대과거)**을 표현.

❶ **완료**: 과거의 한 시점에서, 어떤 일이 이미 완료된 경우.
　· I had *just* **finished** my lunch *when he came* in.

❷ **경험**: 과거의 한 시점에서의 경험.
　· I had *never* **seen** such a pretty girl *till I came* to Incheon.

❸ **지속**: 과거의 한 시점에서, 어떤 일의 지속 상황.
　· I had **driven** this car *for* 12 years *until it broke* down.

❹ **결과**: 과거의 한 시점에서, 돌이킬 수 없는 일의 상태를 나타낸다.
　· I *found* that she **had gone** to Busan. (가 버리고 없었다)

❺ **대과거**: 과거 일어난 두 사건의 **전후 관계**를 밝힌다. 구체적 시점이 제시되어 오해의 여지가 없으면 굳이 대과거를 **쓰지 않는다**.
　· I *knew* (that) it **had rained** there. (비가 왔음을 알았다)　　　　　　[대과거]
　　**cf** I *knew* (that) it **rained** there. (비가 오는 걸 알았다)　　　　　　　[동시제]
　· I *lost* my camera that I **had bought** last year.
　= I *lost* my camera that I **bought** last year.　　　　　　　　　　[굳이 대과거 안 씀]

❻ **관용구**: No sooner A(과완) than B(과거); hardly A(과완) when(before) B(과거) (A 하자마자 곧 B)
　· *No sooner* I **had come** out *than* it **began** to rain. (나오자마자 비가 왔다)
　　[직역: 비가 오기 시작한 것보다 난 더 일찍 나오질 못했다]
　= I had **hardly** come out **when(before)** it began to rain.
　= *As soon as* I came out, it began to rain.

※ 이외에 조동사 will과 완료형을 결합해 **미래 완료** 구문 등 여러 시제를 만들 수 있다. 하지만, 잘 안 쓰이는 시제들은 굳이 연습할 필요가 없다.
　· Next year, I **will have finished** my study.　　　　　　　　　　　[미래 완료]

### 연습문제 46

괄호 속 단어들 중 알맞은 것에 ○표하라.

1. This train starts (yesterday, tomorrow).
2. Next year, you (are going to, shall) be sixteen.
3. Let's go on a picnic if it (is, will be) fine tomorrow.
4. Do you know what time she (will, does) come?
5. The concert is (about, next) to finish.
6. (Did, Have) they play soccer last night?
7. He (has, had) already left when I came here.
8. Yesterday I (have seen, saw) Sally in the park.
9. I knew he (would go, had gone) to New York the next day.
10. Dad is planning to buy a new car (just now, next year).
11. It (has been, is being) cold since last Sunday.
12. Have you ever been to Paris?   /   Yes, I (did, have).
13. Have you ever (been, gone) to L.A.?
14. Tom insulted me in the party, so I (did, have done) with him.
15. Jane had hardly come home (before, since) she started to cry.
16. No sooner the news had started (as, than) the fire broke out.
17. Recently, he (studies, studied) Chinese very hard.

## 종합문제 13

**01 다음 문장에서 어색한 부분을 찾아 바르게 고치라.**

1. I have bought this phone in Busan last year.
2. Yesterday, Mary was reading the book she has borrowed from me.
3. Have you ever play tennis with Jane?
4. The train will leave already when we reach the station.
5. When I met Bill in the park, it is about to rain.
6. Wherever he goes, John bought fancy souvenirs.
7. He couldn't understood what I told.
8. We are planned to travel abroad next week.
9. Mary is living in Seoul for three years.
10. I knew he has worked for 3 hours without a break.
11. John has gone to New York twice.
12. I have finished my homework just now.
13. Didn't you know the earth was moving around the sun?
14. You have been studied English for 6 years.
15. Five years has passed since he died.
16. It is very warm since last weekend.
17. I brush usually my teeth before I go to bed.
18. He recently goes to London to see his mother.
19. You have promised to come early, didn't you?
20. I wondered when she will come.

**02 괄호 속에 있는 말을 이용해 다음 우리말을 영작하라.**

1. 그는 결코 서울을 떠나려 하지 않았다. (would leave)

2. 나는 숙제를 다 마친 다음에 축구를 할 것이다. (have finished, soccer)

3. 내가 방문했을 때, Tom은 점심을 먹고 있었다. (have lunch)

4. 지난 금요일 이후로 계속 눈이 오고 있다. (has, since)

5. 그녀가 언제 집에 올지 너 아니? (know, when)

6. 내가 대학을 졸업한 지 3년이 지났다. (since)

7. 영어로 말해본 적 있니? (have, ever, in English)

8. 밥 먹는 동안에는 말하지 마라. (speak, while, eating)

9. L.A.에 도착할 때까지 그는 8시간 동안 운전했다. (driven, till)

10. 나는 눈이 그렇게 많이 왔다는 걸 알지 못했다. (so much)

**눈보다 빠른 혀:** 과거에 TOEFL Listening 연습을 할 때 필수 교재가 AFKN(American Forces Korean Network) Radio News 원고였다. 그 아나운서의 말하는 속도가 어찌나 빠른지 우리가 눈으로 따라갈 수 없을 정도였다. 나는 종종 영어를 배우는 학생들에게 Text를 최대한 빨리 읽도록 훈련시킨다. 이렇게 해야 TOEFL 혹은 TEPS Listening을 해결할 수 있기 때문이다. 지금은 AFKN 방송이 없어졌으므로, 그다지 빠르진 않지만 CNN 방송을 통해 빠른 announcing에 대한 적응을 하는 게 좋다. 속독 훈련! 이는 Listening 고득점을 위한 필수 코스이다.

# Unit 18 수동태 (Passive Voice)

주어가 동사의 행위를 다른 대상에게 가하는 것을 '능동(active)', 주어가 **동사의 행위를 당하는 것을** '수동 혹은 피동(passive)'이라 부른다. 따라서 수동태는 자동사에는 없고 목적어를 갖는 **타동사에만 적용**된다.

## A 수동태 만드는 법: be + *p.p.*(과거분사) + by

능동태 문장에서 **목적어를** (주격으로 바꿔) **동사로** 앞으로 내놓고 동사를 be+p.p. 형으로 바꾼다. 원래의 주어는 전치사 by와 함께 (목적격으로 바꿔) 동사 뒤로 보낸다. 이때 do 이외의 조동사는 변하지 않는다.

· He teaches *her*. (능동태) ⇒ *She* is taught *by him*. (수동태)

· He *does not* teach her.  ⇒  She is *not* taught *by him*.
· He *can* teach her.  ⇒  She *can* be taught *by* him.
· He *cannot* teach her.  ⇒  She *cannot* be taught *by* him.
· I allowed him to teach her.  ⇒  He was allowed to teach her *by* me.

### 1. by+(행위자)의 생략

능동태 문장의 주어(행위자)가 **일반 주어**(we, you, they, people, someone 등)일 때, 수동태에서 by+(행위자)는 생략될 수 있다. 행위자가 누군지 불분명할 때도 이를 생략한다.

· *They* speak English here. ⇒ English is spoken here (*by them*).
· *We* can see stars at night ⇒ Stars can be seen at night (*by us*).
· He was killed in the Korean War.　　　　　　[행위자가 불분명]
· This house was built in 1880.　　　　　　　　[행위자가 불분명]

### 2. 의문문의 수동태

❶ 의문사가 있으면 의문사는 그대로 두고 나머지 어순만 정리한다.
　· When did you make the box? ⇒ When was the box made (by you)?
　· Why did you make the box? ⇒ Why was the box made (by you)?

❷ **의문사가 주어인 경우**
  · *Who* **made** this box? ⇒ *By whom* **was** this box **made**?
  · *What* **scared** this dog? ⇒ *By what* **was** this dog **scared**?

❸ **의문사가 없으면** do조동사를 없애고 be동사를 도치시켜 수동태를 만든다.
  · Did you **draw** *this picture*? ⇒ **Was** *this picture* **drawn** by you?

### 3. 수여동사 문형(S+V+IO+DO)의 수동태
**두 개의 목적어** 중, 대개 뒤에 나오는 **직접목적어(DO)**를 주어로 쓰고 간접목적어(IO) 앞에는 전치사(to, for)를 붙인다. 오해의 여지가 없는 경우, 간접목적어를 주어로 쓸 수도 있다.

· He *gave* me the pen. (= He *gave* the pen *to* me.)
  ⇒ The pen *was given* (to) me *by* him. (○)          [to는 생략 가능]
  = I *was given* the pen *by* him. (○)
· He *bought* me a doll.
  ⇒ A doll *was bought* (for) me *by* him. (○)
  ⇏ I *was bought* a doll by him. (✕)      [I was bought···에 "인신매매"로 오해할 수도!]

▌**연습문제 47**
다음 문장들을 수동태로 바꾸라.
1. Bill wrote the book two years ago. ⇒
2. We will never leave her alone. ⇒
3. You cannot take pictures in this church. ⇒
4. They built this tower 300 years ago. ⇒
5. Where did they find her bag? ⇒
6. What did you give her on Valentine day? ⇒
7. Did Mary wrote this book? ⇒
8. Mother bought me a hamburger. ⇒
9. Who broke this window? ⇒
10. What made you angry? ⇒

## B 특수한 수동태 용법

### 1. by를 쓰지 않는 수동태
수동태에서 행위자를 나타내는 by 대신 다른 전치사를 쓰는 경우가 있다. 이런 경우는 능동태로 잘 쓰이지 않는다.

**예** be surprised at(~에 놀라다), be disappointed in(~에 실망하다), be pleased with(~에 기뻐하다), be satisfied with(~에 만족하다), be interested in(~에 흥미를 느끼다), be known to(~에게 알려지다), be tired with(from)(~로 지치다), be tired of(~에 싫증나다), be covered with(~로 덮이다), be filled with(~로 가득 차다), be crowded with(~로 붐비다), be scared of(~할까 봐 두렵다), be surrounded with(~로 둘러싸이다)

- I **was surprised at** the news. ⇐ The news *surprised* me.
- Dad **was pleased with** my gift. ⇐ My gift *pleased* dad.
- They **were satisfied with** the result. ⇐ The result *satisfied* them.

### 2. 수동태를 쓰지 않는 타동사
have(갖고 있다), lack(결여하다), become(어울리다), escape(탈출하다), take(시간이 … 걸리다), resemble(닮다), fit(적합하다), cost(비용이 … 들다) 등.

- She **has** red hair. ≠ Red hair *is had* by her. (✕)
- This dress **becomes** you. ≠ You *are become* by this dress. (✕)
- They **escaped** North Korea. ≠ North Korea *was escaped*. (✕)

### 3. (자동사)+(전치사)로 이뤄진 관용구는 타동사처럼 취급해 수동태를 만든다.
- A bike **ran over** the cat. ⇒ The cat **was run over** by a bike.
- She **laughed at** me. ⇒ I **was laughed at** by her.

### 4. 사역동사(make)나 지각동사(see, hear, watch 등)가 부정사를 수반할 때 to를 생략하는데(원형부정사), 수동태를 만들면 to가 다시 나타난다. 사역동사 중 have와 let은 수동태를 잘 만들지 않는다. (☞ 20. 부정사 D (3))

- He **made** me *finish* it. ⇒ I **was made** to *finish* it by him.

▌ **연습문제 48**

괄호 속 단어들 중 알맞은 것에 ○표하라.

1. The ship with many passengers (was, were) sunk in the sea.
2. The book was (reading, readed, read) by Sally.
3. I was surprised (by, at) the news.
4. This company was (found, founded) in 1998.
5. This book is very (interesting, interested).
6. She was (interesting, interested) in this book.
7. I was tired (with, of) this cap, so I changed it.
8. The boy was (took, taken) to the hospital.
9. John was (reading, read) newspaper in the park.
10. The room was filled (at, with) bad smells.
11. This wine was made (by, from) Greek grapes.
12. This wine was made (by, from) Greek masters.
13. She was made (clean, to clean) the room.
14. The accident was known (by, to) everyone in the town.
15. The garden was covered (by, with) fallen leaves.

## ⓒ 중간태 동사(Middle Voice Verbs)

영어의 동사 중에 형태는 능동태이면서 수동의 의미를 갖는 것들이 있는데 이를 편의상 중간태 동사라 부른다. 이 중간태 동사들은 자동사로서, 대체로 부사와 함께 쓰이지만 진행형은 부사 없이 쓸 수도 있다.

예 bake(구워진다), build(지어진다), catch(잡힌다), clean(청소된다), compare, cook, cut, eat, feel, keep, lock, open, print, read, rent, sell, tear, wash, wear, photograph, handle, peel 등.

- This bread **bakes** fast. (= This bread *is* baked fast.)
  → This bread **bakes**. (✗)　　　　　　　　　　　[부사 없이 단독으로는 안 됨]
- The tower is **building**. (○) (지어지고 있다)　　　　[진행형은 단독으로 가능]
- My foot **caught** in the hole. (구멍에 빠졌다)
- The surface of this table **cleans** easily. (쉽게 청소된다)
- Eels can't **catch** easily. (쉽게 잡을 수 없다)

- No artificial light can **compare** with daylight. (비교될 수 없다)
- Eggs **cook** more quickly than potatoes. (더 빨리 요리된다)
- This cake **cuts** easily. (쉽게 잘린다)
- Rust had **eaten** into the metal. (녹슬었다)
- This kind of food won't **keep** long. (오래가지 않는다)
- This cloth **feels** rather rough. (다소 거칠게 느껴진다)
- The door **locked** of itself. (저절로 잠겼다)
- This paper **prints** badly. (인쇄 질이 나쁘다)
- His novel is **printing**. (인쇄 중이다)
- This book **reads** easily. (쉽게 읽힌다)
- This studio **rents** at 200 dollars. (월세 200불로 빌릴 수 있다)
- The magazine **sells** 20,000 copies a week. (2만부씩 팔린다)
- The Sun is the best **selling** newspaper in the U.K. (가장 잘 팔리는)
- These clothes **wash** well. (잘 세탁된다)
- The book **tore** up in two parts. (둘로 쪼개졌다)
- The color of this china **wears** well. (오래 간다)
- This car **handles** well even in bad weather. (운전하기 좋다)
- The paint is **peeling** off my bike. (칠이 벗겨진다)

## ▌연습문제 49

괄호 속 단어들 중 알맞은 것에 ○표 하라.

1. Cathy (resembles, is resembled) her friend Jenny.
2. This novel is the best (selling, sold) book in the store.
3. The bus was crowded (by, with) children.
4. The tower in the island is (building, constructing) fast.
5. This sweater (is feeling, feels) good.
6. His novel cannot (read, study) easily.
7. He was made (work, to work) in the tunnel.
8. The door was (locked, locking) by Sam.
9. His song cannot (compare, compared) with Jane's.
10. Your clothes (are washing, washed).

# 종합문제 14

**01 다음 문장에서 어색한 부분을 찾아 바르게 고치라.**

1. Tom was become a computer programer.
2. I was resembled my grandfather.
3. This train was arrived at 7:00 PM.
4. Whom was this picture drawn?
5. The wounded soldiers were send to the hospital.
6. He was seen go upstairs few minutes ago.
7. This flower should water once a day.
8. The boy born in this house was risen by his aunt.
9. What was told by him was turned out to be true.
10. Mary was made clean the bathroom.

**02 다음 문장들을 수동태로 만들라.**

1. Who made the girl cry?
   ⇒
2. Snow has covered the roof.
   ⇒
3. No one could hear him sing.
   ⇒
4. His failure disappointed me.
   ⇒
5. The mouse surprised my sister.
   ⇒

**03 괄호 속에 있는 말을 이용해 다음 우리말을 영작하라.**

1. 이 책은 프랑스어로 씌어져 내가 읽을 수 없다. (written, in French)

2. 1956년에 지어진 저 건물은 우체국이다. (built)

3. 그는 꼭대기가 눈으로 덮인 산으로 걸어갔다. (covered)

4. 이 거북이는 어디서 발견되었습니까? (discover)

5. 그녀는 매를 맞은 것처럼 보인다. (look, beaten)

6. 그 일은 약 3시간 후에 완료될 것이다. (completed, about)

7. 저 문제는 끝내 풀리지 않았다. (solved, to the end)

8. 나는 그 결과에 만족할 수 없다. (satisfied)

9. 너는 누구에게서 영어를 가르침 받았느냐? (taught)

10. 그 도둑은 경찰에 붙잡혀 감옥에 보내졌다. (caught, sent)

---

**중간태:** 중간태는 그리스어 같은 고대 언어에 존재하던 동사 활용 형태인데, 능동태와 수동태의 중간 형태를 말한다. 쉽게 설명하면, 어떤 행동이 타자가 아닌 자기 자신에게 미치는 재귀동사 같은 경우이다. 실제로 영어에는 이런 태가 존재하지 않고, 그 상황은 재귀 대명사로 표현한다.

# Unit 19 부정사 (Infinitive)

부정사란 활용 이전의 동사 원형(original form)을 가리키는데, **be동사** 이외의 일반 동사에서 현재형(3인칭 단수 예외)과 모양이 동일하다. 부정사에 전치사 to를 붙이면 **명사, 형용사, 부사**로 사용될 수 있다.

## A to(부정사)의 용법

**1. 명사적 용법:** '~하는 것'이란 의미를 가지며, 주어, 목적어, 보어로 사용됨.

- **To know** is one thing and **to teach** is another. (아는 것과 가르치는 건 별개)　　[주어]
- I *want* **to master** English.　　[목적어]
- My goal is **to master** English.　　[보어]

❶ 가주어, 가목적어: 주어나 목적어가 너무 긴 경우, 이해를 돕기 위해 주어, 목적어 자리에 it을 쓰고 진짜 주어나 목적어는 뒤로 보낸다.

- **To master** English *is* very hard.　　[주어]
  = *It* is very hard **to master** English.　　[가주어–진주어]
- I found *it* difficult **to learn** English.　　[가목적어–진목적어]

❷ (의문사)+to(부정사): 의문절의 축약형

- It is important **what to learn**. (무엇을 배울 것인가)
- Let me see **where to go**. (어디로 가야할지)
- Did you decide **when to go**? (언제 갈지)
- I don't know **how to go** there. (어떻게 가야할지)
- Tell me **who to go** with us. (누가 갈건지)
- We haven't decided yet **whether to go** or not. (갈건지 말건지)

**2. 형용사적 용법:** 명사 뒤에 와서 '~하기 위한, ~할만한'이란 의미를 갖는다. 수식하는 명사의 역할에 따라 전치사를 수반할 수도 있다.

- I want *a book* **to read**. (읽을 책)　　[a book은 read의 목적어]
  **cf** I read *a book*.
- I need *a pen* **to write** *with*. (가지고 쓸 펜)　　[a pen은 with의 목적어]
  **cf** I write *with a pen*.
- ※ a paper **to write** *on*(그 위에 쓸 종이); a friend **to play** *with*(함께 놀 친구)

## 3. be + to(부정사)의 용법

be동사 바로 다음에 to(부정사)가 나오는 경우가 종종 있다. 이는 다음과 같은 관용구에서 to(부정사) 앞의 형용사가 생략된 경우인데, 문맥에 따라 어떤 형용사가 생략되었는지 파악해야 한다.

❶ be (allowed) to: ~하도록 허용되다
- Teachers should **be to** monitor students' behaviors.

❷ be (able) to: ~ 할 수 있다
- Not a man was **to be** seen on the street. (한 사람도 볼 수 없었다)

❸ be (supposed) to: ~하도록 일정이 잡히다
- We **are to** meet Mr. Smith at 6. (만나게 되어 있다)

❹ be (obliged) to: ~할 의무가 있다
- You **are to** obey your parents. (순종해야 한다)
- She **is to** blame. (그녀는 비난받아야 한다)

❺ be (destined) to: ~하도록 운명 지어지다
- We **are to** die in the end. (우리는 결국 죽게 되어 있다)

❻ be (necessary) to: ~할 필요가 있다
- You **are to** see a doctor for your health. (진료 받을 필요가 있다)

❼ be (intended) to: ~할 의도(목적)를 갖고 있다(수동)
- This test **is to** check the capacity of your lung. (점검하기 위함이다)

❽ be (intending) to: ~할 의도를 갖고 있다(능동)
- If you **are to** be rich, you should be more diligent. (부자가 되려면)

❾ be (good) to: ~하기에 적당하다
- This program is *not* **to** educate the young students. (교육하기에 적합지 않다)

### 4. 부사적 용법: to+(부정사)는 동사, 형용사, 다른 부사를 수식할 수 있다.

❶ **목적**: '~하기 위하여, 하고 싶어' (=in order to, so as to)
- I came here **to see** you. (너를 보기 위해서)
- The project was planned (in order) **to help** the homeless.

❷ **원인**: '~하니까, ~하기 때문에'
- I am *glad* **to see** you. (너를 보니까)            [감정의 원인]
- He *must be* stupid **to do** such a thing. (하는 걸 보니)   [판단의 근거]

❸ **결과**: '~되다'
- She grew up **to be** a pianist. (자라서 피아니스트가 되었다)
- He worked hard *only* **to fail**. (일해도 실패만 했다)
- Grandpa lived **to be** ninety. (90세까지 사셨다)

❹ **정도**: '~하기에'
- She is too *young* **to learn** English. (영어 배우기에 너무 어리다)
- I am old *enough* **to live** alone. (혼자 살기에 충분히 나이 들다)

❺ **독립적 용법**: to tell the truth(사실대로 말해), to begin with(우선), to be sure(확실히), to say nothing of ~(~은 말할 것도 없고)
- **To be frank,** I have no money. (솔직히 말해)
- **To make matters worse,** the car was broken. (설상가상으로)
- He is, **so to speak,** a romantist. (말하자면)

### 5. to부정사의 의미상 주어

❶ **주어와 일치하는 경우**: to부정사의 의미상 주어가 문장의 주어와 일치하면 굳이 의미상 주어를 쓰지 않는다.
- He loves **to play** soccer.
- I hope **to be** rich.

❷ **목적어와 일치하는 경우**: 목적어 뒤에 그냥 to부정사를 놓는다.
- I want *him* **to go** there. (그가 거기 가길 원한다)
- I hope *you* **to be** rich. (네가 부자가 되길 기대한다)

❸ **for+(목적격)+to(부정사)**: 목적어가 없으면서 부정사의 의미상 주어가 본문 주어와 다를 때는 for+(목적격)을 통해 to부정사의 의미상 주어를 만든다.
  · It is difficult *for me* to master English. (내가 마스터하기엔)
  = I can hardly master English.
  · The stone is too heavy *for him* to lift up. (그가 들어올리기엔)

❹ **of+(목적격)+to부정사:** 사람의 성격을 나타내는 형용사, 즉 nice, kind(친절한), generous(관대한), polite(공손한), clever, foolish, silly, stupid(멍청한), careless(부주의한), careful(주의 깊은), rude(무례한), cruel(잔인한), selfish(이기적인) 등이 오면 for 대신 of로 의미상 주어를 나타낸다.
  · It is *very nice* of you to help me. (당신이 나를 도와주니 나이스!)
  · How foolish of me to trust her! (그녀를 믿다니 내가 바보야!)

※ **부사의 삽입:** 부정사를 수식하는 부사는 **to와 부정사 사이**에 넣는다.
  · Read this book to *wholly* understand his theory.

## ■ 연습문제 50

01. 부정사가 보기와 동일한 용법으로 사용된 경우를 찾으라.

  (보기) To live without car in America is not easy.

① She went to Paris to find her brother.
② To finish her homework, Mary went to the library.
③ I was very glad to meet her again.
④ As it was so hot, I bought something to drink.
⑤ It is hard to find a sincere friend like Bill.

02. 다음 문장 중 부정사의 용법이 나머지 것들과 다른 것을 골라라.

① I like to swim in the lake during the vacation.
② Please tell me how to handle this machine.
③ He wanted me not to give up the study.
④ She set up the plan to spend her vacation.

03. 괄호 안에 알맞은 전치사를 넣으라.

1. I like it better (    ) you to play tennis after school.
2. It is foolish (    ) him to marry Jane.
3. Please bring me a knife to cut the meat (    ).
4. It is right (    ) him to enter the college.
5. We need to find an apartment to live (    ).

04. 괄호 안에 무슨 말이 생략되어 있는지 보기 중에서 찾아 그 번호를 쓰라.

[보기] ① allowed   ② able   ③ supposed   ④ obliged   ⑤ destined
      ⑥ necessary   ⑦ intended   ⑧ good

1. We are (    ) to pay taxes to our country.
2. The email is (    ) to be sent to me by 10 o'clock.
3. The guest is (    ) to arrive here at 5 PM.
4. Today's test is (    ) to check the function of the car.
5. Girls should be (    ) to wear pants even in the school.

05. 괄호 속 단어들 중 알맞은 것에 ○표하라.

1. It is very kind (for, of) you to lend me money.
2. I don't know what (will, to) do now.
3. Bring me a knife to cut (on, with).
4. To (say, tell) the truth, she is not pretty.
5. I want (for him, him) to enter the college.
6. Julia is, (to be sure, so to speak), a bookworm.
7. It is hard (fast to, to fast) solve this problem.
8. Tell me (what, where) to go.

## B to(부정사)의 활용

**1. 부정:** not, never, neither, nor 등의 부사는 to 앞에 붙인다.
- I want you *not* to leave away. (당신이 떠나지 않기를)
- He went to L.A. *never* to return. (가서 다신 돌아오지 않았다)
- She wanted *neither* to go *nor* to come back. (가기도 오기도 싫음)

**2. 과거, 완료 시제:** 말하는 시점보다 앞선 시제는 to have p.p. 로 나타낸다.
- He seems **to have been** rich. (과거에 부자였던 것처럼 보인다)
  = It seems that he **was** rich.
  - **cf** He seems (**to be**) rich. = It seems that he is rich.
- It seems **to have rained** much. (그간 비가 많이 왔던 것처럼 보인다)

**3. 수동태:** to부정사의 수동태는 to be p.p.(과거분사)로 나타낸다.
- I am glad **to be invited**. (초대 받아서 기쁘다)
- I helped him (**to be**) relaxed.

**4. 진행형:** to부정사의 진행형은 to be ~ing(현재분사)로 나타낸다.
- He seems (**to be**) **listening** to music. (음악을 듣고 있는 것처럼 보인다)

## C to부정사의 특별 용법

**1. to be 의 생략:** 뜻이 전달만 된다면 말을 간략하게 하는 게 좋다. 예컨대, 2형식 동사 prove, turn out, seem, appear 다음에 to be **(형용사)** 꼴이 나오면 to be는 종종 생략한다. 5형식 동사의 S+V+O+C 형식에서도 C 앞에 to be가 생략된 상태이다.

- The *rumor turned* out (**to be**) true.
- He *seems* (**to be**) happy.
- I think him (**to be**) happy.

**2. 대부정사:** 반복되는 to부정사는 간단히 to로 대신 받을 수 있다.
- How do you like **to** *go* shopping? / I love **to** (go shopping).
- You may *go* if you want **to** (go).

## 3. 관용적 표현

**❶ too (형/부) to~ = so (형/부) that cannot~** (너무…해서~할 수 없다)
- You are **too** *young* **to** ride a horse. (말을 타기엔 너무 어리다)
  = You are **so** *young* **that** you **cannot** ride a horse.

**❷ (형·부) enough to ~ = so (형·부) that can~** (충분히…해서 ~할 수 있다)
- He ran *fast* **enough to** catch the puppy. (강아지 잡기에 충분히 빨리)
  = He ran **so** *fast* **that** he **could** catch the puppy.
  - **cf** He has **enough** *money* **to** buy a bike.　　　　[enough는 명사 앞에]

## D 원형부정사(Bare Infinitive)

**지각동사**와 **사역동사**에선 목적 보어로서 to 없는 **원형부정사**를 쓴다.

### 1. 지각동사: 감각을 표현하는 see, look at, listen to, watch, hear, feel 등.
- I *saw* him **swim** in the river.
   = I *saw* him **swimming** in the river.
- I didn't *hear* him **come** in. (그가 들어오는 소리를 듣지 못했다)
- We *felt* the car **move** by itself. (저절로 움직이는 걸 느꼈다)

### 2. 사역동사: 타인에게 행동을 하도록 시키는 let, have, make, help. 단, help는 to를 쓸 수도 있다.
- *Let* him **clean** his room. (제 방을 청소하게 하라)
- He *made* me **keep** silent. (떠들지 못하게 했다)　　　　[강한 사역의 의미]
- I *had* my dog **follow** me. (날 따라오게 했다)　　　　[make 보다 약한 의미]
- He *helped* me **(to) carry** it. (나르는 걸 돕다)

### 3. 지각동사와 사역동사의 수동태: 수동태를 만들기 위해 목적어가 앞으로 나가면 동사 간의 충돌을 막기 위해 **원형부정사** 앞에 to를 다시 넣어준다.
- They *saw* him **go** out.　⇒　He *was seen* **to go** out.
- Mom *made* me **study**.　⇒　I *was made* **to study** by mom.
- He *let* me **drink** water.　⇒　I *was allowed* **to drink** water by him.
  [let은 수동태에서 대개 allow로 바꿔 쓴다.]

## 4. 원형부정사를 쓰는 관용적 표현

**❶ cannot but + 원형:** '~이외엔 도리가 없다', 즉 '~하지 않을 수 없다'
- I **could not but** *give* him money. (주지 않을 수 없었다)
  = I **could not help** *giving* him money.

**❷ had(would) better + 원형:** '~하는 편이 낫다' (☞ 가정법)
- You'd **better** *go* now. (지금 가는 게 좋겠다)
- You'd **better** *not go* now. (지금 가지 않는 게 좋겠다)

**❸ let go of:** '~을 가게 하다, 포기하다'. 이와 유사하게 사역동사 make, help도 목적어 없이 원형부정사와 사용될 수 있다.
- She never *let* **go** of his dream. (결코 꿈을 놓지 않았다)
- Please *let* **go** of me! = Please let me go.

> cf  I'll *make* **believe** I didn't hear you (못 듣는 척 흉내를 내겠다)
>     = I'll *pretend* I didn't hear you.
> cf  This drug can help (to) lower blood pressure.

**❹ Why not (원형)…?:** Why don't you…?의 축약형
- **Why not** *give* it a try? = Why don't you give it a try? (한 번 해 봐)

**❺ go, come + (원형):** 자주 사용되는 말 뒤에 to를 생략하곤 한다. (구어체)
- *Come* **see** me anytime. = Come *to* see me anytime.

▌**연습문제 51**

**01.** 다음 문장들을 지시에 따라 고쳐 쓰라.

1. Mary was too proud to beg for food. (so~that을 사용)

_____

2. He was so rich that he could buy the car. (enough to를 사용)

_____


**02.** 괄호 속 단어들 중 알맞은 것에 ○표하라.

1. They decided (not to go, to go not) back to their homeland.
2. Jerry seems to (have been, be) fat at that time.
3. He was lucky to (be saved, save) from the fire.
4. Mary is too young (to enter, entering) the school.
5. Let me (to ask, ask) you a question.
6. Jim was (strong enough, enough strong) to hold up the box.
7. I saw her (to study, studying) in the library.
8. He could not but (help, helping) his sister.
9. You'd better not (eat, to eat) the rotten apple.
10. Why not (join, to join) us on a hike?
11. The mother would never let go (of, to) her son.
12. You can play the guitar if you want (do, to).


**03.** 다음 각 문장에서 불필요한 단어를 골라 지우라.

1. She seemed be happy when she came back home.
2. I watched him to go out of the room after lunch.
3. Nobody can let me to kneel down before my enemy.
4. You can eat any food in this room, if you want to do.
5. Tom is so too short to buy the bicycle.

# 종합문제 15

**01 다음 문장에서 어색한 부분을 찾아 바르게 고치라.**

1. He want you carefully to handle the picture.
2. Mary hurried to not be late for school.
3. I had Tom taking a picture of dad.
4. He saw me to walk along the stream.
5. It is silly for you to tell a lie to me.
6. Don't forget to not change the password.
7. I could not but helping my brother.
8. I want for you to bring the box.
9. I was made watching the boys in the yard.
10. You'd not better break your promise.
11. I think him having been rich in China.
12. Bill is enough smart to solve the problem.
13. You need to make friends to study.
14. She is careless enough to take care of the baby.
15. Tell me whom to go with Tom?

**02 괄호 속에 있는 말을 이용해 다음 우리말을 영작하라.**

1. 그녀는 아무 것도 몰랐던 것처럼 보인다. (seem)

2. 너는 지금 잠을 자지 않는 것이 낫다. (would better)

3. Tom은 너무 뚱뚱해 그 옷을 입을 수 없다. (too, put on)

4. 그는 자전거를 탈만큼 충분히 건강하다. (enough)

5. 나는 함께 야구할 친구를 찾고 있다. (to play with)

6. 우리는 하늘이 어두워지는 걸 느꼈다. (feel, get dark)

7. 공항까지 마중 나오시니 참 친절하시군요. (kind, meet)

8. 너와 함께 공부하게 되어 매우 기쁘다. (happy)

9. 우선, 우리는 달성할 목표를 정해야 한다. (begin, to achieve)

10. 빵은 말할 것도 없고, 우리는 마실 물도 없다. (say nothing)

11. 나는 나중에 그녀를 데리러 갈 것이다. (go get)

12. 솔직히, 나는 그녀를 사랑한다. (frank)

---

**구어체**: 본 문법책에는 구어체가 가끔 소개된다. 예컨대, "Go get her!(가서 그녀를 데려와)", "I know the girl who John loved before.(나는 John이 전에 사랑한 소녀를 안다)" 등은 실제로 많이 쓰이는 말이지만, 문법 문제에 나오면 아직은 틀리다고 봐야 한다. 우리 말에서 "너에 것"이라 말해도 다 알아 듣지만 "너의 것"이 맞듯이!. 단, 숙어로 굳어져 신문 컬럼에 나오는 경우라면 문법적으로 맞다고 봐야 한다.

· Go get her!(×) ⇒ Go to get her! (○)

· I know the girl who John loved.(×) ⇒ I know the girl whom John loved. (○)

# Unit 20 동명사 (Gerund)

to(부정사)는 명사 노릇을 해도 전치사의 목적어 구실을 못하므로 **(동사원형)+ing**로 동명사를 만들게 되었다. **동명사 만드는 법**은 **현재분사 만드는 법**과 동일하다. (☞ 17 동사의 시제, **C**) 한편, **동명사**는 주로 **과거** 혹은 **현재** 일을 가리키는 반면, **to(부정사)는 장래 일**을 나타내는 경향이 있다.

## A 동명사의 용법

**1. 동명사의 구실:** 동명사는 명사이므로 원칙적으로 명사가 하는 역할, 즉 주어, 목적어(전치사 목적어 포함), 보어의 구실을 다 할 수 있다.

- **Speaking** English *is* not easy.　　　　　　　　　　　　　　　　　[주어]
- She *likes* **speaking** English.　　　　　　　　　　　　　　　　　　[목적어]
- The problem *is* **speaking** English.　　　　　　　　　　　　　　　[보어]
- I am interested *in* **speaking** English.　　　　　　　　　　　　　　[전치사 목적어]
- Thank you *for* **listening**. (들어줘서 감사!)　　　　　　　　　　　　[전치사 목적어]

**2. 동명사의 의미상 주어:** 필요한 경우, 동명사의 주어는 **소유격**으로 나타내는데, 구어에선 간혹 목적격을 쓸 수도 있다.

- I heard of *Tom's* **inviting** my mon. (Tom이 엄마를 초대한 것)
- He stopped *my* **swimming**. (내 수영을 금했다)
  - **cf** He stopped *me* **swimming**.　　　　　　　　　　　　　　[구어]

**3. 동명사의 부정:** 동명사를 부정할 때는 not을 동명사 앞에 놓는다.
- I am disappointed with *his* **not coming**. (그가 오지 않은 것)

**4. 동명사의 시제:** 동명사의 행위가 주절의 시점보다 과거이면 having+p.p.
- Do you know his **inviting** her? (그녀를 초대하는 것)
- Do you know his **having invited** her? (초대했다는 것)

**5. 동명사의 수동:** 동명사의 수동태는 being+p.p.
- Do you know her **being invited** by him? (초대되는 것)
- Do you know her **having been invited**? (초대된 것)

## 6. 동명사만 목적어로 취하는 동사

아래 동사들은 대체로 **장래** 일보다 **과거 혹은 현재** 일을 받기 때문에 to부정사 대신 동명사 목적어를 갖는다.

**예** avoid, imagine, admit, practice, escape, consider, suggest, finish, enjoy, deny, postpone, mind, forgive, give up, quit, stop, put off 등.

- Did you enjoy **watching** TV?
- He gave up **working** in the factory.
- I stopped **smoking**. (흡연하기 그만 두었다)
  **cf** I *stopped* **to smoke**. (흡연하기 위해 멈춰 섰다)      [장래 일, 부사]
- He *tried* **smoking**. (흡연을 시도해 보았다)      [흡연을 실제로 함]
  **cf** He *tried* **to smoke**. (흡연을 위해 노력했다)      [흡연을 아직 안 함]
- Jim *practiced* **playing** the guitar.
- He *postponed* **replying** to me.
- Would you *mind* my **smoking** here? = Mind if I smoke here?
  [대답] No, go ahead. (괜찮아요, 피세요) / Yes, I do(예, 좀 꺼려지네요.)

## 7. 부정사만 목적어로 취하는 동사

주로 장래 일에 관한 언급을 하는 동사들이다.

**예** agree, ask, want, hope, decide, plan, promise, choose, expect, learn, mean, offer, refuse, pretend, afford, manage 등

- I *want* **to go** out.    **cf** I want going out. (✗)
- I *decided* **not to go** out.
- She *managed* **to escape** from the burning car. (겨우 빠져나왔다)

## 8. 동명사와 부정사 목적어를 모두 취하는 동사

like, love, hate, begin, continue, intend, neglect, attempt 등은 동명사와 부정사를 모두 목적어로 취할 수 있지만, 간혹 과거/미래에 대한 시간적 규제가 생길 수 있다.

- The baby *began* **crying(to cry)**.
- She *likes* **playing(=to play)** cards. (카드놀이를 좋아한다)
  **cf** I would like you to come. (○) (네가 오면 좋겠다)      [미래적 의미]
       I would like you coming. (✗)

## 9. 동명사 목적어와 부정사 목적어의 뜻이 다른 경우

remember, forget, regret 등에서 to**부정사**는 앞으로 **행할[미래]** 일을 의미하고 **동명사**(-ing)는 **이미 행한[과거]** 일 혹은 **행하고 있는[현재]** 일을 의미한다.

- I *regret* **to tell** you this sad news. (슬픈 소식을 전하게 되어 유감이다)
- I *regret* **telling** you that sad news. (그 소식 전했던 걸 후회한다)
- I almost *forgot* **to tell** you the news. (그 소식 전하는 걸 잊을 뻔했다)
- I *forgot* **telling** you the news. (이미 그 소식 전했다는 걸 잊었다)
- *Remember* **to tell** him the news. (그에게 소식 전하는 걸 기억해라)
- I *remembered* **telling** him the news. (그에게 소식 전한 걸 기억한다)

## 10. 동명사를 대신하는 가주어, 가목적어

가주어/가목적어 it은 주로 to부정사와 같이 쓰나, 동명사와 쓰이기도 한다.

- It is no good(use) **crying** over spilled milk.    [It = crying 이하]
- It was nice **meeting** you.    [It = meeting 이하]

### ■ 연습문제 52

괄호 속 단어들 중 알맞은 것에 ○표하라.

1. (To talk, Talking) is easier than doing.
2. While camping in the forest, we use a (sleepy, sleeping) bag.
3. Dad quit (to smoke, smoking) for his health.
4. I hope you (to pass, passing) the entrance exam.
5. The taxi driver stopped (resting, to rest) after a long driving.
6. Did you enjoy (to surf, surfing) on the beach?
7. Buddhists avoid (to eat, eating) meat.
8. You should avoid stress (to keep, keeping) yourself healthy.
9. He escaped (to be, being) drowned in the pool.
10. Tom pretended (to be, being) a doctor.
11. Don't forget (to send, sending) this letter tomorrow.
12. (It, That) was nice seeing you.

## B 동명사 관련 관용 표현

### 1. 전치사 to가 동명사를 목적어로 갖는 경우
contribute to(~에 기여하다); look forward to(~하기를 고대하다);
be accustomed to(~에 익숙해지다); be used to(~에 익숙해지다);
be opposed to(~에 반대하다)

- I *look forward to* seeing you.
- We are *opposed to* raising taxes.
- He has much *contributed to* developing Korean economy.
- He is *used to* taking a nap after lunch.
  - **cf** This tool *is used* to pull out the screw. (~에 사용된다)

### 2. in~ing (~을 하면서, ~하는 데에): in은 자주 생략된다.
- He *spends(wastes)* much time (in) playing games.
- I had a *hard time* (in) finding jobs.
- We have *no trouble* (in) speaking English.
- I was *busy* (in) writing a book.
  - **cf** He *spends* much money *to develop* his country. (나라를 발전시키기 **위해** 많은 돈을 쓴다)
  
  [목적의 의미로 to부정사를 쓸 수 있다]

### 3. cannot help ~ing (~하지 않을 수 없다): = cannot but (동사원형)
- I couldn't help laughing.   =   I couldn't but laugh.

### 4. keep(prevent)+(목)+from ~ing (~가 ~하는 걸 막다)
- The snow *kept me from* going to school. (학교 가는 걸 막았다)

### 5. feel like ~ing (~하고 싶다): 간혹 **feel like to**부정사를 쓰기도 한다.
- I *feel like* having dinner with you. (너와 저녁 먹고 싶다)

### 6. go ~ing(~하러 가다):
go fishing(낚시 가다); go skiing(스키 타러 가다); go camping(캠핑 가다)

- Do you want to *go* hunting or *go* on a picnic?
- Let's go shopping after swimming.

## 7. How(What) about ~ing? (~하는 건 어때?)

· *How(What) about* **having** dinner with me?

**cf** how와 what은 종종 바꿔 쓸 수 있지만 do you think 가 삽입되면 그럴 수 없다.

· **What** do you think about shopping? (○)
≠ **How** do you think about shopping? (✕)   [생각하는 방법에 대한 물음]

## 8. On ~ing(~하자마자) = As soon as

· **On hearing** the news, she burst out crying.

## 9. There is no ~ing(~하는 건 있을 수 없다)

· *There is no* **staying** at home in this fine weather.

## 10. be worth ~ing(~할 가치가 있다)

· His book is not worth reading. (그의 책은 읽을 가치가 없다)

### ■ 연습문제 53

괄호 속 단어들 중 알맞은 것에 ○표하라.

1. I am looking forward to (see, seeing) your new car.
2. Sam is not accustomed to (be, being) alone in the dark.
3. This tool is used to (punch, punching) the plate.
4. She used to (spend, spending) a lot of money in shopping.
5. The vitamins will keep you (for, from) aging.
6. (In, On) getting off the bus, he ran to the rest room.
7. I feel like (watch, watching) movies at home.
8. Jane is used to (keep, keeping) a diary.
9. He spends every Saturday (to play, playing) soccer.
10. I couldn't help (laugh, laughing) at the weird scene.
11. Anyhow, there is (no, not) going back in time.
12. How about (to go, going) fishing after lunch?

## 종합문제 16

**01** 다음 문장에서 어색한 부분을 찾아 바르게 고치라.

1. We finished to build a dog house in the back yard.
2. To speaking English is not easy.
3. I want him taking part in the seminar.
4. We are looking forward to see you soon.
5. How about to see the movies this Saturday?
6. I am not used to talk with foreigners.
7. Would you mind me opening the window?
8. We are opposed closing the old theater.
9. I want to take a walk instead of stay at home.
10. Yesterday Jane went to shopping with her sister.
11. Mom asked me take care of my kid brother.
12. I regret to blame you in the class yesterday.
13. John has contributed to build the art center.
14. On seeing me, the girl began to weeping.
15. Tom denied to have cheated in the last test.
16. He managed passing the exam.
17. I could not but crying at the news.
18. Don't forget calling me tomorrow morning.
19. This game is no worth to comment on.
20. The microscope is used magnifying small things.

**02** 괄호 속에 있는 말을 이용해 다음 우리말을 영작하라.

1. 너는 그가 독감으로 입원했다는 걸 아느냐? (his, hospitalized)

2. 이 책은 읽을 가치가 있다. (worth)

3. 나는 숙제하는 걸 거의 잊을 뻔했다. (forget)

4. 그는 책들을 쓰느라 많은 시간을 보냈다. (spend)

5. Mary는 바이올린 연주를 시도해 보았다. (try)

6. 과거의 실수를 후회해도 아무 소용없다. (no use, regret)

7. 방과 후에 테니스를 치고 싶다. (feel like, play)

8. 이렇게 추운 날 밖에서 잔다는 건 있을 수 없다. (there is no)

9. 그는 자신이 거짓말했음을 인정했다. (admit, having)

10. 많은 실패에도 불구하고 그는 그림 그리기를 포기하지 않았다. (give up)

---

**help 의 용법:** make, have, let과 함께 사역동사로 꼽히는 help는 특이한 용법을 갖는다. 우선, make, have, let는 대개 명사 목적어가 나고 그 다음에 원형 부정사를 쓰는 반면, help는 명사 목적어 없이 단독으로 원형 부정사를 목적어로 쓸 수 있다.
· This book will help (to) understand Darwin.
또, help는 부정사뿐 아니라 동명사도 목적어로 가질 수 있는데, 그때는 "...을 피하다"라는 의미를 가지며 보통 can 혹은 cannot과 함께 쓰인다.
· I could not help crying. (울음을 피할 수 없었다)
 = I could not but cry.

# Unit 21 분사 (Participle)

분사는 현재분사와 과거분사로 나뉜다. 문장에서 형용사나 부사의 역할을 하는데, 분사를 만드는 방법은 ☞ 17. 동사의 시제, **B**와 **C**

## **A** 분사의 용법

**1. 한정적 용법:** 명사의 앞/뒤에서 명사를 수식하는 형용사 역할을 한다.

❶ **현재분사**: 진행(~하고 있는) 및/혹은 능동(~행하는)의 의미를 갖는다.
- I saw a **barking** *dog* on the street.      [능동+진행의 의미]
- I saw a *dog* **barking** at a cat. (고양이에게 짖고 있는 개)
- He is, so to speak, a **walking** dictionary.      [능동적 의미]
- a **sleeping** baby = a baby who *is sleeping*      [진행의 의미]
  - **cf** a **sleeping** bag = a bag *for sleeping*      [동명사]

❷ **과거분사**: 완료(~을 마친) 및/혹은 수동(~을 당하는)의 의미를 갖는다.
- I collected **fallen** *leaves* in the basket.      [완료]
- I collected the *leaves* **fallen** on the car. (차 위에 떨어진 낙엽)      [완료]
- I eat only **cooked** fish.      [수동+완료]
- I saw the *fish* (being) **cooked** in the oven. (오븐에서 조리되는)      [수동]

**2. 서술적 용법:** 분사는 형용사로서, 주격 및 목적격 보어 역할을 한다.

❶ **현재분사**: 대개 능동과 진행의 의미를 동시에 갖는다.
- The dog is **barking** at the cat.      [주격 보어]
- I saw her **playing** the piano.      [목적격 보어]

❷ **과거분사**: be동사와 함께 쓰이면 **수동**, have동사와 함께 쓰이면 **완료**.
- He *is* frequently **beaten** by his friends.      [수동 주격 보어]
- I never saw *him* **beaten** by his friends.      [수동 목적격 보어]
- All the leaves *have* **fallen**. (다 떨어졌다)      [완료]
- I saw *the leaves* **fallen** on the ground. (떨어져 있는 걸)      [완료]
- I had my hair **cut**. (머리를 깎았다)      [수동]

▌ **연습문제 54**

괄호 속 단어들 중 알맞은 것에 ○표하라.

1. In the 1970s, Korea was a (developing, developed) country.
2. Many scientists were (inviting, invited) to the meeting.
3. Tom stole a black van (parking, parked) in front of the bank.
4. I am (interesting, interested) in this (excited, exciting) game.
5. She picked up the letter (falling, fallen) on the floor.
6. The roof was (covered, covering) with snow.
7. This picture is really (scared, scaring).
8. The information center, (opening, opened) last week, is helpful.

## B 분사구문(Participial Construction)

분사가 접속사 역할을 함께 하는 구문으로, 이는 부사절의 접속사와 주어 등을 거추장스런 말들을 생략해 문장을 **간소화**시키는 데 목적이 있다. 만약 이들을 생략했을 때 **문장 의미**가 모호해지면(특히 **양보** 구문) 굳이 분사구문으로 만들지 않는다. **조동사**가 포함된 절도 분사구문으로 잘 만들지 않는다.

### 1. 부사절을 분사구문으로 바꾸는 법(주절은 그대로 둠)

첫째, 부사절의 **접속사를 없앤다**. (의미를 명확히 하려면 남겨도 됨)
둘째, 부사절의 **주어를 없앤다**. 부사절과 주절의 주어가 다르면, 부사절의 주어를 남겨둔다.
셋째, 부사절의 **동사를 분사**로 만든다.
주절과 시제가 같으면 **–ing**를 붙이고, 주절보다 앞선 시제이면 **having + p.p.** 형으로 바꾼다. **not**이나 **never**는 분사 앞에 붙인다. 수동태 구문에선 being이나 having been을 생략하고 **과거분사만** 남길 수 있다.

· When we finished our work, we went to play soccer.
⇒ **Finishing** our work, we went to play soccer. [접속사, 주어 생략]

· As the cat was not fed well, it is very weak.
⇒ **Not having been** fed well, the cat is very weak. [앞선 시제]

· As he did not sleep well, Tom feels tired now.
⇒ **Not having slept** well, Tom feels tired now. [having 생략 가능]

- *Before I left* my office, I gave him a call.
  ⇒ Before **leaving** my office, I gave him a call. [접속사 남김]
- *Though he was* poor, he became a mayor. [양보]
  ⇒ **Though being** poor, he became a mayor. [though 없인 뜻이 모호]
- *As it was* rainy, I didn't go outside.
  ⇒ **It being** rainy, I didn't go outside. [주절의 주어와 다름]
- *If there is* not a shop here, you can buy it online.
  ⇒ **There not being** a shop here, you can buy it online. [There 절]
- *As Jack was beaten* so hard, he could not move.
  ⇒ **(Being) Beaten** so hard, Jack could not move. [being 생략 가능]
- *As he was born* in L.A., he is a US citizen.
  ⇒ **(Having been) Born** in L.A., he is a US citizen. [Having been 생략]

## 2. 분사구문을 부사절로 바꾸기

첫째, 접속사 찾기: 분사구문을 부사절로 바꿀 땐 when, while, as 등의 시간, 원인 접속사를 주로 쓰나, 주절과의 관계를 고려해 적당한 접속사를 고른다.

둘째, 주어 찾기: 주절의 주어를 가져다 쓰는데, 간혹 일반주어를 쓸 수도 있다.

셋째, 시제: 대체로 주절의 시제에 따르되 전후관계를 따져서 바꿀 수도 있다.

- **Walking** down the street, I met John.
  ⇒ *While(As, When) I walked* down the street, I met John. [시간]
- **Turning** to the left, you can find the school.
  ⇒ *If you turn* to the left, you can find the school. [조건]
- **(Having) fallen** on the road, the leaves were swept away.
  ⇒ *After they had fallen* on the road, the leaves were swept away.
- **Admitting (that)** you are right, I will not go with you.
  ⇒ *Though I admit* **(that)** you are right, I will not go with you. [양보]
- **Waving** his hand, he got on the bus.
  ⇒ *While he was waving* his hand, he got on the bus. [동시상황]
- **Sent** to the island, he became lazy.
  ⇒ *After he was sent* to the island, he became lazy. [수동]

▎연습문제 55

01. 다음 밑줄 친 부분을 분사구문으로 바꾸라.(시제에 주의)

1. As I played outside, I am so tired. ⇒ _____
2. After he graduated from school, he married Jane. ⇒ _____
3. If there are no helpers, call your teacher. ⇒ _____
4. Though I was dumped by Jack, I don't hate him. ⇒ _____
5. If you are not busy, you can come here. ⇒ _____

02. 다음 밑줄 친 부분을 부사절로 바꾸라.

1. Having learned from John, I became his assistant. ⇒ _____
2. It being rainy tomorrow, I will stay here one more day. ⇒ _____
3. Brought up in India, he can speak English very well. ⇒ _____


## C 분사의 특별 용법

1. **독립 분사구문**: 부사구가 일반 주어(you, we, they, it 등)를 갖는 경우로, 주절과 주어 일치가 되지 않는 관용적 표현이다.
   - **Strictly speaking,** she is not a genius. (엄격히 말하면)
     ⇒ *When we strictly speak,* she is not a genius.
   - You may use the calculator, **if necessary.** (필요하면)
     ⇒ You may use the calculator, *if it is necessary.*

2. **전치사처럼 사용되는 분사**: 일종의 독립 분사구문
   - **Considering** our budget, this plan is impossible. (감안할 때)
   - **Judging from** his face, he must be sick. (판단컨대)
   - **Notwithstanding** the risk, he invested in the company. (불구하고)
   - **Given** such a situation, we have to be very careful. (감안할 때)
   - She has many friends **including** Sally and Tom. (포함하여)
   - The movie was made **based on** his life. (기초로 하여)

3. **with+(명사)+분사**: 동시상황으로, (명사)가 분사의 의미상 주어가 됨.
   - He looked at me *with his arms* **folded**. (팔짱을 낀 채)
     ⇒ He looked at me *while his arms were* **folded**.
   - She ran to me *with her scarf* **flapping**. (스카프를 펄럭이며)
     ⇒ She ran to me *while her scarf was* **flapping**.

4. **부대상황**: 어떤 일이 동시에 혹은 연속으로 일어나는 상황을 나타내는데, 접속사 **as, while** 혹은 **and then** 등이 생략된 경우다. 대개 주절 뒤에 분사 구문이 덧붙는다.
   - She ate the sandwich, **reading** the newspaper.
     ⇐ She ate the sandwich, *while she was reading* the newspaper.
   - Tom took the train at two, **arriving** in Seoul at five.
     ⇐ Tom took the train at two, *and then arrived* in Seoul at five.

### ▌연습문제 56

**01.** 다음 밑줄 친 부분의 용법이 나머지와 다른 것을 골라라.

① A monkey is <u>sleeping</u> on the tree.
② A dog barked at the <u>sleeping</u> cat.
③ While camping in the mountain, I slept in the <u>sleeping</u> bag.
④ He studied hard, <u>sleeping</u> four hours a day.

**02.** 괄호 속 단어들 중 알맞은 것에 ○표하라.

1. (Gone, Going) to the park, I saw many interesting buildings.
2. He stayed up all night, (watched, watching) the soccer game.
3. (Not receiving, Receiving not) a reply, I sent an e-mail again.
4. (Giving, Given) the time schedule, you have to be hurry.
5. (Being, It being) fine tomorrow, we can go on a picnic.
6. She stared at me with tears (flowing, flown) down her cheeks.
7. (Judging, Judged) from this evidence, it is clear Jack is the criminal.
8. Strictly (speaking, spoken), he is not the author of the book.

## 종합문제 17

**01** 밑줄 친 부분의 용법이 나머지와 다른 것을 찾으라.

① Waiting for my friend, I watched a webtoon on the phone.
② He was once called a walking dictionary.
③ I saw a cow grazing in the pasture.
④ Do you know where she is studying now?
⑤ Parking in this area is not permitted.

**02** 다음 문장에서 어색한 부분을 찾아 바르게 고치라.

1. Did you see the old man walked in the park?
2. He was fixed a broken chair in his room.
3. This book is so excited that I cannot stop reading it.
4. They got boring with the long lecture.
5. Once there was a boy naming Jack.
6. I was very surprising to know the fact.
7. Do you know the girl slept on the sofa now?
8. This bike was make in Korea.
9. They have been built the church for 5 years.
10. If it is giving more attention, this plant will grow better.
11. When visiting at night, this street is fantastic.
12. Before taken a walk in the park, we had lunch.
13. Bill stood before me with his arms folding.
14. Strictly spoken, you are not handsome.

**03** 괄호 속에 있는 말을 이용해 다음 우리말을 영작하라.

1. 나는 물고기들이 강에서 수영하는 것을 보았다. (see, swim)

2. 아침식사 전에는 손을 씻어야 한다. (have, washed)

3. 중국에서 만들어진 이 손목시계는 고장 났다. (made, broken)

4. 운동장에서 놀고 있는 아이들은 누구냐? (who, playing)

5. 하늘에서 날고 있던 새가 그물에 걸렸다. (flying, caught in)

6. 숙제를 마치고 나서, 나는 TV를 봤다. (having)

7. 너희의 능력을 감안할 때, 이 일은 가능하다. (considering)

8. 저 모퉁이에서 왼쪽으로 돌면, 서점을 찾을 수 있다. (turning)

9. 감옥에 갇힌 후, 그는 법을 공부하기 시작했다. (taken)

10. 그는 새 한 마리가 땅에 떨어져 있는 걸 보았다. (fallen)

---

**고등 수식의 표현:** 수식 읽기의 보충

$\sqrt[2]{x}$ : square root of x  $\qquad$ $\sqrt[3]{y}$ : cubic root of y

$\sqrt[4]{x}$ : fourth root of z  $\qquad$ m/n : m over n

# Unit 22 비교 (Comparison)

형용사와 부사는 정도를 표현하기 위해 **원급, 비교급, 최상급**으로 변화한다.

## A 원급: '~와 같은'

as 혹은 not so ~ as 등을 이용해 두 대상이 **같음을 보여주는 표현**으로, as + **(형용사, 부사)** + as **(비교 대상)** 형식으로 쓴다. 여기서 앞의 as는 부사이고 뒤의 as는 **접속사**이므로 (비교대상)은 **주격이 원칙**이지만 구어에선 목적격도 쓴다. as는 **유사 관계대명사**(☞ 13. 관계대명사 A. ❺)로도 쓰인다.

### 1. 동등 비교
- He is *as* old *as* I (am old). (he와 I는 같은 나이) = He is the same *age* as I.
- He is **not so(as)** *old* as I.　　　　　　　　　　　　　　　　[so는 강조적 의미]
- He runs **as** *fast* as I.
- He bought the **same** *pen* as I have.　　　　　　　　　　　[as는 유사 관계대명사]

### 2. 배수 표현
- Father is **twice** as *old* as I.
- She has **three times** as *many* shoes as I.

### 3. 관용적 동급 표현

❶ **as long(far) as I know**: 내가 아는 한(한계)
- As *long(far)* as I know, he is honest.

❷ **may as well**: ~하는 편이 좋다, ~할 수도 있다
- You **may as well** study English. (배우는 편이 좋다)
- Noise **may as well** cause the headache. (두통을 유발할 수도 있다)

❸ **as good as**: ~와 다름없는, 못지않은
- He is as *good* as dead. (죽은 것과 다름없다)
- Your guess is as *good* as mine. (네 생각이 내 생각이다)

❹ **as well as**: 뿐만 아니라, 게다가
- I as well as you *was* wrong.　　　　　　　　　　　　　　　　[동사는 I를 받음]

❺ 강조의 as ~ as: 무려, 불과
　· I woke up as *early* as 4 o'clock. ⇐ I woke up early at 4 o'clock.
　· Here, the temperature went up as *high* as 42 degrees Celsius.

❻ as ~ as possible: 가능한 한 ~하게
　· He eats food as *slowly* as *possible*. (가능한 한 천천히)
　　= He eats food as *slowly* as *he can*.

❼ as ~ as (one) can: 더할 나위 없이(주로 비인칭 주어의 경우)
　· The weather is as *fine* as (it) can be.

❽ not so much A as B: A보다는 B가 더 낫다
　· He was **not so much** a father **as** an actor.
　　= He was **not** a father **so much as** an actor.
　　= He was *less* a father than an actor.
　　= He was *good as* an actor, but *not so good as* a father.

❾ not so much as ~: 심지어 ~하지 않다(강조)
　· She can**not so much as** write her own name.
　　= She can**not even** write her own name. (심지어 자기 이름조차 못씀.)

▌**연습문제 57**

괄호 속 단어들 중 알맞은 것에 ○표하라.

1. Please come home (as, so) soon as possible.
2. Tom can run twice as (fast, faster) as I.
3. The rumor is not true as (long, short) as I know.
4. You may as (good, well) go back home now.
5. These shoes are as (good, well) as brand new.
6. I can't hear you. Please tell me as (fast, slowly) as possible.
7. I have never seen such a nice watch (as, so) Tom has.

## B 비교급: '~보다 더 ~한'

두 대상의 **우열을 비교할 때** 사용하며, **than** (비교대상)과 함께 쓴다. than 다음엔 주격이 나오는 게 원칙이지만 구어체에선 목적격도 쓴다.

**1. 비교급 만들기:** 형용사나 부사 다음에 ~er을 붙이는데, e로 끝나는 말엔 -r만 붙인다.
- The elephant is large but the whale is larger than it.
- He had more guests than are expected.     [than은 유사관계대명사]

❶ **(단모음)+(자음)**으로 끝나는 말은 그 끝 자음을 한 번 더 반복한다.
- Seoul is *hot*, but Busan is **hotter** *than* it.

❷ **(자음)+y** 로 끝나는 말은 -y 대신 -ier로 비교급을 만든다.
- I am happy, but my cat is happier than I(me).
- Today, he got up earlier than yesterday. (어제보다 더 일찍)

❸ **2음절**(-y로 끝나는 단어는 예외) **이상**의 긴 형용사/부사는 **more**를 붙여 비교급을 만든다.
- difficult → more difficult
- diligent → more diligent
- famous → more famous
- precise → more precise

❹ **과거분사(p.p)**나 -ly, -ful 등의 접미사로 품사 전환된 말엔 **more**를 붙임.
- toughly → more toughly
- awful → more awful
- used → more used
- bent(p.p) → more bent

❺ **열등비교**를 나타내는 **less**는 **단음절** 형용사/부사에도 사용한다.
- I am less *strong* than he(him). (덜 강하다)

❻ **–or+to 비교급**: 라틴어에서 온 prior, junior, senior, inferior, superior, anterior(이전의) 등은 than 대신 to를 쓴다. 이런 형용사는 more ~ than 형태로도 쓸 수 있다.
- This duty is **prior** *to* all others. (이 의무가 무엇보다 먼저다)
- This machine is **superior(inferior)** *to* that.
- He is **junior(senior)** *to* me.     [me 대신 I 는 못씀]
 = He is more **junior(senior)** *than* I(me).

## 2. 비교급의 특별 용법

**❶ the+비교급, the+비교급의 용법: ~하면 할수록, 더 ~해진다**
  · The more you eat, the fatter you become. (더 먹을수록 더 비만해짐)
   = As you eat more, you become fatter.
  · The more, the better. (많을수록 더 좋다)

**❷ 비교급 and 비교급: '점점 ~된다'**
  · It is getting colder and colder. (점점 추워진다)

**❸ 차이의 표현: 비교급 앞에 차이를 나타내는 말을 둔다.**
  · This car is *much(far)* more expensive than that.　　　　　　　[very는 안 씀]
  · This is *three times* bigger than that. (세 배 더 큰)
  · Tom is *two inches* taller than I(me). (2인치 더 큰)
   = Tom is taller than I(me) *by* two inches.

**❹ more than (형용사) to~: ~하게 되어 더없이~하다**
  · I am more than *happy* to help the poor. (돕게 되어 더없이 행복하다)

**❺ not more than: ~이하**
  · I *have* not more than 5 cars.　　　　　　　　　　　　　[5대 이하로, 둘 셋도 가능]

**❻ no more than: 기껏 그 정도(=only)**
  · I have no more than *5 cars*. (겨우 5대)
  · The media were no more than puppets of the government.

**❼ no more A than B : B 못지않게 A가 아닌**
  · A whale *is* no more a fish than a horse is. (말이 어류가 아니듯이)
   = A whale is not a fish any more than a horse is.

**❽ rather than(~보단 차라리): 형용사, 부사 이외의 것을 비교할 때 사용**
  · I will die bravely rather than live cowardly.　　　　　　　　[동사 비교]
  · I will rather be a soldier than a teacher.　　　　　　　　　[명사 비교]

❾ **no longer = not any longer**: 더 이상 ~이 아닌
  · I am **no longer** a baby. (더 이상 ~이 아닌)
  = I am not a baby **any longer**.

❿ **more often than not**: 이따금씩(없는 것보다는 더 자주)
  · I meet her **more often than not**. (간혹 그녀를 만난다)

⓫ **sooner or later**: 조만간(조금 이르거나 늦게)
  · I will call you **sooner or later**. (조금 늦거나 일찍, 조만간)

⓬ **prefer A to B**: A 보다 B를 더 선호한다
  · He **prefers** pizza **to** hamburger.

⓭ **than usual**: 평상시보다 더 ↔ **as usual** (평상시처럼)
  · Mary is *prettier* than usual.

## ▌연습문제 58

괄호 속 단어들 중 알맞은 것에 ○표하라.

1. It is (hoter, hotter) than yesterday.
2. She was (happier, more happy) than ever.
3. This picture is (awfuller, more awful) than that.
4. James is two year senior (than, to) me.
5. Tom is more junior (than, to) me.
6. Roy is (very, much) older than his brother.
7. John is stout (rather, better) than fat.
8. (A, The) more you have, the more you get worried.
9. It will rain sooner (and, or) later.
10. More (usual, often) than not, they fight with each other.
11. I prefer country music (than, to) rock'n roll.
12. Do not eat more salt (that, than) is necessary.

## C 최상급: '~가운데 가장 ~한'

여럿 중 으뜸을 나타낼 때 사용하며, (최상급)+of(in) 집단 의 형태로 쓴다.

### 1. 최상급 만들기
형용사나 부사 뒤에 –est를 붙인다. [붙이는 원칙은 비교급 –er 과 동일.] 최상급 명사엔 a(n) 대신 (최고의 것이 여럿 있을 수 없으므로) the가 붙는다. 단, one of the~ 다음엔 **최상급 복수형**을 쓸 수 있다. '지역이나 단체' 중에서는 in, '같은 종류' 중에서는 of를 주로 쓴다.

- Mary is **(the) youngest** *in* the class.
- Mary is *one of* **the youngest** students in the class.
- This apple is **(the) biggest** *of* them.
- This is one of **the biggest** apples in the farm.

### 2. 원급과 비교급을 통해 최상급 의미 나타내기
- He is **the tallest** boy *in* the class.
  = **No (other) boy** *in* the class is as *tall* as he.
  = **No (other) boy** in the class is **taller than** he(him).
  = He is **taller than** *any other* boy(s) *in* the class.

### 3. 최상급의 특별 용법

❶ 강조: **much, the very, by far** 등을 사용할 수 있다.
  - His score is **much(by far)** *the best*. (2등과 많이 차이나는 1등)
  - He is **the very** *best*. (정말로 1등)

❷ 서수와 함께 쓰는 최상급: **second best, third largest** 등
  - Tom is **the** *third* **tallest** in his class. (세 번째로 키가 큰)

❸ **the last to~**: '~할 마지막 사람'이란 뜻에서 '결코 ~하지 않을 사람'
  - John is **the last (one) to** *tell a lie*. (결코 거짓말하지 않을 사람)

❹ **first thing in the morning**: 내일 아침 제일 먼저 할 일(구어)
  - I'll call him **first thing in the morning**. (일어나자마자 전화할게)

❺ 기타 관용 어구

at last: 마침내, 결국
at (the) most: 많아 봐야, 최대한
at (the) least: 적어도, 최소한

at (the) best: 기껏, 아무리 애써도
at (the) worst: 최악의 경우라도
at (the) latest: 늦어도

표 19. 불규칙 비교급, 최상급 변화

| 원급 | 비교급 | 최상급 | 원급 | 비교급 | 최상급 |
|---|---|---|---|---|---|
| good/well | better | best | ill/bad | worse | worst |
| many/much | more | most | prius | prior | prime |
| little | less, lesser[1] | least | up | upper | upmost, uppermost |
| old | older | oldest(나이) | out | outer | outmost, outermost |
|  | elder[1] | eldest(형제) | in | inner | inmost, innermost |
| late (늦은) | later | latest(시간) | far | father | farthest(거리) |
|  | latter | last(순서) |  | further | furthest(정도, 거리) |

주: 1. lesser(더 작은), elder(더 나이든)는 대개 한정적 용법으로 쓰인다.
  · My **elder** brother is 2 years **older** than I(me).

### 연습문제 59

괄호 속 단어들 중 알맞은 것에 ○표하라.

1. However tall you may be, you can't be (taller, tallest) of all.
2. Peter is one of the smartest (boy, boys) in the world.
3. Which do you like (better, best), basketball or baseball?
4. Jack found out the second (better, best) answer.
5. Which of the three dolls is (pretiest, prettiest)?
6. Neptune is the (innermost, outermost) planet in the solar system.
7. Henry is the best dresser (in, of) my friends.
8. The raw fish is the (last, least) thing I want to eat.
9. Mary was the (much, very) best in the contest.
10. The prize is given to one or at (least, most) three players a year.
11. Jim stayed in Africa at (last, least) for 10 years.
12. At (best, worst), you may lose your life in this battle.

# 종합문제 18

**01** 다음 문장에서 어색한 부분을 찾아 바르게 고치라.

1. Jack is two years old than me.
2. Tom can run twice as faster as I.
3. He is a shortest of all the students in the class.
4. The Nile is one of the long rivers in the world.
5. Monkeys are very smarter than rabbits.
6. There is no highest mountain than Everest.
7. Jim is richest than any other man in this island.
8. The more you eat, the more fat you get.
9. I think Jack is as strong as usually.
10. She is two years elder than me.
11. He smokes lesser than before.
12. In the quality, my car is superior than yours.
13. Mary's life became more bad after marriage.
14. I want to learn farther about the life of Edison.
15. They climbed higher for higher to reach the summit.
16. I am more than happier to participate in this project.
17. You are not a child no longer.
18. Jim collected shellfish by farther the most among us.
19. Bill is faithful. He is the latest one to betray us.
20. You have to come back home at last 10 o'clock.

**02** 괄호 속에 있는 말을 이용해 다음 우리말을 영작하라.

1. 내가 아는 한, 그는 건강하다. (as far as)

2. 이 강은 한강보다 두 배 길다. (as, twice, the Han River)

3. 사람은 배우면 배울수록 더 겸손해진다. (the more)

4. 필요한 것보다 더 많은 돈을 가지려 하지 마라. (try, more, than)

5. 이 상품은 기대했던 것만큼 싸지 않다. (chief, as expected)

6. 나는 연필을 두 자루밖에 갖고 있지 않다. (no more)

7. Bill은 그의 반에서 두 번째로 빠르다. (second, fastest)

8. 그녀는 더 이상 우리의 지도자가 아니다. (no longer)

9. 나는 적어도 다섯 개의 사과가 필요하다. (at least)

10. John은 사과를 기껏해야 5개밖에 못 먹을 것이다. (at most)

---

**자주 등장하는 라틴어 약어:**
cf.: confer(비교) i.e.: id est (that is, 즉)
e.g.: exempli gratia (for example) etc.: et cetera (기타 등등)
no.: numero (번호)

# Unit 23 가정법 (Subjunctive Mood)

고대엔 직설법, 명령법, 가정법에서 사용되는 동사의 형태가 다 달랐다. 다행히 영어에선 직설법과 명령법에서 쓰는 동사 형태가 동일하고, 가정법에서도 별 차이가 없다(was 자리에 were 쓰는 정도). 그러나 이 작은 형태적 차이가 큰 의미적 차이를 가지므로 가정법의 형태에 유의하여 문장을 정확히 이해해야 한다.

## A 가정법의 종류

흔히 영어에서 가정법이 여러 종류인 것처럼 말하지만, 실은 딱 둘뿐이다: **가정법 과거형, 가정법 과거완료형**. 가정법에선 조건접속사 if를 주로 사용하지만, **if가 나온다고 다 가정법은 아니며** if로만 가정법을 만드는 것도 아니다. 가정법의 판단은 **동사의 형태**에 있으므로, 동사 변화에 유의하자.

### 1. 가정법 과거형

**현재와 미래의 불가능한 혹은 불확실한 상황이나 소원**을 언급할 때 사용하며, 이때엔 동사의 **과거형**을 쓴다. 다만 be 동사는 인칭/수에 관계없이 항상 were를 쓴다. 형태는 과거형이지만 **과거의 의미는 전혀 없다**.

- (직설법) If I **am** not tired, I **will** come to you. (피곤하지 않으면)
- (가정법) If I **were** a bird, I **could** fly to you. (내가 새라면)

❶ **불가능한 현재 사실과 상황의 표현:**
- *If* I **were** to be young again, I **could** be an actor.
  = *As* I am not to be young again, sadly I *cannot* be an actor.
- *Even if* the sun **rose** in the west, he **would** remain calm.
- *Though* Mary **were** a witch, I **would** still love her.

❷ **현재와 미래의 불확실한 상황**
현재나 미래의 상황에 대해 자신 있게 말하기 어려울 때 사용.

- If he **were** a wise man, he **would** not do so.　　　　[현명한지 불확실]
  = A wise man **would not** do so.

❸ **완곡한 표현:** 부드럽게 권면, 예측 등을 할 때 **가정법 과거형**을 쓴다. 현재적 상황에서 쓰는 would, could, should는 모두 이런 용법이다.

- *Can* you open the door? (문 열 능력 있니?)          [직설법]
  ⇒ **Could** you open the door? (문 열 의향이 있으세요?)     [가정법]
- **Would** you mind if I *smoke* here?(혹시라도 꺼려하실 건가요?)
  [if 다음엔 직설법을 쓰는데, 이는 실제로 그렇게 할 의향이 있기 때문이다.]
- You *shall* be careful. (반드시 조심하라)          [엄격한 경고]
  ⇒ You **should** be careful. (되도록이면 조심하라)      [격식 있는 권면]
- I didn't expect that your wife **(should)** object. (설마 반대할까)
- If I **should** die, bury me in my country. (혹시나 죽게 되면)
- Breathing **could** be difficult on the high mountain.     [불확실한 예측]

## 2. 가정법 과거완료형

**과거 사실의 반대 상황** 혹은 **과거의 불확실한 상황**을 언급할 때 사용하며, 이때는 동사의 **과거완료형**을 쓴다. 과거 사실에 대한 **예의적 표현**에도 쓴다.

- If I **had worked** harder, I **could have succeeded**.
- If the war **had not broken**, he **could have survived**.
- It's a gift for you. / Oh, you **shouldn't have done** this!   [예의적 표현]

## 3. 가정법 복합시제형

상황에 따라 가정법 과거형과 과거완료형, 직설법 등을 함께 쓸 수 있다.

- If I **had worked** out harder[가과완], I **would be** healthy now[가과].
  ⇒ As I **did not** work out harder, I **am not** healthy now.
- If the earth **were** flat[가과], he **couldn't have reached** India[가과완].
  ⇒ As the earth is **not** flat, he **could** reach India.
- If it **should rain** tomorrow[가과], I **will not go** out[직미래].

## 4. 가정법의 직설법 전환

가정법을 직설법으로 전환할 때는 대개 느낌을 표현하는 문구를 넣는다.

- *If* I **were** a millionaire, I **could** buy you a car.
  ⇒ *As* I **am not** a millionaire, *sadly* I **cannot** buy you a car.

■ 연습문제 60

괄호 속 단어들 중 알맞은 것에 ○표하라.

1. If I had enough money, I (can, could) buy you a diamond ring.
2. Would you mind if I (close, closed) the window?
3. Though the world (is, were) ruined now, I would not leave you.
4. Though I (may, might) fall to death, I will climb up the tree.
5. (If, Unless) he were a genius, he couldn't have solved the problem.
6. If I (had known, knew) the fact, I would not have come here.
7. A faithful man would not (tell, have told) a lie in that situation.

## B 다양한 가정법 표현들

**현재 상황을 말하면서 과거형 동사**를 쓴다면 이는 완곡한 가정법 표현이다.

1. **I wish + 가정법**: ~하고 싶은데 (하지 못해) 아쉬워하다
   I wish는 대개 가정법과 함께 쓰이고, 직설법을 쓸 땐 hope를 사용한다.

   · I *wish* I **could go** with you.                    [지금은 같이 갈 수 없는 상황]
   · I *wish* I could have gone with you.                 [과거에 같이 갈 수 없던 상황]
   　cf I hope (that) I can go with you.                  [지금 같이 갈 수도 있는 상황]

2. **as if(as though) + 가정법**: (사실과 다른데) 마치 ~인 듯이

   · He tells *as if(though)* he **knew** everything. (아는 것처럼)
   · He tells *as if(though)* he **had seen** everything. (본 것처럼)

3. **If it were not (had not been) for~**: ~이 없(었)다면

   · **If it were not for** the sun, no one **could survive**.
     = *Without(But for)* the sun, no one **could survive**.
   · **If it had not been for** the war, my father **could have survived**.
     = *Without(But for)* the war, my father **could have survived**.

4. **would (should)like to~**: (가능하다면) ~하고 싶다   [주어의 정중한 희망]
   · I **would like to** take a rest a while. (잠시 쉬고 싶다)
   · I **should like** Kim **to** study hard. (Kim이 열심히 공부하면 좋겠다)

5. **would rather ~**: (가능하다면) 차라리 ~하고 싶다   [주어의 정중한 의지]
   · I **would rather** not eat than be fat. (살찌느니 먹지 않겠다)

6. **would better ~**(= had better): ~하는 게 좋다   [주어에 대한 정중한 충고]
   · You **would better** not go now. (지금 안 가는 게 좋겠다)

7. **as it were**(= so to speak): 말 그대로
   · All we are**, as it were,** in a same boat.

### ▌연습문제 61

**01.** 괄호 속 단어들 중 알맞은 것에 ○표하라.

1. I wish I (win, won) the lottery.
2. I hope you (can, could) go with us anyway.
3. He orders me as if he (was, were) a king.
4. If it (were not, had not been) for your help, I would have failed.
5. I (will, would) like to have beef rather than chicken.
6. You'd better (not be, be not) noisy.
7. I would (better, rather) study than work.
8. You are, (as, so) it were, a mouse in a trap.

**02.** 다음 가정법 문장을 보기에 따라 직설법으로 바꾸라.

> If I were free, I could go to L.A. with you.
>    ⇒ I feel sorry I cannot go to L.A. with you because I am not free.

1. If the phone were not so expensive, I could buy it for you.
   ⇒ _____
2. I wish you could have played the guitar better.
   ⇒ _____

## 종합문제 19

**01 다음 문장에서 어색한 부분을 찾아 바르게 고치라.**

1. If I was an American, I could teach you English.
2. If I knew the fact, I could have informed it to you.
3. I wish I can go back to my childhood.
4. If the sun rose in the west, I would not stop my daily job.
6. As it is late at night, you'd better going home.
7. I'd rather to be a hammer than a nail.
8. I wish everything will go fine tomorrow.

**02 다음 직설법 문장을 가정법으로 바꿔 쓰라.**

1. I feel sorry I cannot buy the house because I'm not rich enough.

2. I feel sorry I could not meet you because I was sick.

3. I feel sorry I cannot sing well. (wish를 사용)

4. I feel sorry I could not win the lottery. (wish를 사용)

5. I feel happy I could succeed in the business with his advice.

6. Though not being an artist, he talks like an artist.

**03** 괄호 속에 있는 말을 이용해 다음 우리말을 영작하라.

1. 만약 아빠가 그때 담배를 끊었다면, 지금 건강하실 텐데. (if)

2. 내가 다시 어린애가 되면 좋겠다. (wish)

3. 내가 지금 미국에 있다면, 나이아가라에 가보고 싶다. (if, would like)

4. 그의 충고가 없었다면, 나는 그 대학교에 가지 않았을 것이다. (but for)

5. 내가 설사 부자라도, 그런 차는 사지 않을 것이다. (though)

6. 만약 내가 과거로 돌아갈 수 있다면, 그녀를 살릴 수 있었을 텐데. (if)

7. Mary는 마치 자신이 한 때 공주였던 것처럼 행동한다. (behave, as if)

8. 내일 세상이 멸망해도, 나는 오늘 한 그루 사과나무를 심겠다. (though)

9. 나는 코끼리 꼬리가 되느니 차라리 말의 머리가 되겠다. (would rather)

10. 그 경기에 졌을지라도, 우리는 다시 일어설 수 있었을 것이다. (even if)

11. 지금은 네가 미국으로 가야 할 적기이다. (high time, should)

12. 너는 앞으로 그녀를 안 만나는 게 좋겠다. (would better, from now on)

13. 제가 창문을 닫아도 될까요? (mind, if)

14. 건강한 사람은 거기서 넘어지지 않을 것이다. (healthy man)

# Unit 24 일치와 화법 (Agreement & Narration)

## A 서술 형태의 일치(Parallelism)

영어에서는 서술형태의 일관성을 문법의 중요한 요소로 본다.

### 1. 명사들 간의 형태 일치

- I like **reading** books, **cooking** and **to watch** movies. (×)
  ⇒ I like **reading** books, **cooking** and **watching** movies. (○)

### 2. 동사들 간의 형태 일치

- Some children were **playing** games, and others made cookies. (×)
  ⇒ Some children were **playing** games, and others (were) **making** cookies. (○)

### 3. 명사와 대명사 간의 형태 일치

- While staying in Seoul, **Mary** lost **his** own passport. (×)
  ⇒ While staying in Seoul, **Mary** lost **her** own passport. (○)
- As **you** have finished the work, **one** can take a rest. (×)
  ⇒ As **you** have finished the work, **you** can take a rest. (○)
- After acquiring **the information**, we will use **them** for the test. (×)
  ⇒ After acquiring **the information**, we will use **it** for the test. (○)

### ▌연습문제 62

괄호 속 단어들 중 알맞은 것에 ○표하라.

1. Yesterday, I studied English, mathematics and (science, scientist).
2. I went to a park with Jim, where (they, we) rode the bumper cars.
3. People in the land lived by fishing, hunting and (collecting, collection).
4. Which do you prefer, cooking or (to do, doing) the dishes?
5. Some went shopping, and others (playing, to play) badminton.
6. A herd of goats is coming to the meadow with (its, their) shepherd.
7. If you find the cat, please bring (them, it) to me.
8. If Tom lives in Seoul, his mother must also live (there, that).

## B 주어와 동사의 일치

**1. 인칭의 일치:** be동사 변화와 일반동사의 3인칭 단수 현재 변화에 유의

- *I* am a boy and *you* are a girl.
- *He* was 8 when *you* were 6.
- *I* like blue but *Jane* likes red.

**2. 수의 일치:** 주어의 수에 따라 동사의 활용이 달라짐.

- *Tom and I* are good friends.　　　　　　　　　　　　[and로 연결된 명사는 대개 복수]
  - cf The *bread and butter* is delicious. (버터 바른 빵)　　　　　　[단수]
- A *number* of birds **were** captured.
  - cf 10 *miles* is a long distance.　　　　　　　　　　　[단위는 단수 취급]

**3. or, nor, but also 로 연결시:** 동사와 가까운 단어의 인칭/수에 일치시킴

- *Either* you *or* I *am* in charge. (너 혹은 나에게 책임이 있다)
- *Neither* you *nor* I *am* rich. (너나 나나 부자가 아니다)
- *Not only* you *but also* he *is* smart. (너뿐 아니라 그도 똑똑하다)
  = He *as well as* you *is* smart.　　　　　　[as well as you는 삽입구]

**4. every~, each~: 항상 단수 취급**

- *Every* boy and girl *was* present. (모두 참석했다)
- *Each* of the girls *has* the flower. (각 소녀들)

### ▌연습문제 63

괄호 속 단어들 중 알맞은 것에 ○표하라.

1. The United States (is, are) the strongest in the world.
2. One third of children (was, were) awake during the nap time.
3. Each of the people (was, were) given a piece of cake.
4. All the chicken in the freezer (was, were) used up.
5. Every boy and girl (was, were) not so happy.
6. Neither you nor I (am, are) from England.
7. Not only you but also Tom (want, wants) to meet her.
8. Tom as well as his friends (love, loves) the game.

## 🅲 시제의 일체

종속절을 가진 문장에서, 주절 동사와 종속절 동사의 시제는 일치해야 한다. 이에 대한 자세한 내용은 아래 🅳. 화법의 전환을 참조하라.

· When I left the city, it has begun to rain. (×)
⇒ When I left the city, it began to rain. (○)


## 🅳 화법의 전환(Conversion of Narration)

say 동사와 따옴표(" ")를 이용해 화자의 말을 직접 인용하는 것을 **직접화법**이라 하고, 따옴표 안의 내용을 접속사 that이나 의문사 등을 이용해 전달하는 것을 **간접화법**이라 한다.

### 1. 직접화법을 간접화법으로 바꾸는 방법

첫째, 콤마(,)와 따옴표(" ")를 없앤다. 둘째, 전달동사를 알맞게 바꾼다 (예, said → told). 셋째, 접속사와 함께 전달하는 내용을 기술한다. 이때 시제를 일치시키는 것이 중요하다. 시간, 장소 등의 부사는 말을 전달하는 상황에 맞게 바꾼다. 일반적으로는 다음과 같이 바꾼다.

> <부사의 전환>
> now → then; this → that; here → there; ago → before; today → that day; next week(year) → the next week(year); tomorrow → the next day; yesterday → the previous day; last night → the previous night

❶ **평서문**의 전달: said to → told; 접속사 that(생략 가능)

· She **said to** me, "*I* love *you*."
⇒ She **told** me (that) *she* loved *me*.
· She **said to** me, "*I will love you* forever."  [내용상, 약속임]
⇒ She **promised** me (that) *she* would love *me* forever.
· She **said to** me, "I saw you *last night*."  [앞선 시제]
⇒ She **told** me (that) she had seen me *the night before*.

❷ **의문사 있는 의문문의 전달**: said to → asked; 의문사 + S + V

- She **said to** me, "*Where* **are** *you* from?"
  ⇒ She **asked** me *where I* **was** from?
- He **said to** her, "How **did** you come here?"
  ⇒ He **asked** her how she **had come** there.  [앞선 시제]

❸ **의문사 없는 의문문의 전달**: if 혹은 whether를 사용

- He **said**, "Is she happy *now*?" (지금 행복하니?)
  ⇒ He **asked** *if* she **was** happy *then*? (그때 행복했는지)
- She **said to** me, "**Were** you *here last* Sunday?"
  ⇒ She **asked** me *if* I **had been** *there* the *previous* Sunday.  [앞선 시제]

❹ **명령문의 전달**: said to → told, asked, ordered 등; 동사 → to부정사

- He **said to** us, "Don't be *noisy here*."
  ⇒ He **ordered**(asked) us **not to be** noisy *there*.
- He **said to** me, "*Please*, give me some food."
  ⇒ He **begged** me **to give** (him) some food.
- He **said to** me, "*Would you open* the door?"
  ⇒ He *politely* **asked** me **to open** the door.
- He **said to** me, "*You'd better not leave* here."
  ⇒ He **advised** me **not to leave** there.
- He **said to** me, "*Let's have* hamburger for lunch."
  ⇒ He **suggested**(proposed) me **to have** hamburger for lunch together.

❺ **감탄문의 전달**: said → cried, shouted, admired, exclaimed; 감탄문은 어순 그대로 쓰거나 very 등을 보충해 평서문으로 고침.

- She **said**, "*What* a pretty dog it is!"
  ⇒ She **exclaimed** *what* a pretty dog it was.
  ⇒ She **said** it was a very pretty dog.

## 2. 시제 일치의 예외

**❶ 일반적 진리**: 동사는 항상 현재 시제

· He **said to** us, "The earth **is** round." ⇒ He **told** us (that) the earth **is** round.

**❷ 현재적 습관**: 과거의 습관이 현재까지 이어지면 동사는 현재 시제

· He **said to** me, "I **get up** at 6:00."
⇒ He **told** me (that) he **gets up** at 6:00.  [현재도 6시에 일어남]

**❸ 역사적 사실**: 동사는 항상 과거 시제

· He **said to** me, "The Titanic **sank** in 1912."
⇒ He **told** me (that) the Titanic **sank** in 1912.

**❹ 동시에 일어난 두 사건을 전달할 땐 시제일치를 시키지 않는다.**

· Bill **said to** me, "I **was** sleeping when my wife **was** cooking."
⇒ Bill **told** me he **was** sleeping when his wife **was** cooking.

**❺ 시간적 전후 관계가 명백**하고 오해 소지가 없을 경우, had를 반복하는 번거로움을 피하기 위해 시제일치를 시키지 않을 수 있다.

· Tom **said**, "It **began** raining before I **left** school."
⇒ Tom **said** it **began** raining before he **left** school.

**❻ 가정법**: 애초에 **다른 유형의 동사 활용**을 하므로 **시제 일치 해당 안 됨**.

· She **said to** me, "*Would* you like coffee?"
⇒ She **asked** me if I *would* **like** coffee.
· He **said to** her, "If I *were* you, I *would* never stay here."
⇒ He **told** her (that) if he *were* her, he *would* never stay there.

**❼ must 구문**: 과거형은 have to(의무), must have p.p.(추측)로 바꿔 쓰되, 오해의 여지가 없으면 그냥 must로 쓰기도 한다.

· He **said to** me, "You **must** leave now." (떠나야 한다)
⇒ He **told** me (that) I **must**(had to) leave then.
· He **said to** me, "You **must be** hungry now." (배고픔에 틀림없다)
⇒ He **told** me (that) I **must**(must have been) hungry then.

■ 연습문제 64

괄호 속 단어들 중 알맞은 것에 ○표하라.

1. As soon as I (had come, came) in the tent, it began to rain.
2. After dad went out for work, mon (has watched, watched) TV.
3. I didn't know she (was, had) died already.
4. Roy told me Korean war (broke, had broken) out in 1950.
5. Teacher asked me if I (have, had) finished my homework.
6. We found out the island (lies, lay) in the south of Taiwan.
7. Mom said she (was, had been) ill when Korean War broke out.
8. I found he (was, had been) born after his father died.

# 종합문제 20

## 01 다음 문장에서 어색한 부분을 찾아 바르게 고치라.

1. Every couples were seated side by side.
2. Tom and I am good friends.
3. The village people didn't believe the earth was round.
4. Ten years are not a long term when compared with our history.
5. This Saturday, we were going to have a party on the beach.
6. A number of members was present at the meeting.
7. A pair of new shoe was delivered to me.
8. On her way home, Jane's brother saw a crow.
9. If you have some sugar, lend them to me please.
10. They love jogging, hunting, picnicking and to hike.
11. Either you or Jack have to come to help me.
12. Roy's pants was really awesome.
13. Eggs and ham are my favorite dish.
14. She ordered me if I would like to have lunch.
15. Yesterday Tom said he had nothing to do now.

**02** 괄호 속에 있는 말을 이용해 다음 우리말을 영작하라.

1. Mary는 나에게 언제 돌아올 거냐고 물었다. (when)

2. 너나 나나 부자가 아님을 모든 사람이 알고 있었다. (neither, nor)

3. 우리는 그녀가 미국으로 가버린 걸 알지 못했다. (had gone)

4. Tom은 네가 그를 배신하지 않으리라 믿었다. (would)

5. 나는 미국 남북전쟁이 왜 일어났는지 몰랐다. (Civil War)

6. 우리는 그가 예전에 의사였음을 기억했다. (once)

7. 아빠는 나에게 그 소녀를 만나지 말라고 명하셨다. (order)

8. 나는 우주가 팽창하고 있음을 알지 못했다. (universe, expand)

9. 그녀는 곧 다시 돌아오겠다고 내게 약속했다. (promise)

10. James는 자신이 한국인이면 좋겠다고 말했다. (wish)

# Unit 25 기교적 표현 (Technical Expression)

여기선 도치, 생략, 삽입 등 영어의 기교적 표현을 다룬다.

## A 도치(Inversion)

강조를 위해 목적어, 보어, 부사어 등을 문두로 보내는 경우, 종종 주어와 동사의 순서를 뒤바꾼다. 타동사의 경우, do를 대신 써서 도치시킨다.

### 1. Here, There 구문: 단, 대명사인 경우는 주어 - 동사 위치가 바뀌지 않는다.
· **Here** *is* your change. (여기 거스름돈 있어요.) ⇒ **Here** it *is*.
· **There** *is* a postman. ⇒ **There** he *is*!(그가 저기 있네!)

### 2. so, neither, nor 구문
· I *am* thirsty. / **So** *am* I.   · I *will* wait. / **So** *will* I.
· I *don't* like broccoli. / **Neither(Nor)** *do* I.

### 3. 부정어구: hardly, no, never, seldom, rarely, little, only then 등
· **Never** *did* I know the fact.
· Under **no** circumstances *will* I quit. (어떤 경우에도 포기 않겠다)
· **Hardly** had I reach the port when the ship started. (항에 도착하자마자)

### 4. 장소, 방향의 부사구
· **Under the tree** *was lying* a lion.
· **Along the river** *came down* a group of ducks.

### 5. So-형용사/부사, Such + that 구문
· **So beautiful** *was* Jane **that** everyone wanted to see her.
· **So fast** *was* the car **that** I could not see well its driver.
· **Such** *was* his power **that** no one could oppose to him.

### 6. 직접화법에서 인용부호(" ") 다음에 화자가 올 때
· "I am sorry," **said** John. = "I am sorry," John.

### 7. 가정법에서 if의 생략

- *If* he **were** my son, I would scold him hard.
  = **Were** he my son, I would scold him hard.
- *If* I **had recognized** the fact, I would never have allowed it.
  = **Had** I **recognized** the fact, I would never have allowed it.

### 8. as, though 등의 양보절

- **Though** he is a little *boy*, he is very gentle.
  = *A little boy* **as**(**though**) he is, he is very gentle.
- **Whatever** you *may say*, they will not accept it.
  = *Say* what you *may*, they will not accept it.
- **However** you *may try*, you cannot succeed.
  = *Try* **as** you *may*, you cannot succeed.

## B 강조(Emphasis): 도치 이외의 방법

### 1. It ~ that 구문: 사람이면 who, whom을 쓸 수도 있다.

- I met Jane yesterday in the park.
  ⇒ It was *Jane* that(whom) I met yesterday in the park.  [사람 강조]
  ⇒ It was *yesterday* that I met Jane in the park  [날짜 강조]
  ⇒ It was *in the park* that I met Jane yesterday.  [장소 강조]

### 2. do 이용한 동사의 강조

- I **do** love you. (정말 사랑해)
- I **did** love you. (정말 사랑했다)

### 3. 재귀대명사 통한 주어의 강조

- I made the furniture **myself**.
  = I **myself** made the furniture. (내가 직접 만들었다)

### 4. very를 통한 명사의 강조

- He is the **very** man (that) I was looking for. (바로 그 사람이다)
- This is the **very** fact (that) we have to know.

## 연습문제 65

괄호 속 단어들 중 알맞은 것에 ○표하라.

1. Never (I did, did I) recognized it was a fake.
2. May I see your passport? / Here (are you, you are).
3. Along the road (down walked, walked down) the children.
4. He can run fast. / So (I can, can I).
5. (I were, Were I) rich, I would go abroad for study.
6. "I will stay here," (said, told) Jack.
7. Rich (as, if) George was, he didn't stop working.
8. (That, It) was Steve that asked me to come here.
9. He (did, was) do his best in the game.
10. He is the (much, very) player we've been looking for.

## C 생략과 대체(Omission and Substitution)

미국인은 말의 반복을 싫어해 종종 이를 생략하거나 다른 간단한 어구로 대체한다.

### 1. 동일 어구의 생략 및 대체

- Some *cats* ate meat and *others* (ate) fish.　　　　　[others = other cats]
- **Come** if you want to (come).
- I hate to **be late** for school but frequently **am** (late for school).
- Did you *have lunch*? / Yes, I **did**.　　　　　　　　[did = had lunch]
- I have been (sincere) and will be sincere to you.

### 2. 비교 구문에서의 생략

- Tom is **as tall as** I *am tall*. (×)　　　　　　　　　[Redundancy]
  ⇒ Tom is as tall as I(me).
- Tom is **taller than** I *am tall*. (×)　　　　　　　　[Redundancy]
  ⇒ Tom is taller than I(me).
- The sooner (*it is*), the better (*it is*). (빠를수록 좋다)

## 3. 부사절에서 (주어+be동사)의 생략

- When *(I was)* young, I was very shy.
- Though *(he was)* very sick, Tom went to school.
- He was sitting on the couch as if *(he were)* dreaming.

## 4. 관용적 생략: 문맥상 알 수 있는 경우, 가급적 생략한다.

- What *(would happen)* if I should fail the exam?
- Correct errors, if *(there are)* any. (있으면 틀린 걸 고치라)
- I will help you if *(it is)* possible.
- Can you help me? / I'm afraid not. (아무래도 안 될 것 같다)
  (= I'm afraid I can't *help you*.)
- Will it be cold? / I hope not. (= I hope *it will* not *be cold*.)
- Do you like it? / Of course not. (= I do not *like it*.)
- I can't go. / Why not? (=Why can't *you go*?)
- No pain, no gain. (아픔이 없으면 얻는 게 없다)
  = *If there is* no pain, *there is* no gain.

## 5. 가주어, 가목적어: 주어나 목적어가 길어지면 그 대신 it을 쓰고 주어나 목적어는 뒤로 보냄.

- It is difficult to find ways in Seoul.(= To find ways in Seoul is difficult)
- You will find it easy to buy the subway ticket.

## 6. 불필요한 반복(Redundancy): 다음과 같은 반복은 문법적으로 틀린 것으로 간주된다.

- Each and every boy was given a pen. (×)
  → Each(*or* Every) boy was given a pen. (○)
- This is an actual fact. (×) → This is a fact. (○)
- We have to collaborate together. (×)
  → We have to collaborate(*or* work together). (○)
- The telephone was first invented by G. Bell. (×)
  → The telephone was invented by G. Bell. (○)
- The dog followed after me. (×)
  → The dog followed(*or* came after) me. (○)
- It is a free gift for you. (×) → It is a gift for you. (○)
- Why don't you join us together? (×)
  → Why don't you join us? (○)

- This hat has a unique **outward appearance**. (×)
  → This hat has a unique **appearance**. (○)
- Do you know the **past history** of this country? (×)
  → Do you know the **history** of this country? (○)
- Please **repeat again** after me. (×)
  → Please **repeat** after me. (○)
- There are **various different** types of pasta. (×)
  → There are **various** types of pasta. (○)
- Tom is a **wellknown famous** movie star. (×)
  → Tom is a **famous** movie star. (○)
- He spent his money **uselessly in vain**. (×)
  → He spent his money **in vain**. (○)

## D 삽입과 동격(Interpolation and Apposition)

1. **삽입**: 앞뒤에 콤마(,)를 넣어 삽입구를 만든다.
   - He is, **so to speak**(=as it were), a fish out of water. (말하자면)
   - Life is, **I think**, just a dream. (내 생각에)
   - Take this pill, **if necessary**, when you go to bed. (만약 필요하면)

   ※ **의문사**를 가진 의문문에 do you think(believe, imagine, guess, suppose 등)가 삽입될 때는 콤마를 사용하지 않는다.
   - *What* do you think this sign means?
   - *Why* do you believe she is greedy?(왜 탐욕스럽다고 믿니?)
   - cf Do you know *whom* she is waiting for?

2. **동격**: 콤마(,)를 넣어 동격을 만들며, 콤마 뒤에 or를 덧붙이기도 한다. 동격절을 만들 때는 that을 쓴다.
   - Mr. Kim, **our homeroom teacher**, is handsome. (담임인 김 선생님)
   - Obama, **the former President of America**, is black.
   - Fasting, **or not eating**, is not recommended for you.
   - He raised the price by 2 dollars, **or 10 percent**, to 22 dollars.
   - I was shocked at the *news* **that he was killed**.

■ 연습문제 66

**01.** 괄호 속 단어들 중 알맞은 것에 ○표하라.

1. Did you have breakfast yet?  /  Yes, I (did, have)
2. Are you ready to go?  /  I'm (not afraid, afraid not).
3. If she doesn't go, (not, neither) do I.
4. You may enter the room if you want (do, to).
5. I will not eat anything.  /  Why (will, not)?
6. Please send my money back soon, if (necessary, possible).
7. Who do you (know, think) the girl is?
8. Gauchos, (and, or) Argentine cowboys, looked romantic.
9. Did you hear the news (which, that) John passed the exam?
10. (This, It) is hard for me to understand the question.
11. (How, What) if the bus does not arrive on time?

**02.** 다음 중 불필요한 부분을 찾아 지우라.

1. He made a big hit by combining art and science together.
2. James first discovered this island in 1892.
3. Do they have any future plan for economic growth?
4. I read the past history of Spain in the library.
5. When do you think Jim will return back?
6. We took the whole entire products out of the storage.
7. The two boys looked both alike in uniform.
8. The plane left for Seoul at 8 AM in the morning.

# 종합문제 21

**01 다음 문장에서 어색한 부분을 찾아 바르게 고치라.**

1. It were 50 dollars that I borrowed from Bill last month.
2. It was through Jane who I got to know Mary.
3. It was John that I want to see most.
4. Near the river the house was in which he was born.
5. As he was poor, Tom was always clean and tidy.
6. We were very happy to see you.   /   So did I.
7. John was helpless and he was disappointed at that time.
8. Can you come to the party?   /   Yes, I'm afraid not.
9. Mr. Smith, and my homeroom teacher, is very friendly.
10. Do you think why Mike came here?
11. I will learn to play tennis.   /   So do I.
12. I am not interested in the classical music   /   So am I.

**02 다음 문장을 지시에 따라 고쳐 쓰라.**

1. Yesterday I bought a camera in the Town Mall. (Town Mall 강조)

2. I was so hungry that I went into a restaurant. (so hungry 강조)

3. Anybody could not solve this problem. (nobody를 이용)

4. Irrational as it was, Tom believed the UFO story. (though 이용)

5. I have never seen such a beautiful car. (never를 강조)

## 03 괄호 속에 있는 말을 이용해 다음 우리말을 영작하라.

1. 내가 할머니를 방문한 것은 지난 주였다. (it, that)

2. 나는 정말 유명해지고 싶다. (do)

3. 우리는 바로 이 방에서 이야기를 나눴다. (very)

4. Bill은 인도를 방문한 적이 있으며, 그의 여동생도 그렇다. (so)

5. 그녀는 내게 직접 칠면조를 요리해 주었다. (herself, turkey)

6. 네가 먹지 않으면, 나도 먹지 않겠다. (neither)

7. 그는 말하자면 이 시대의 양심이다. (so to speak, conscience)

8. 테니스를 칠 때, 만약 필요하면, 이 모자를 써라. (if necessary)

9. 그의 월급은 10% 즉 200달러 올랐다. (went up, or)

10. 나는 그가 시험에 떨어졌다는 사실에 매우 실망했다. (fact that)

# 실전문제 (미국 SAT 문법 변형 문제)

**밑줄 친 부분에서 문법상 틀린 말 혹은 구절을 찾으라.**

1. The ①identities ②of them who have ③been called ④as witnesses will ⑤be released by the district attorney.

2. We ①hope that training the high school students ②to compete in debate contest ③will help prepare them ④to become ⑤a successful scholar.

3. The fishermen ①saw that ②a school of ③bluefish ④were coming ⑤near the reef.

4. In consideration ①about his long service, the education committee ②made a special presentation ③honoring Mr. Kim who had ④recently retired ⑤from the school.

5. The girls ①comprising 30% of the class ②is represented by ③only one member ④out of 5 ⑤on the class council.

6. ①Neither the students ②nor the teacher ③were satisfied ④with the project ⑤made by the school.

7. The workers ①who I see in the factory ②every evening ③seem ④tired and ⑤dejected.

8. The report ①was rejected ②because of its length, ③verbosity ④and ⑤its one-sidedness.

9. Mr. Smith's ①decision to retire ②came ③as a shock to all ④that ⑤respects his ability.

10. ①A large quantity of ②clothing and ③of valuable jewelry ④were stolen ⑤from Mary's room.

11. ①Between the small shops of Greenwich and the large ②department stores of Manhattan ③lie the ④residential neighborhood ⑤of Chelsea.

12. ①Rowing ②vigorous the ③sinking boat, we managed ④to remain ⑤afloat.

13. We ①had ought to finish ②our trip before ③dark because ④it ⑤goes very cold after sunset.

14. The success of ①recent art exhibitions ②illustrate a ③shift in ④both scholarly assessment ⑤and public taste.

15. ①Just as some people ②adore cell-phone games, so ③others condemn ④it as ⑤a waste of time.
16. I ①should like you and ②she to supply the ③necessary data for the ④annual report ⑤to present in the next meeting.
17. ①After the space shuttle explosion, ②where 7 crew members ③were killed, the NASA program ④underwent a ⑤massive examination.
18. Twenty ①restless ②6-year-olds were drawing ③on the blackboard and ④called one another while their teacher ⑤was out.
19. ①Before taking the musical to Broadway, the producer tried ②getting the show with all ③its actors ④booked in summer stock theaters for ⑤last revisions.
20. If you buy ①a condominium, you ②will have ③less work than ④owning a house ⑤is required.
21. We ①have come to the conclusion ②that we can ③end this crisis by providing ④more water and ⑤to develop local resources.
22. Despite ①lived in ②the US ③for more than 50 years, he continued ④writing novels ⑤in Swedish.
23. The ancient concept which ①states that ②the sun ③revolves around Earth ④is questioned by Copernicus ⑤in the 16th century.
24. The opera members, ①which ②ranged from manager to conductor, joined ③forces to pay ④tribute to ⑤retiring tenor Pavarotti.
25. ①Both teams – ②each eager ③to dominate this year's National League competition – ④has reviewed the game ⑤videos of last year.
26. This scholarship ①is given to ②whomever in the class ③has done the ④most ⑤to promote goodwill in the community.
27. The two parties ①interpreted the contract condition ②differently, ③so they ④needed a judge to settle ⑤its dispute.
28. ①All of the club members, ②except him, ③is practicing ④twice as long to ⑤enter pro teams.
29. Everybody ①but Tom ②has paid ③their dues. We ④must seek ways ⑤to persuade the guy.
30. The data ①that you presented ②is not ③pertinent to the ④issue ⑤under discussion.

**31.** ①In order for ②she and I to be able to ③enter the concert, we ④will need to get the tickets ⑤within the week.

**32.** ①A new production of the opera *Aida* will be ②sang ③on an ④outdoor stage with ⑤live animals.

**33.** ①Unless three ②or more members ③object to ④him joining our club, we ⑤shall have to accept him.

**34.** Bill ①made history by ②becoming the first ③black general when he was ④appointed of this position ⑤by President Johnson.

**35.** ①What ②may be the world's ③largest rodent is the capybara, ④which is found throughout ⑤many of South America.

**36.** ①Despite the ②thorough investigation, ③surprising little is ④known of the motivations of the ⑤serial killer.

**37.** Cream, ①like other dairy goods that ②spoils ③easily, ④needs to be kept ⑤under refrigeration.

**38.** ①During the 1920s, they began to show ②much interest in the movement of black writers ③who ④came to be ⑤known as the Harlem Renaissance.

**39.** ①Initially, Roy made ②heavy use of the internet to raise funds; ③latter he ④went on to ⑤more conventional methods.

**40.** The differences ①between my world view and ②that of Tom ③arise less from a dispute about the function of government ④but from a dispute about the ⑤nature of humankind.

연습문제 1

1. (1) You→you, jane→Jane (2) how→How, i→I (3) there→There, han river→Han River, seoul→Seoul 2. *Dear my friend please help me. I am in a trouble.*

연습문제 2

2, 3, 6, 12

연습문제 3

1. ③ 2. ④ 3. ③ 4. ① 5. ④ 6. ② 7. ② 8. ① 9. ④ 10. ②

연습문제 4

1. ② 2. ① 3. ④ 4. ② 5. ④ 6. ③ 7. ④ 8 ①

연습문제 5

1. ① 2. ④ 3. ① 4. ④ 5. ① 6. ② 7. ④ 8. ① 9. ④ 10. ③

연습문제 6

1. ③ 2. ④ 3. ③ 4. ⑤ 5. ② 6. ① 7. ④ 8. ③ 9. ② 10. ④ 11. ② 12. ②

연습문제 7

1. ① 2. ③ 3. ① 4. ③ 5. ② 6. ① 7. ② 8. ④ 9. ④ 10. ④ 11. ③ 12. ① 13. ④  14. ③ 15. ① 16. ③ 17. ② 18. ①

연습문제 8

1. ③ 2. ④ 3. ③ 4. ① 5. ③

연습문제 9

1. tópic, cémetery, báckpáck, behínd, móbile, mediterránean, cashíer, considerátion, cómmíttee, employée, cóncentrate, fígure, detér

2. He was again attacked by Americans who had been amusing themselves.
   히워저   개너   택트바이어   메리칸스   후드비너   뮤징   뎀셀브스

연습문제 10

1. sugar 2. are 3. coffee 4. the 5. are 6. Cokes 7. information 8. is

연습문제 11

1. foxes 2. churches 3. pianos 4. potatoes 5. photos 6. candies, babies 7. boys, toys 8. loaves 9. leaves, roofs 10. Wives, knives 11. children 12. Thieves, safes 13. axes 14. theses, oxen 15. teeth, feet 16. geese 17. mice 18. deer, bison 19. sheep, Japanese 20. is 21. are 22. is 23. is 24. those 25. are 26. passers-by 27. forget-me-nots 28. is 29. horse 30. hundred

연습문제 12

1. (1) three (2) twice (3) hundred (4) is (5) to

2. (1) duchess  (2) waitress (3) stewardess (4) actress (5) princess (6) ewe (7) niece (8) daughter (9) maid-servant (10) she-goat (11) lass (12) female

연습문제 13

1. He 2. me 3. her 4. my 5. girls' 6. today's 7. is 8. a friend of mine 9. that bike of Tom's 10. butcher's

종합문제 1

1. (1) an old my friend → an old friend of mine (2) this Tom's camera → this camera of Tom's (3) scissor → scissors (4) ten-years-old → ten- year-old (5) in 1990s → in the 1990s

(6) Tom's and Jerry's → Tom and Jerry's (7) hour's → hours' (8) nineth → ninth (9) the China → China (10) waters are → water is
2. (1) John's (2) hero (3) today's (4) one (5) landlady (6) is (7) are (8) queen (9) she (10) hers
3. (1) I cannot forget this old friend of mine. (2) 10 dollars is not enough to buy this bike. (3) The train started after 20 minutes' delay. (4) The Smiths went to China by plane yesterday. (5) Tom's family are tall. (6) Tom's family is from Canada. (7) I saw the handbag of the girl with a red hat. (8) One third of my friends are Americans.

연습문제 14
1. an 2. a 3. the 4. the 5. the 6. the 7. the 8. was 9. were 10. was

연습문제 15
1. smart a 2. quite a 3. double the 4. bed 5. cancer 6. arm

종합문제 2
1. (1) A sun, a moon → The sun, the moon (2) a breakfast → breakfast (3) an → a (4) a tennis → tennis (5) piano → the piano (6) the double price → double the price (7) are → is (8) is → are (9) How → What 혹은 a lovely flower → lovely a flower (10) a such → such a (11) The both → Both the (12) a hand in a hand → hand in hand (13) A water → Water 혹은 The water (14) the my → my (15) the all → all the (16) this a pen → this pen (17) this your friend → this friend of yours (18) a → the (19) a → an (20) a Sunday, a bus → Sunday, bus
2. (1) He plays the guitar from morning till night. (2) They elected Trump president of the USA. (3) We go to bed at 10. (4) He is an actor and writer. (5) Who made such a big pizza? (6) They make 100 cars a year. (7) Monday is the second day of a week. (8) The old man died of malaria. (9) She was a famous actress in the 1980s. (10) John is as handsome a boy as his brother.

연습문제 16
1. our 2. mine 3. herself 4. me, his 5. them 6. mine 7. hers. 8. They 9. yourself 10. of

연습문제 17
1. It 2. it 3. it 4. it 5. It 6. it true

연습문제 18
1. This 2. this 3. that 4. those 5. this

연습문제 19
1. ones 2. one 3. None 4. Each 5. some 6. another 7. the other 8. it 9. Both 10. anything

연습문제 20
1. (1) What (2) Whom (3) Whose (4) Who (5) Which(What) (6) Who (7) What (8) Whose (9) whom (10) Whom (11) What (12) Which(What)
2. (1) Who is (2) Whose (3) What (4) Whom (5) What

종합문제 3
1. (1) were → was (2) your → yours (3) him → himself (4) oneself → myself (5) That → It (6) round → long long → round (7) the other → another (8) those → these (9) neither →

none (10) his → their (11) a book → book (12) who → whom (13) one → other (14) Where → What (15) something → anything (16) This my picture → This picture of mine (17) every → one (18) some → any (19) that → those (20) neither → none 혹은 are → is
2. (1) On Valentine Day we give presents to our beloved ones. (2) Please pour some water into the bowl. (3) I didn't eat all the cake. (4) I gave some of cake to Tom and the rest to Jane. (5) People in the room are shaking hands one another. (6) I am an old friend of Bill's but I don't know everything about him. (7) He doesn't know anything about this plan. (8) None of them are fat. (9) Whomever should we sent for this duty? (10) May I have your name?

### 연습문제 21
1. from 2. On 3. under 4. along 5. out of 6. through 7. between 8. around

### 연습문제 22
1. at 2. on, in 3. by 4. for 5. during 6. within 7. through

### 연습문제 23
1. by 2. Without 3. with 4. by 5. for 6. at 7. in 8. on 9. but 10. for 11. about 12. in spite

### 연습문제 24
1. (1) for (2) for (3) behind (4) to (5) with (6) over (7) at (8) after (9) of (10) of (11) to (12) of (13) with (14) with (15) in
2. (1) with (2) for (3) with (4) on (5) from (6) for (7) of (8) to (9) for (10) of

### 종합문제 4
1. (1) On today → Today (2) to home → home (3) on everyday → everyday (4) On the morning → In the morning (5) L.A. → in L.A. (6) think → think of (7) music → to music (8) in → at (9) to → for (10) by → at (11) him with → with him (12) by → in (13) this → from this (14) reach at → reach (15) laughed to → laughed at (16) with → of (17) by → with (18) after → for (19) for → in (20) with → to
2. (1) His room is filled with old books. (2) We walked along the river for about an hour. (3) The girl was around 4 years old. (4) Buds are coming out from beneath the ground. (5) This plastic is made from petroleum. (6) Yesterday he was absent from school because of illness. (7) Dad is getting rid of weeds in the yard. (8) He heard a strange sound coming from behind the door. (9) Every living cannot live without air. (10) Yesterday I came home on foot.

### 연습문제 25
1. to school 2. home 3. are 4. was 5. deeply 6. soft 7. arrived 8. am is 9. were 10. English 11. good 12. well 13. happy 14. true 15. nice 16. looks 17. bad 18. sad 19. sick 20. straight

### 연습문제 26
1. entered 2. waiting 3. me 4. a man 5. the

### 연습문제 27
1. (1) I sent a letter to Mary yesterday. (2) They sold a broken car to him. (3) Will you cook a steak for me? (4) She asked two questions of me. (5) You played a trick on her.
2. (1) I will show you the way to the station. (2) Father left me nothing. (3) The test will

take you about 3 hours.

### 연습문제 28
1. (1) five dollars to me → me five dollars (2) of his success → his success 혹은 him (for) his success (3) two weeks to the refugee → the refugee two weeks (4) 10 dollars to me → me 10 dollars (5) 100 dollars to the smuggler → the smuggler 100 dollars
2. (1) on (2) on (3) with (4) with (5) to (6) of (7) of (8) of (9) of (10) of

### 연습문제 29
1. smart 2. sad 3. him 4. working 5. open 6. barking 7. called

### 종합문제 5
1. (1) went → went to (2) down → down on (3) bad → badly (4) marry with → marry(marry는 타동사) (5) to there → there (6) slow → slowly(자라는 상태를 보여주므로 부사여야 한다) (7) silent → silently (8) redly → red (9) looked → looked at (10) to me → for me
2. (1) a great job to me (2) a whole day for us (3) a lot of work to me (4) a math book for me (5) a question of you.
3. (1) I found the question very difficult. (2) He played me a trick. (3) We elected her president. (4) He sold me a lemon. (5) Don't ask me such a question. (6) We called John a living legend. (7) Mary kissed me on the cheek. (8) Don't require him too much. (9) I felt hungry after school. (10) Please show me the way to the subway station. (11) This coupon saves us 5 dollars. (12) Please forgive me my rudeness.

### 연습문제 30
1. can 2. doesn't 3. will 4. has 5. go 6. cross 7. is going 8. Would 9. Shall 10. Don't 11. dare 12. would 13. Need 14. would 15. May

### 종합문제 6
1. (1) goes → go (2) Do you can → Can you (3) finished → finish (4) be able to 삭제(중첩) (5) to go → go (6) to fight → fight (7) come → to come (8) be going to 삭제(중첩) (9) make → to make (10) do loves → do 삭제 혹은 does love (11) may → might(시제일치) (12) was → did (13) to take → take (14) went → go (15) helping → help (16) must not → need not (17) have been → be (18) may → must, shall 혹은 should (19) would → will (10) got → get
2. (1) She would not listen to me. (2) It is about to rain. (3) You don't have to come to the library tomorrow. (4) Would you like some coffee? (5) I will love that beautiful mountain forever. (6) Could you talk with me just for an hour? (7) Shall we go to see the movies after dinner? (8) You may well get angry at me. (9) He cannot steal the friend's money. (10) She must have been rich in the past.

### 연습문제 31
1. loving 2. golden 3. What 4. each 5. sung 6. friendly 7. enlarge 8. saddening 9. easy 10. drink

### 연습문제 32
1. lonely 2. older 3. awake 4. sleeping 5. general 6. long 7. are 8. was 9. money 10. a few 11. a lot of 12. some 13. were 14. was(chicken은 닭고기) 15. much

연습문제 33

1. something 2. anything 3. with 4. downstairs 5. else 6. Sejong the Great 7. Two

종합문제 7

1. (1) many → much (2) much → many (3) silveren → silver 혹은 silvern (4) the Alexander Great → Alexander the Great (5) cold something → something cold (6) these my two dogs → these two dogs of mine (7) interested → interesting (8) write to → write on (9) money enough → enough money (10) vainly → vain (11) an alive → a live (12) particularly → particular (13) asleepy → asleep (14) exciting → excited (15) two his → his two (16) few → little (17) were → was (18) bored → boring (19) sleepy → sleeping (20) annoying → annoyed

2. (1) The man upstairs seems very lonely. (2) Look at that baby sleeping on the bed (3) No dogs are left in the park. (4) These two big African elephants are sick. (5) Please give me some water to drink and a hat to put on. (6) He has little money to spend for game. (7) The poor are not always unhappy. (8) Whose is the book in the bag? (9) The members present at the meeting were Koreans. (10) Nobody else can dance so beautifully.

연습문제 34

1. nice 2. truly 3. hard 4. well 5. strongly 6. enough 7. late 8. loudly 9. for it 10. close

연습문제 35

1. What 2. Why 3. How 4. Luckily 5. it off 6. an only

연습문제 36

1. very 2. so 3. set 4. yet 5. it up 6. neither 7. too 8. before 9. took 10. gave

종합문제 8

1. (1) enough kind → kind enough (2) off it → it off (3) awfully → awful (4) In last → Last (5) goes often → often goes (6) surprised → surprise (7) was → were (8) to meeting → to meet 혹은 meeting (9) lately → late (10) hard → hardly (11) kind → kindly (12) happy → happily (13) ago seven years → seven years ago (14) too → neither (15) yet → already (16) away it → it away (17) terrible → terribly (18) loud → loudly (19) close → closely (20) very → much

2. (1) I was once a student of this school. (2) Every Saturday he visits the nursing home. (3) We met him at the library in Seoul at 2 PM last Monday. (4) He lives alone but does not feel lonely. (5) Tom no longer stays here but Mary still does. (6) Haven't you fixed my computer yet? (7) When I arrived at the airport, mom came to pick me up. (8) We wear glasses to make up the bad eyesight. (9) I live at A-(dash) 308 Jemulpo Apt 6-11 Subongro Namgu Incheon. (10) If you do not give up I won't either.

연습문제 37

1. and 2. or 3. but 4. however 5. or

연습문제 38

1. so 2. that 3. when 4. whether 5. When 6. why 7. before 8. because 9. Though 10. or 11. If 12. Unless 13. am 14. Whenever 15. since 16. long 17. as soon as 18. so 19. Whoever 20. than 21. lest 22. Even 23. that 24. that 25. that

종합문제 9

1. (1) and → or (2) or → and (3) where → when 혹은 while (4) and a nurse → a nurse and (5) and → but (6) When everytime → Whenever 혹은 Everytime (7) so a fine → such a fine 혹은 so fine a (8) and → or (9) were → was (10) or Tom → Tom or (11) so → but (12) Whatever → However

2. (1) He was so short that he could not ride the horse. (2) I studied hard so that I might pass the exam. (3) If you read my letter, you will understand why I left you. (4) While I was fishing in the river, I saw a crocodile. (5) It was such a cold day that she could not go shopping.

3. (1) Mary is not a nurse but a doctor. (2) While mom was doing dishes, dad read the news paper. (3) Until I see it with my own eyes, I will not believe it. (4) Whoever you meet, be kind to him or her. (5) Now that it stopped raining, let's go out to play basketball. (6) Though the time was over, the train did not start. (7) As far as I know, he is not rich. (8) Wherever you go, I can find you. (9) I was so busy that I could not have lunch. (10) This fruit is not only delicious but also looks good.

연습문제 39

1. (1) whose (2) who (3) which (4) whose (5) that(who의 반복을 피하기 위해) (6) that (7) which (8) of which (9) as (10) than

2. (1) I have a friend who has five bulldogs. (2) We visited Jane whose mother was a cook. (3) Look at the house, of which the wall is painted in red. (4) There was a queen in England whom all the people loved. (5) Do you know what Tom gave me last night? (6) I know them all that came from China.

연습문제 40

1. who 2. which 3. in which 4. which 5. who 6. whom 7. on which 8. at (look up to는 '존경하다') 9. who 10. which I looked for (for which I looked after school은 '개를 위해 학교를 돌본다'로 오해될 수도 있다) 11. in which 12. which

종합문제 10

1. (1) whom → who (2) which → whose 혹은 of which the windows (3) the bike of which → whose bike (4) what → that (5) whom → which (6) who → which (7) which → what (8) what → that (9) that → than (10) gave it → gave (11) girl can → girl who(혹은 that) can (12) of which ~ afraid → which ~ afraid of (13) in which ~ interested → which ~ interested in (14) for which ~looked → which ~ looked for (15) which ~been beyond → beyond which ~ been

2. (1) who is (2) 없음 (3) that (4) who (5) that

3. (1) Who knows that man (that is) standing at the door? (2) I know that old man whose two sons live in Japan. (3) Do you see the house whose roof is covered with snow? (4) The girl who(m) you looked at in the park yesterday is my sister. (5) This is the middle school from which I graduated. (6) He gave me all the money that he had. (7) What he really need is love. (8) There is no one but doesn't love her.

연습문제 41

1. why 2. where 3. when 4. where 5. which 6. way 7. when 8. where 9. why 10. how

종합문제 11

1. (1) when → which 혹은 that (2) which → where (3) ,why → why(콤마 생략) (4) when → where(즐거운 시간을 보낸 건 concert 때문이므로) (5) when → which (6) which → where (7) why → how 혹은 that (8) while → where (9) how → where (10) Hurray → Alas

2. (1) This is the garden where Jack planted the magic bean. (2) Bill died in 2016, when there was a great famine. (3) Do you know the way (how) she survived the cold winter? (4) I don't know (the reason) why Mary does not answer my phone. (5) I arrived in Busan at 2 PM, when it began to rain.

3. (1) I went to the park today, where I met Tom. (2) Tell me why he was absent from school today. (3) He visited me in the afternoon when it rained hard. (4) The house where he had once lived became a hotel now. (5) I came home at 4 PM yesterday, when Jane called me. (6) Tom told me how he opened the door. (7) We don't know when and where he was born. (when, where는 의문대명사) (8) Oh my god, we have a flat tire! (9) Ouch, my foot was caught in the door! (10) Oops, I'm sorry. / That's OK.

연습문제 42

1. was 2. doesn't 3. has 4. is not 5. can 6. there 7. No 8. Who 9. played 10. made you 11. or 12. she is 13. Who do you think 14. you did 15. me

연습문제 43

1. isn't 2. doesn't 3. won't 4. ain't 5. weren't 6. it 7. shall 8. can he 9. will 10. there

연습문제 44

1. (1) it is (2) What (3) How (4) Don't be (5) let us (6) Why (7) and (8) awesome 2. (1) How heavy this stone is! (2) What a tall building it is! (3) What a fast runner Kim is!

종합문제 12

1. (1) flower pretty → pretty flower (2) Who do you know → Do you know who (3) I ain't → I'm not (4) you are → are you (5) has → have (6) didn't → haven't (7) won't → will (8) did you go → you went (9) did he → he did (10) What do you know → Do you know what

2. (1) will you (2) is it (3) haven't you (4) isn't it (5) shall we (6) doesn't she (7) is he (8) aren't there (9) won't she (10) ain't I

3. (1) Don't be angry at me because of money. (2) How cold it is today! (3) What a smart student Tom is! (4) Where do you think Mary is now? (5) Do you know when Mary bought this book? (6) Why don't you go swimming with us? (7) She must be sick right? (mustn't she?를 쓸 수도 있지만 잘 안 쓴다) (8) Follow me quickly, or you will get lost.

연습문제 45

1. (1) (play)-plays-played-playing (2) (have)-has-had-having (3) (get)-gets-got- getting (4) (arrive)-arrives-arrived-arriving (5) (marry)-marries-married-marrying (6) (lie)- lies-lied-lying (7) (visit)-visits-visited-visiting (8) (fall)-falls -fell-falling (9) (run)- runs – ran –running (10) (set) - sets – set - setting

2. (1) played (2) wrote (3) stopped (4) dying (5) was (6) spread (7) hurt (8) belongs (9) feels

(10) was having (11) catch (12) eating (13) lay (14) studies (15) is used

### 연습문제 46
1. tomorrow 2. will 3. are going to 4. is 5. will 6. about 7. Did 8. had 9. saw 10. would go 11. next year 12. has been 13. have 14. has rained 15. been 16. have done(절교) 15. before 16. than 17. studied

### 종합문제 13
1. (1) have bought → bought (2) has → had (3) play → played (4) leave → have left(미래완료) (5) is → was (6) goes → went (7) understood → understand (8) planned → planning (9) is living → has lived (10) has worked → worked (11) gone → been (12) have finished → finished (13) was → is (14) studied → studying (15) has → have (16) is → has been (17) brush usually → usually brush (18) goes → went (19) didn't → haven't (20) will → would
2. (1) He would never leave Seoul. (2) I will play soccer after I have finished my homework. (3) When I visited him, he was having lunch. (4) It has been snowing since last Friday. (5) Do you know when she will come home? (6) Three years have passed since I graduated from college. (7) Have you ever spoken in English? (8) Don't speak while you are eating. (9) He had driven for 8 hours till he reached L.A. (10) I didn't know that it had snowed so much.

### 연습문제 47
1.The book was written by Bill two years ago. 2. She will never be left alone (by us). 3. Pictures cannot be taken in this church. 4. This tower was built 300 years ago. 5. Where was her bag found? 6. What was given (to) her by you on Valentine day? 7. Was this book written by Mary? 8. A hamburger was bought for me by mother. 9. By whom was this window broken? 10. By what were you made angry?

### 연습문제 48
1. him 2. was 3. read 4. was 5. whom 6. at 7. founded 8. interesting 9. interested 10. of 11. taken 12. reading 13. with 14. from 15. by 16. selling

### 연습문제 49
1. resembles 2. selling 3. with 4. building 5. feels 6. read 7. to work 8. locked 9. compare 10. are washing

### 종합문제 14
1. (1) was become → has become 혹은 became (2) was resembled → resembled (3) was arrived → arrived (4) Whom → By whom (5) send → sent (6) go → to go (7) water → be watered (8) risen → raised (9) was turned → turned (10) clean → to clean
2. (1) By whom was the girl made to cry? (2) The roof has been covered with snow. (3) He could not be heard to sing by anybody. (4) I was disappointed in his failure. (5) My sister was surprised at the mouse.
3. (1) As this book was written in French, I can't read it. (2) The building (which was) built in 1956 is the post office. (3) He walked to the mountain whose peak was covered with snow. (4) Where was this turtle discovered? (5) She looks like beaten. (6) This work will be completed about 3 hours later. (7) The problem was not solved to the end. (8) I cannot be

satisfied with the result. (9) By whom were you taught English? (10) The thief was caught by police and sent to prison.

연습문제 50

1. ⑤ (명사적 용법, 나머지는 부사적 용법) 2. ④ (형용사적 용법, "방학을 보낼 계획", 나머지는 명사적 용법) 3. (1) for (2) of (3) with 4. (1) ④ (2) ⑥ (3) ③ (4) for (5) in 4. (1) of (2) to (3) with (4) tell (5) him (6) so to speak (7) to fast (8) where

연습문제 51

1. (1) Mary was so proud that she could not beg for food. (2) He was rich enough to buy the car. 2. (1) not to go (2) to have been (3) be saved (4) to enter (5) ask (6) strong enough (7) studying (8) help (9) eat (10) join (11) of (12) to.
3. (1) be (2) to (3) to (4) do (5) so

종합문제 15

1. (1) carefully to handle → to carefully handle (2) to not → not to (3) taking → take (4) to walk → walk 혹은 walking (5) for you → of you (6) not change → not to change (7) helping → help (8) for you → you (9) watching → to watch (10) not better → better not (11) having → to have (12) enough smart → smart enough (13) to study → to study with (14) careless enough → too careless (15) whom → who
2. (1) She seems to have known nothing. (2) You would better not sleep now. (3) Tom is too fatty to put on the clothes. (4) He is healthy enough to ride a bike. (5) I am looking for a friend to play the baseball with. (6) We felt the sky get dark(er). (7) It's very kind of you to meet me at the airport. (8) I am very happy to study with you. (9) To begin with, we have to decide the goal to achieve. (10) To say nothing of bread, we have no water to drink. (11) I'll go to get her later. (12) To be frank, I love her.

연습문제 52

1. Talking (뒤의 doing과 맞춤) 2. sleeping 3. smoking 4. to pass 5. to rest 6. surfing 7. eating 8. to keep 9. being 10. to be 11. to send 12. It

연습문제 53

1. seeing 2. being 3. punch 4. spend 5. from 6. On 7. watching 8. keeping 9. playing 10. laughing 11. no 12. going

종합문제 16

1. (1) to build → building (2) To speaking → To speak 혹은 Speaking (3) taking → to take (4) see → seeing (5) to see → seeing (6) talk → talking (7) me → my (8) opposed → opposed to (9) stay → staying (10) went to → went (11) take → to take (12) to blame → blaming (13) to build → building (14) weeping → weep (15) to have → having (16) passing → to pass (17) crying → cry (18) calling → to call (19) to comment → commenting (20) magnifying → to magnify
2. (1) Do you know his being hospitalized because of flu? (2) This book is worth reading. (3) I almost forgot to do my homework. (4) He spent a lot of time writing books. (5) Mary tried playing the violin. (6) It is no use regretting past mistakes. (7) I feel like playing tennis after school. (8) There is no sleeping outdoors on this cold day. (9) He admitted his having

lied. (10) In spite of many failures, he didn't give up drawing pictures.

연습문제 54

1. developing 2. invited 3. parked 4. interested exciting 5. fallen 6. covered 7. scaring 8. opened

연습문제 55

1. (1) Having played outside (2) Having graduated (3) There being no helpers (4) Though having been dumped (5) Not being busy
2. (1) After he (had) learned (2) If it is rainy (3) As he was brought up

연습문제 56

1. (3) 2. (1) Going (2) watching (3) Not receiving (4) Given (5) It being (6) flowing (7) Judging (8) speaking

종합문제 17

1. ⑤ (동명사 나머지는 분사) 2. (1) walked → walking (2) fixed → fixing 혹은 was → has (3) excited → exciting (4) boring → bored (5) naming → named (6) surprising → surprised (7) slept → sleeping (8) make → made (9) built → building (10) giving → given (11) visiting → visited (12) taken → taking (13) folding → folded (14) spoken → speaking
2. (1) I saw the fish swim in the river. (2) Before breakfast, you must have your hands washed. (3) This watch made in China was broken. (4) Who are the children playing on the ground? (5) The birds flying in the sky were caught in the net. (6) After having finished the homework, I watched the TV. (7) Considering your ability, this work is possible. (8) Turning left at that corner, you can find the book store. (8) After (having been) taken into prison, he began to study laws. (10) He saw a bird fallen on the ground.

연습문제 57

1. as 2. fast 3. long 4. well 5. good 6. slowly 7. as

연습문제 58

1. hotter 2. happier 3. more awful 4. to 5. than 6. much 7. rather 8. The 9. or 10. often 11. to 12. than

연습문제 59

1. tallest 2. boys 3. better 4. best 5. prettiest 6. outermost 7. of 8. last 9. very 10. most 11. least 12. worst

종합문제 18

1. (1) old → older (2) faster → fast (3) a → the (4) long → longest (5) very → much (6) highest → higher (7) richest → richer (8) more fat → fatter (9) usually → usual (10) elder → older (11) lesser → less (12) than → to (13) more bad → worse (14) farther → further (15) for → and (16) happier → happy (17) no → any (18) farther → far (19) latest → last (20) last → latest
2. (1) As far as I know, he is healthy. (2) This river is twice as long as the Han River. (3) The more humans learn, the humbler they get (4) Do not try to have more money than is necessary. (5) This product is not so cheap as expected. (6) I have no more than two pencils. (7) Bill is the second fastest in his class. (8) She is no longer our leader. (9) I need

at least 5 apples. (10) John will be able to eat at most 5 apples.
연습문제 60
1. could 2. closed 3. were 4. might 5. Unless 6. had known 7. have told
연습문제 61
1. (1) won (2) can (3) were (4) had not been (5) would (6) not be (7) rather (8) as 2. (1) I feel sorry I cannot buy the phone for you because it is so expensive. (2) I feel happy (that) living things could emerge on the earth thanks to the air.
종합문제 19
1. (1) was → were (2) knew → had known (3) can → could (4) If → Even if, Even though (5) going → go (6) to be → be (7) will → would
2. (1) If I were rich, I could buy the house. (2) If I had not been sick, I could have met you. (3) I wish I could sing well. (4) I wish I could have won the lottery. (5) If it had not been for his advice, I couldn't have succeeded in the business. (6) He talks as if he were an artist.
3. (1) If dad had quit smoking then, he would be healthy now. (2) I wish I could become a child again. (3) If I were in the USA, I would like to go to Niagara Fall. (4) But for his advice, I would not have entered the university. (5) Though I were rich, I would not buy such a car. (6) If I could go back to the past, I could have saved her life. (7) Mary behaves as if she had once been a princess. (8) Though the world would perish tomorrow, I would plant an apple tree today. (9) I would rather be a horse head than an elephant tail. (10) Even if we had been defeated in the game, we could have risen again. ((11) You would better not meet her from now on. (12) Would you mind if I close the window? (13) A healthy man would not fall down there.
연습문제 62
1. science 2. we 3. collecting 4. doing 5. playing 6. its 7. it 8. there
연습문제 63
1. is 2. were 3. was 4. was 5. was 6. am 7. wants 8. loves
연습문제 64
1. (1) came (2) watched (3) had (4) broke (5) had (6) lies (7) was (8) was
2. (1) You told me that either you or I was going to be the chairman. (2) Bill asked me not to forget to give him a call the next day. (3) She told me that she had seen me in that cafe the day before. (4) Dad asked me if I would go with him to his office. (5) Roy told Jane that she was very pretty in that dress. (6) Tom told me that the world is not fair. (7) He told me that even if this world ruined then, he would love me. (8) She told me that she wished I could go to Paris. (9) She suggested me to go to see her parents the next week. (10) Mary told me that I must be in love with Jane. (11) Jack told me he was listening to music when I called him. (12) Mom said she was very pretty when she was Jane.
종합문제 20
1. (1) couples were → couple was (2) am → are (3) was → is (4) are → is (5) were → are (6) was → were (7) shoe → shoes (8) her → his (9) them → it (10) to hike → hiking (11) have → has (12) was → were (13) are → is (14) ordered → asked (15) now → then

2. (1) Mary asked me when I would come back. (2) Everybody knew that neither you nor I was not rich. (3) We didn't know that she had gone to America. (4) Tom believed that you would never betray him. (5) I didn't know why the Civil War broke out. (6) We remembered that he was once a doctor. (7) Dad ordered me not to meet the girl. (8) I didn't know the universe is expanding. (9) She promised me she would come back soon. (10) James said he wished he were a Korean.

연습문제 65
1. did I 2. you are 3. walked down 4. can I 5. Were I 6. said 7. as 8. It 9. did 10. very

연습문제 66
1. (1) did (2) afraid not (3) neither (4) to (5) not (6) possible (7) think (8) or (9) that (10) It (11) What
2. (1) ~~together~~ (2) ~~first~~ (3) ~~future~~ (4) ~~past~~ (5) ~~back~~ (6) ~~whole~~ (7) ~~both~~ (8) ~~AM~~

종합문제 21
1. (1) were → was (2) who → whom (3) together → ~~together~~ (4) the house was → was the house (5) As → Though 혹은 Poor as he was (6) did → was (7) and he was disappointed → and disappointed  Redundancy  (8) Yes → No (9) and → or (10) Do you think why → Why do you think (11) do → will (12) So → Neither
2. (1) It was in the Town Mall that I bought a camera yesterday. (2) So hungry was I that I went into a restaurant. (3) Nobody could solve this problem. (4) Though it was irrational, Tom believed the UFO story. (5) Never have I seen such a beautiful car.
3. (1) It was last week that I visited my grandma. (2) I do want to be famous. (3) We talked with each other in this very room. (4) Bill has been to India and so has his sister. (5) She herself cooked me the turkey. 혹은 She herself cooked the turkey for me. (6) If you won't eat neither will I. (7) He is so to speak the conscience of this age. (8) Put on this cap if necessary when you play tennis. (9) His salary went up 10% or 200 dollars. (10) I was very disappointed with the fact that he failed in the test.

《미국 SAT 문법문제》
(1) ② → of those (2) ⑤ → successful scholars (help는 원형부정사를 목적어로 가질 수 있다) (3) ④ → was ((4) ① → of (5) ② → are (6) ③ → was (7) ① → whom(see의 목적어) (8) ⑤ (its 는 생략: Redundancy) (9) ⑤ → respect 혹은 respected (10) ④ → was (11) ③ → lies (12) ② → vigorously (13) ① → ought (14) ② → illustrates (15) ④ → them (16) ② → her (17) ② → in which(explosion은 장소가 아니므로 where로 받지 못한다) (18) ④ → (were) calling (19) ② → to get(장래 일이므로) (20) ⑤ → requires(주택 소유가 요구하는 것보다) (21) ⑤ → developing (22) ① → living 혹은 having lived(전치사의 목적어) (23) ④ → was (24) ① → who (25) ④ → have (26) ② → whoever (27) ⑤ → their (28) ③ → are (29) ③ → his or her (30) ② → are(data는 복수형) (31) ② → her and me (32) ② → sung (33) ④ → his joining (34) ④ → appointed to (35) ⑤ → much(many of 다음엔 항상 복수형) (36) ③ → surprisingly(놀랄 만큼 적은 양) (37) ② → spoil (38) ③ → which(선행사가 movement) (39) ③ → later (40) ④ → than from

memo

# 멘토링 영문법
- 최고로 치는 남자의 [멘토링 영문법(Mentoring English Grammer)]

| | |
|---|---|
| 인쇄 · 발행 | 2022년 1월 25일 |
| 지은이 | 최치남 |
| 펴낸 곳 | 꿈과 비전 |
| 발행 · 편집인 | 신수근 |
| 편집디자인 | 한미나 |
| 등록번호 | 제2014-54호 |
| 주소 | 서울 관악구 관악로 105 동산빌딩 403호 |
| 전화 | 02-877-5688(대) |
| 팩스 | 02-6008-3744 |
| 이메일 | samuelkshin@naver.com |

ISBN 979-11-87634-23-2 부가기호 13700
정가 15,000원